1994

EMOTION IN ORGANIZATIONS

EMOTION IN ORGANIZATIONS

Edited by

STEPHEN FINEMAN

SAGE Publications
London • Newbury Park • New Delhi

SAGE Publications Ltd
6 Bonhill Street
London EC2A 4PU

SAGE Publications Inc
2455 Teller Road
Newbury Park, California 91320

SAGE Publications India Pvt Ltd
32, M-Block Market
Greater Kailash – I
New Delhi 110 048

British Library Cataloguing in Publication Data

Emotion in Organizations
  I. Fineman, Stephen
  658.3

  ISBN 0-8039-8733-1
  ISBN 0-8039-8734-X pbk

Library of Congress catalog card number 93-084332

Typeset by Mayhew Typesetting, Rhayader, Powys
Printed in Great Britain by Biddles Ltd, Guildford, Surrey

Contents

Contributors

Stephen Fineman Reader in Organizational Behaviour, School of Management, University of Bath

Helena Flam Assistant Professor, Faculty of Administration, University of Konstanz

Yiannis Gabriel Lecturer in Organizational Behaviour, School of Management, University of Bath

Jeff Hearn Reader in Sociology and Critical Studies on Men, Department of Applied Social Studies, University of Bradford

Arlie Hochschild Professor of Sociology, University of California, Berkeley

Heather Höpfl Director of Research and Reader in Organizational Behaviour, Bolton Business School, Bolton Institute

Nicky James Senior Lecturer, Department of Nursing and Midwifery Studies, University of Nottingham

Steve Linstead Hong Kong University of Science and Technology

Dennis K. Mumby Associate Professor of Communication, Purdue University

Wendy Parkin Senior Lecturer in Sociology and Social Work, School of Human and Health Sciences, University of Huddersfield; and social worker in a Family Centre, Kirklees Metropolitan Council

Linda L. Putnam Professor of Communication, Purdue University

Howard S. Schwartz Professor of Organizational Behavior, School of Business Administration, Oakland University

Acknowledgements

My special thanks to Sue Jones at Sage, whose active and constructive support for this book helped it to come about, and also to my colleague, Yiannis Gabriel, whose views and feedback have helped me enormously.

Preface

Arlie Hochschild

Imagine a large bakery. It is an 'organization' in the sense that it coordinates a complex series of tasks so as to sell 30,000 loaves of bread each day and earn a yearly profit of £4 million. The organization purchases supplies. It hires and trains and supervises workers. Workers oversee machines which whip and fold the batter; they bake, check, wrap and deliver the bread. For each task in the organization, we may envision someone doing something. A forklift driver unloads bags of flour from a delivery truck. A personnel manager talks to a worker. An advertising agent sits in a meeting brainstorming good ideas for an ad.

At first glance, we might assume that the operation of the bakery has little to do with human emotion. Why? Because it is not the purpose of the employees of the bakery to feel or express emotion but rather to make bread and earn money. The dominant principle of the place is, or should be, to pursue these goals efficiently. We associate efficiency with the public domain, public wage earning, and often with manhood, itself associated (as Jeff Hearn observes in Chapter 7) with level heads and moderate-sounding tones of voice.

To be sure, social psychologists who study organizations have explored such issues as worker satisfaction, job-related stress and attitudes toward the workplace. Yet often they study opinions and attitudes that exist 'on top of' an emotion-free machine. To the extent that the emotion enters in at all, the social psychologist imagines it to appear in idiosyncratic and not routine ways, to be disruptive not constructive in its consequence, and to be basically marginal, not central, to life at work. Paradoxically, in assuming all this, analysts of the workplace seem to convert to the belief that the workplace holds of itself.

This path-breaking volume, edited by Stephen Fineman, tunes a fine ear to this paradox, and opens the way to exploring the idea that, among other things, it is emotion that is 'organized'. The volume has the spirit of a busy workshop. It lays out basic theoretical approaches, an array of exciting working concepts. In a series of highly imaginative essays and research reports, the authors gathered here show what insights can emerge when we change the premises mentioned above into questions. Is emotional expression an unexpected departure from workaday routines, or is it part of the inner wiring of them? Are emotions temporary disruptions or part of the permanent functioning of a place? If they are a permanent aspect of the workplace, what follows from that? Are the informal lore and ritual, the formal training and supervision of workers – which inspire and maintain emotions – basic to the production of bread and to the creation of profit?

What questions would we ask of the workers in our bakery if we began to comprehend it through the minds in this book?

Let us return to the forklift driver, the personnel manager and the advertising agent. What, we could ask, are the 'real-time emotions' or 'work feelings' of the forklift driver? (Fineman's and Mumby and Putnam's terms respectively). How does he feel, for example, about the new woman forklift operator who got hired over his best buddy? How does he manage his fear about the decline of his union and rumours of layoffs? How big a part of 'himself' is related to his job and his company? (an issue Helena Flam treats thoughtfully in Chapter 3). Is he proud of his company? Is pride, indeed, a feeling he seeks or expects to experience? Yiannis Gabriel would also ask of him what metaphors fit his experience of the company. Does he see it as a football team? A madhouse? A family? A conveyor belt? And what is the structure behind his work feelings? What social conditions influence him and his relations to others? What are the 'emotional zones' in the company within which he has to 'look busy' or can 'blow off steam'? The lunchroom, the bathroom, the water-cooler, the boss's office, the entrance way, have, after all, very different 'feels' to them, as Jeff Hearn points out.

Like the forklift driver, the personnel manager has 'real time emotions' on the job. But in addition, as part of his job, he has to do what I called in my book, *The Managed Heart* 'emotional labor'. Expanding that notion here, I would argue that emotional labour includes knowing about, and assessing as well as managing emotions, other people's as well as one's own. (Who does what kind of emotional labour is partly marked – and partly hidden – by the conventional division of labour at work, as Nicky James' chapter shows.) Thus, as part of the personnel manager's emotional labour, he has to learn the company's 'emotional map'. He learns where, along a continuum of outgroup jokes, the laughter begins in a luncheon meeting at the executive club, in the computer room where the engineers eat their packed lunches, in the cafeteria where the truck drivers have a smoke. He has to know where, along an accelerating array of insults, it becomes OK to take offence without too much counter-offence. He has to understand what various expressions 'mean' for a worker with a given biography, disposition, reputation and status within the company. On an overlay map, so to speak, he learns to trace patterns of emotional attribution (for example the secretaries may say their boss is mad today while his own boss doesn't think so at all).

As part of emotional labour, the manager also assesses feeling. Every time a manager handles an office quarrel, an inter-departmental rivalry, a family emergency, he functions as a mini-judge – deciding when a worker is under 'too much' stress, feels 'too angry' or 'too jealous'. He decides which feelings seem 'healthy' and which seem 'sick' (as Wendy Parkin has noted). He tries to draw the line between harmless flirting, harassment and a difficult office affair. (See Putnam and Mumby on this.) When is a mother who feels guilty for leaving a young child at a day nursery for nine hours to be offered shorter or more flexible hours because her guilt is interfering with her work? How much working-parent guilt and anxiety passes for 'normal' in this company? And how flexible can it get before a manager feels anxious that he or she is losing control? 'Company culture' sets the social boundaries between the right and wrong thing to do. Managers infer the corresponding emotional boundaries between the right and wrong way to feel in a range of contexts – both those of others and of themselves.

The manager's emotional labour also involves regulating feeling – his own and that of other people. This may include absorbing the feelings of others (active but non-reactive listening when an employee is 'blowing up' at one). It may include inducing or inspiring feeling, as when a manager tries to 'motivate' listless, discouraged or cynical employees. It includes attempts at inhibiting or rechannelling feelings. Ideally, emotional labourers come to understand the feelings of workers of a variety of statuses, reputations and backgrounds.

The advertising agent, like the personnel manager, does emotional labour. But she may have to know more about feelings and perhaps manage them less. The personnel manager deals with 'internal customers' (as employees at the company I am currently studying call regular workers). The ad agent deals with 'external customers' – but often from a distance. Apart from getting along with fellow workers, the emotional job is to appraise the 'mood' of the buying public. A benign but peremptory ad such as 'Eat Mother's Bread' may appeal to a sense of duty and guilt. 'Delightfully Nutty, Slimming and Nutritious' may appeal to an ambivalence between desires to be carefree and careful. Insofar as capitalism depends on expanding, if not inventing, the market it fills, it relies heavily on someone's labour reading people's feelings.

All in all, we can think of emotion as a covert resource, like money, or knowledge, or physical labour, which companies need to get the job done. Real-time emotions are a large part of what managers manage and emotional labour is no small part of what trainers train and supervisors supervise. It is a big part of white-collar 'work'. This is true for manufacturing firms, like the bakery, but it is far more true in the rapidly expanding service sector – in department stores, airports, hotels, leisure worlds, hospitals, welfare offices and schools.

Recommendations for Future Research

This volume pioneers a new perspective on major institutions and opens up a rich new research agenda on organizations, many of which are facing the year 2000 in trouble. We could begin by tracing a set of links between organizational dilemmas (such as determining how to distribute rewards), the emotional consequences of them (such as some workers' envy of other workers) and organizational mechanisms designed to avert or contain such potential consequences (secrecy of personnel records, compensatory rewards for losers, rituals of solidarity 'for us all'). The success and failure of these solutions we can relate, in turn, to the real-time emotions of workers who try to reconcile what the company wants of them with what they want for themselves. This set of links fleshes out the context for the rich variety of forms and variations of emotional labour.

In the years ahead, we could have a growing body of careful, grounded, highly nuanced studies that allow us to piece together a coherent portrait of emotion in organizations. In the research to come, Stephen Fineman wisely counsels us to study actors in their local contexts. I would add that it would also be wise to start by addressing specific concrete issues (such as work–family balance, the introduction of high-performance teams, the effect of new technology). Since emotion is a topic which requires subtlety of grasp, we should also refrain from counting things before we know precisely what they are.

Once we have a good body of work, we can enrich it by adding a comparative dimension. With emotions in mind, we can compare companies of different types and sizes, with different company cultures and differently placed in the global market. Within the company, we can compare working parents supervised by two kinds of managers – one who becomes anxious and suspicious when a worker leaves the least bit early to pick up a child from a carer, and one who relies on cooperation and trust to get the job done. These are the sort of vital issues this book invites us to explore. It is an exciting beginning, with a big future.

Introduction

Stephen Fineman

A book about feelings should not seem strange to anyone who has worked in an organization. It should not seem odd to those who have tried to organize others, or have been subjected to management efforts. Emotions are within the texture of organizing. They are intrinsic to social order and disorder, working structures, conflict, influence, conformity, posturing, gender, sexuality and politics. They are products of socialization and manipulation. They work mistily within the human psyche, as well as obviously in the daily ephemera of organizational life.

Although we might know this, it seems to be uncomfortable knowledge. Writers on organizations have successfully 'written out' emotions, to the extent that it is often impossible to detect their existence. A scan of the indexes of recent texts on organizational behaviour reveals no direct entries under 'feelings' or 'emotions'. We teach and preach on organizational life and management, usually acknowledging that our subject matter can be a bit messy – because people are not like machines. But at the same time we fail to square up to the essential emotionality of organizational processes, much of which is, and is likely to remain, unmanaged.

The fear, it seems, is that organization as we know it will collapse if we cannot de-emotionalize emotions – make them seem rational in terms of organizational goals and management purpose. This volume brings together writers who explore and challenge this view. They take emotions to the forefront of organizational studies, drawing upon rich seams of theory and research from different corners of the human sciences. They are united in their belief that emotions are central to the constitution of the realities that we so readily take for granted in our working and organizing. Once we strip the facade of rationality from organizational goals, purposes, tasks and objectives, a veritable explosion of emotional tones is revealed. When we look more closely at cognitions, they are not fully comprehensible without a recognition of the feelings that drive and shape them. When we examine the way organizational order is achieved and undone, the management and mobilization of emotions are pivotal.

This book is not one which dissects emotion as if it were tissue under the surgeon's knife. As lived experiences, firmly contexted in organizational life, feelings are portrayed in qualitative discourse – illustrations, stories, interview accounts and the authors' own personal experiences. Our aim has been to appeal to students and researchers of organizations who, up to now, may not have considered emotion to be part of their subject matter – be they from the ranks of sociology, psychology, anthropology, organizational behaviour or management. In doing this, we hope that we will bring emotion a step closer to becoming a normal feature of organizational studies – where it rightly belongs.

The Structure and Content of this Book

Outside of organizational studies, the literature on emotion is vast. Consequently Part I of the book takes a long slice through this material and pulls out some of the significant perspectives and concepts which make the case for organizational emotion. It offers the reader a broad introduction to the field, raising many of the key questions and debates. Parts II and III focus on more specific illustrations of some of the themes so far identified. Finally, in Part IV, directions for researching organizational emotion are explored.

Part I The Emotional Organization

There are two chapters in this section. In the first I examine key features of organizational emotion through two complementary conceptual lenses – social constructionism and psychodynamic theory. In different ways each explains how emotions form, deform, and direct organizational processes. Social constructionism provides insights into how emotions shape, and are shaped by, the social arrangements, rules and languages used. The much popularized concepts of culture and politics are revealed to be quintessentially emotional. Organizational order depends on feelings of togetherness and apartness, while organizational control would be hard to conceive without the ability to feel shame, anxiety, fear, joy or embarrassment.

Social constructionism opens other emotion doors: such as to gender rules of emotional display, and the way that specific social roles determine what we should or should not feel, or show we feel. Arlie Hochschild's distinction between emotion work and emotional labour is germane in this respect (and is used by many of the contributors to this book). Emotion work is the effort we put into ensuring that our private feelings are suppressed or re-presented to be in tune with socially accepted norms – such as looking happy and enthusiastic at a friend's party, when we actually feel tired or bored. Emotional labour is the commercial exploitation of this principle; when an employee is in effect paid to smile, laugh, be polite, or 'be caring'. An essential feature of the job is to maintain the organizationally prescribed demeanour or mask. This can be fun; an exquisite drama. It can also be stressful and alienating.

The counterpoint to social constructionism (although still markedly 'social' in its origins) is psychodynamics. Here, a largely invisible world of personal anxieties, fears and yearnings can be seen to underpin some of the routines and rituals of work organization and behaviour. Or, to turn the logic around, our deepest existential fears are camouflaged by the very act of work-ing and organizing.

In Chapter 2 Linda Putnam and Dennis Mumby harness the concept of emotional labour to suggest that our emotions in organizations have been controlled to a far greater extent than is normally recognized. This is because of the stranglehold of bureaucracy and the reification of rationality. Indeed, it is hard to find a managerial text which does not pay homage to bureaucracy in some form or another, or offer prescriptions on how to improve rationality. Emotional labour, argue the authors, is unavoidable, and is often pernicious, because the very nature of corporate life as we know it marginalizes our personal feelings. Feelings get in the way of organizational effectiveness. But what if we reverse the reasoning? What if we assume that work feelings are central to effective human interaction, and the expression of 'real' feeling is quite consistent with corporate excellence? Putnam and Mumby suggest that such a scenario is quite possible, especially if we reframe our concept of organization through feminist theory. They challenge us to explore new ways of knowing and relating.

Part II Emotion Work

In this part of the book, specific organizational settings are used to show something of the variety, and poignance, of emotion work and labour.

Helena Flam (Chapter 3) offers a powerful exposition of the effects of fear in corporate life, and the emotion work that changes it into something that is organizationally acceptable. She presents her argument in an unusual manner. Firstly she illustrates, from her researches on the Polish communist party, how fear in an institutionalized setting can subvert moral judgement. She then switches to the corporate business world to draw disturbing comparisons. Fear and anxiety have been underworked in organizational theorizing; obscured, perhaps, by the positive thinking and feeling expected for many work transactions. The fear of loss of face, prestige, position, favour, fortune or job focuses the corporate actor's mind and sharpens his or her political vision and skills. Such anxieties are readily transformed into a socially acceptable work enthusiasm or drive, which ambitious organizational members soon learn to display.

In Chapter 4 Heather Höpfl and Steve Linstead examine the people whose business it is to shape the displays of enthusiasm and drive – management consultants and marketing experts. Such people provide the fuel for others' emotional labour. The authors employ a dramaturgical frame – well suited to the staging, performance, scripts and general razzmatazz of emotional manipulation and display. They delve into the fine detail of dramatism to show how the organizational actor's emotions are intricately related to social settings and audiences. Theatre acting and life performances carry very different risks, yet there is much in the theatre metaphor which advances our understanding of organizational emotion.

Nicky James (Chapter 5) takes us into the painful world of the cancer hospital to explore the tense mix of emotion work and labour when different people attempt to deal with the anxiety of cancer. Who discloses what to whom? When and how do the patients and their relatives get 'informed' by the medical and paramedical establishment? What is communicated? We return again to fear and its effects – in a very specific sense. In James' terms, the various parties learn skills of emotional regulation commensurate with their organizational positions and roles. The emotional labour is tougher for some than for others, depending on their level of involvement with, and personal closeness to, the cancer victim. But, as James shows in her graphic case accounts, it is often the patient and his/her relatives who become caught and confused in a web of divisions of emotional labour – as one carer or professional is careful not to 'say too much' before another has said his or her piece. These arrangements are not immutable, suggests James. In taking the patient's position in this manner, James could be seen as presenting the other side to the psychodynamic view that medical staff *need* their deference rituals to protect *themselves* from the anxiety associated with the morbidity of their work.

In Chapter 6 Yiannis Gabriel explores the individual emotion work which transforms the harsh tones of current organizational experiences into a picture of a warm, ideal past. Gabriel points to an unexpected discovery from his field research on organizational humour: the majority of his industrial respondents would lapse into reverie, recalling glorious leaders, remarkable colleagues, 'characters', and buildings which were 'meant for real people'. The past was fine and good; the present is sad and disappointing. Why enrich the past? Why such nostalgia? Because, suggests Gabriel, organizations are the sites of more disillusionment and discontent than many us would care to admit. The creation of an idyllic past serves to soothe and console, to convince ourselves that there was once a loving world of which we were a part. In further explanation, Gabriel invokes Freud's concept of the ego ideal – a safe, blissful state where we are central, loved and accepted unconditionally: the world of the infant with its totally devoted mother. But that world, if it ever did exist, can never be recaptured. Work, careers and relationships often disappoint, rarely approaching the vision. Nostalgia, though, offers a way of creating a reality that approaches the ego ideal. It is easier to tolerate an unhappy present if we can boast about an enchanted past.

Part III Emotions and the Politics of Difference

Difference in sex, ethnicity, race, religion, and so forth divide emotions. Emotions are *attributed* to one or another social group according to cultural/role expectations; also people have feelings *about* such groups, based on what they feel their members are 'worth'. In this section we examine these features as they influence emotionality in organizations.

In the first chapters (7 and 8), Jeff Hearn and Wendy Parkin look at the crucial role of gender-linked emotions in organizational settings. Social constructionism regards maleness and femaleness as very much more than physical and biological differences between people of different sex. It is cultural learning that determines what behaviour is appropriate for men and for women. This gendering process is a vital one for emotion – its valuing, its expression and its control. Jeff Hearn confronts 'the myth of unemotional man' through self-reflective accounts and organizational stories – which reveal much that is emotional. Men can be wedded to their organization in distinctly emotional ways – such as for their sexual identity, friendship and bonding with male (or female) colleagues. Sex talk and male narrative affirm the feelings. Yet, in the dominant patriarchal organization, male feelings hardly get recognition in formal affairs, whereas female feelings ('comforting', 'unreliable', 'fickle', 'difficult') become defined in benign to pejorative terms. The social construction is all-important; who does the defining, and their power to do so. Men, argues Hearn, are much involved in the control of others' emotions and in the control of emotion labour.

With slightly broader sociological brush, Hearn speaks of emotionalized zones, places or settings in organizations which become understood in terms of different emotions. So the funeral parlour, pithead bath, shop-floor canteen, are each socially constructed for particular forms of emotional display – solemnity, tears, laughter, joy. . . . The notion of emotionalized zones also reminds us that organizations rarely have homogeneous emotional cultures. Corridors, tea rooms and the corners of workshops offer different degrees of emotional freedom, and can be gendered – maled or femaled – in different ways.

Wendy Parkin, with strong feminist voice, speaks on the neglect of gender and sexuality in organization theory – which connects intimately with emotionality. Some of the driving passions associated with love affairs and sexual liaisons in organizations are problematic in the rational world of work. But, Parkin notes, it is often women who are problematized in these instances – as emotion-mongers; and it is men who dominate the sexual agenda. Parkin goes on to explore the social substrata of gender/sexually linked emotions. As with Hearn's emotionalized zones, she observes the shifts in feelings and emotional expression as she, a woman, moves through different settings which constitute the private and public arenas of her own life. She points to the ambiguities of some settings, such as in residential establishments called 'homes' where there is little that is cosy or homely to help the elderly occupants bear their loss, pain or distress. Or meetings of social work teams where much emotional labour ensures that clients' distresses are objectified and classified, and the social workers' own anxieties are firmly suppressed. The worker's upset, grief, stress or anxiety is channelled into the deeper recesses of the psyche, or, through bureaucratic/managerial device, to the private realm of 'compassionate leave', 'sickness', or 'a holiday'. Many work organizations can best deal with extreme, or uncomfortable, feelings by pathologizing them.

In Chapter 9 Howard Schwartz steps into the sensitive, and shifting, territory of political correctness. Political correctness is the adherence to specific attitudes, behaviour and forms of address which do not deprecate or undermine a particular social group. For Schwartz, political correctness is problematic when it becomes institutionalized, because it can divide people emotionally into very committed, angry, and opposing camps. Schwartz describes the emotional pressure brought to bear on the politically incorrect in universities – like the student who is ostracized for declaring his discomfort about dating someone from another race. If shame and rage shape the values of the university then, suggests Schwartz, something is amiss. As with Gabriel (Chapter 6), the ego ideal figures prominently in Schwartz' analysis. Political correctness reflects the narcissism of the ego ideal because it demands others' unqualified acceptance and love of what one *is* (sex, race, religion, etc.), not what one has achieved. In the university this clashes with the culture of respect based on accomplishment or achievement – the manner by which acclaim is traditionally earned. The inevitable frustration of the ego ideal gives rise to hatred or rage – directed at 'bad' others, or at oneself. Thus, the university is transformed into a battleground between the forces of 'right thought' (the politically correct) and 'wrong thought' (those who refuse to comply).

Part IV Directions

In the final section of the book I offer some thoughts on empiricism, methods and theory for emotion research. We do not need a new theory of emotion for organizations; what is required is the empirical development of specific propositions which arise from existing social constructionist and psychodynamic thought. A primary objective should be an adequate portrayal of the emotionalities of working. Then there are substantive details to explore, such as the way feelings are reworked and culturally incorporated through sharing in everyday work life; the emotional fabric of decision making; the way moral judgements are diluted or re-formed by feelings; the nature and operation of *implicit* feeling rules; the effects of pathologizing certain feelings; and the emotional roots to problems of change. Such research will challenge the way we study organizations and how we engage with our subjects. It opens up different possible discourses through which we can convey the essence of emotion – as it is expressed, felt, managed and controlled.

This book does not present a comprehensive account of organizations and their emotionalities. What is offered, though, is an unfolding picture of some of the passions and perturbations of men and women at work in public and private enterprises, some of whom face extreme circumstances. Overall, we try to give a sense of the way personal feelings vitalize and deflate, become compromised or corrupted, and generally make going to work a pleasurable, dull or mind-numbing experience.

In creating organizations we are, often unwittingly, responding to an emotional agenda which is fundamental to our social existence and personal sense of importance. It is difficult ground to grasp, so much so that our theories of organization have focused their attention elsewhere. Perhaps this can begin to change.

PART I

THE EMOTIONAL ORGANIZATION

1

Organizations as Emotional Arenas

Stephen Fineman

Feelings shape and lubricate social transactions. Feelings contribute to, and reflect, the structure and culture of organizations. Order and control, the very essence of the 'organization' of work, concern what people 'do' with their feelings.[1]

Having said this, the student of work organizations would find little in existing organizational theory to reveal the detail of such phenomena, despite an enormous shift from a strictly rationalistic view of organizations. The Weberian notion of an ideal bureaucracy where efficiency is unsullied by 'love, hatred and all purely personal, irrational and emotional elements' (Gerth and Mills, 1958: 216) has been solidly challenged by the 'human resource' principle.[2] This acknowledges that people with personal needs, goals, skills and preferences will collide, collaborate, resist and comply in ways that make organizational life messier, but much more exciting, than traditional administrative theorists have led us to believe. Our understanding of organizational life has placed human beings and their subjectivity, nearer centre stage (e.g. Argyris, 1964; Likert, 1961; Pfeffer, 1981).

Yet, when we look closely, the people presented are emotionally anorexic. They have 'dissatisfactions' and 'satisfactions', they may be 'alienated' or 'stressed', they will have 'preferences', 'attitudes' and 'interests'. Often these are noted as variables for managerial control. The influential anti-rationalist writings of Peters and Austin (1985) speak boldly and refreshingly of feelings at work, such as of love, empathy, verve, zest and enthusiasm. But their principal interest is in presenting such emotions as 'oughts' for managerial success, as bottled and packaged as the products and services (hamburgers, pizzas, computers, air transport) of the companies they admire. We find little or no mention of how feeling individuals worry, envy, brood, become bored, play, despair, plot, hate, hurt, and so forth. The feelings of *being* organized, *doing* work and organizing are hard to detect. The way feelings are produced, reproduced, camouflaged, communicated and acted upon in organizations are not revealed.

In this chapter I will elaborate the view that organizations can, indeed should, be regarded as emotional arenas. To do so I will explore two complementary streams of thought.

The first concerns the social construction of organization and of emotion. Despite sharing a similar philosophical grounding, these topics tend to be found in separate literatures – the former in organizational theory, the latter in microsociology and social psychology (Albrow, 1992). To a lesser or greater extent, both advocate that reality and its expression is a product of interacting individuals and groups who interpret cultural and subcultural cues as they strive for meaning in their daily activities. This frame fashions organization and emotion in dynamic form.

The second, rather different, perspective is a psychodynamic one. Here, we find explanations of organizational form and practice as a direct reflection of the imported emotional needs of its actors. Early life experiences may influence the way organizational members will organize themselves, and others, and the feelings they display or submerge in their working relationships.

In preparing this chapter my journey crossed many disciplinary boundaries. This is exemplified particularly in the study of emotion which has now been wrested from its traditional guardians – biologically inclined experimental psychologists. Over the past decade anthropologists, social historians, social and psychodynamic psychologists and sociologists have contributed substantially to the thesis that emotions cannot fully be understood outside of their social context. Few of them would dispute that we are physiologically 'wired' for some categories of emotional response; and few would deny that many emotions reflect somatic and endocrinal changes. But, they note, there is so much that is learned, 'social', interpretive, culturally specific, in the meaning and production of emotions, that strictly biological, in-the-body, explanations soon lose their potency.

The Social Construction of Organization – and the Missing Emotion

Social constructionism presumes no natural order to social arrangements. It draws attention to the fragility of many social patterns. Not surprisingly, given the sense of instability and unpredictability that this conveys, we find that texts for managers and primers on organizational theory tend to stress more deterministic approaches to organizational life. They take for granted an organization confronted by an environment of competitors, suppliers, markets and governments (e.g. Hellriegel et al., 1988).

For social constructionists the organizational world is not so easily divided; they question even the boundary between organization and environment (Zucker, 1987). Organizations exist through individual actors. Actors, singly or in groups, can crack the facade of the 'competition', the 'government pressures' or the 'economy' and interpret them, sometimes even re-form them. Organizations are in environments, but environments are also in organizations – an intriguing conundrum. In other words the social structures which influence organizations are human creations but at the same time part of the process of creating new structures and meanings (Aldrich, 1992; Giddens, 1977; Pettigrew, 1979).

Interpretation is a cornerstone to social constructionist thought. It refers to the way actors perceive their life in organizations, how they take into account the constraints of their physical and social environment, and what events *mean* to them. As action – doing work, speaking, collaborating, negotiating – unfolds over time, interpretations and meanings also evolve which coalesce into a system of taken-for-granted rules and structures, and a sense of 'the organization' (Pfeffer, 1982; Fine, 1984). Organizations, so construed, are in-the-head fictions, which are taken *as if* they had material existence. Do they still exist on Sundays when we are not at work? Yes, because their constructed rules say we are not to work on Sundays; rules which are implicitly reinforced when we return to work on Monday (Czarniawski-Joerges, 1992).

Social constructionism has been reflected in various forms in organizational studies but, most relevantly for our present purposes, in the areas of *organizational culture, politics,* and *dramaturgy*. In different ways these link with conceptions of emotion, to be discussed later in the chapter.

Culture

Organizational culture researchers aim to reveal the meaning structures in organizations – the shared, taken-for-granted interpretations that constitute what organizational members value and to which they subscribe (Frost et al., 1985; Turner, 1990). Many investigators will rely on cognitive indicators – how people think about their organizational life, the stories they tell, the language used, the myths which are circulated and cultivated, their descriptions of 'how things are done around here'. Weick (1979) in particular argues that organizations are bodies of thought 'by thinking thinkers' – and a manager's job is to manage the images and symbols. Others will infer cultural themes from observed rituals and ceremonies or work life (Van Maanen and Barley, 1984) – such as during selection, training and apprenticeship.

The cultural approach has been much popularized through the assertion that 'strong' organizational cultures, where a uniform, consensual set of values runs throughout the organization, is a recipe for corporate success (Peters and Waterman, 1982). This application has been challenged by the view that cultural consistency is often illusory. More likely, it has been suggested, are clashing subcultures, or even no fixed consensus at all (Martin and Siehl, 1983; Van Maanen and Kunda, 1989). Aldrich (1992) neatly sums this up by remarking that we have moved from a notion of culture as an area of clarity, a clearing in the jungle of meaninglessness, to one where culture is the jungle itself.

How then do we make meaning in the jungle? Organization and change proceeds through *negotiated order* (Strauss, 1978); continual adjustments to situations through micro-agreements – deals, compromises and tradeoffs. Individuals will continue to perform in this manner because of the fear of uncertainty and chaos that lurks in a unsocially constituted world (Berger and Luckmann, 1966; Clegg, 1983).

Politics
Politics takes us inside negotiated order. It refers to efforts of social actors to mobilize support or oppositions to policies, rules, goals, or means in which they have some stake (Lawler and Bacharach, 1983). In this sense, political actions are *strategic*, thought out, having an internal rationality; they are a means to an end. Through alliances, lobbying, persuading, selectively using information, networking, manipulating rules and image building, organizational members will attempt to create work meanings which reflect their own self-interests. While the form and quality of political activity may vary across different organizations, it is generally regarded as both universal and inevitable (Mintzberg, 1985; Pfeffer, 1978).

Dramaturgy
Dramaturgy is rooted in the social construction of self – the self as defined by others. To express our individuality we have to rely on the language, manners and gestures that are already 'there',

defined by others and in terms of the roles they expect us to play. But exactly what role we are to play, and how, in various organizational encounters, is not always clear (Fontana, 1980). There is risk involved. In the politics of negotiated order there are enemies as well as friends 'out there', and there is the ever present fear that a valued working order may collapse – if we 'get it wrong'. We must therefore attend to how we present ourselves; foster impressions that others will see as normal or acceptable.

The sociology of dramaturgy is detailed in the works of Ervin Goffman (1971) and taken into specific organizational settings by Mangham and Overington (1987) and Giacalone and Rosenfeld (1991). Attention focuses on the performing actor, and how he or she performs on the organizational 'stage'. Skills of concealment, at adopting socially acceptable masks, are paramount.

. . . and Emotion?

The social construction of organizations, as outlined, is intensely subjective and personal. We are informed that work organizations, as well as producing goods and services, are also sites where individuals make meaning for themselves, and have their meanings shaped. The profound emotional basis for this is only hinted at. The anxiety and fear of disorder, of not having a social place, seems to drive people to don masks, seek alliances, accept the prescriptions of others, and generally pick up whatever cultural pieces seem to fit together. Social constructionism does not ask much about what is 'beneath' the actor's actions. Existential and psychodynamic theorists – to which I shall return – have more to contribute here.

In making meaning – constructing reality, negotiating order – there is much stress on the cognitive; the purposeful deliberations of actors. On reading the work of Weick (1969), for example, and other theorists who speak of a cyclical process of applying social 'rules' to sort out organizational disorder, there is a strong sense of the consciously aware actor. But there is other evidence that habits and automatic, taken-for-granted routines are just as likely to operate (Langer, 1978; Abelson, 1976). Moreover, and as significantly, the experience of what *feels* right and comfortable is not addressed. We are left with an impression of organizations as places where there is much head work, but little of the heart – which is ironic in that individuality is so reified. In a short section in Jeffrey Pfeffer's excellent book on organizational theory, he makes this important point, almost as an aside:

The mindlessness and affect and emotion perspectives offer an alternative to the cognitive, quasi-rationalistic perspectives that have come to
dominate the social constructionist approaches to organizational
analysis just as they have been so strongly represented in the dominant,
individual rationality approaches. (1982: 224)

While emotions will play their part in the meaning-making process,
they will also be a constituent of meanings themselves. Thus, one
would expect social activity in organizations to produce as well as
reflect emotions – as most of us know who work in organizations.
Although the early theorizing on social culture embraced emotion
(Parsons, 1951) there is very little in recent constructionist
organizational theory which acknowledges or explains it. We are
left with an image of an actor who thinks a lot, plans, plots and
struggles to look the right part at the right time. But we do not
hear this actor's anger, pain, embarrassment, disaffection or
passion and how such feeling relates to actions – except when it
forms part of the organizational script. So Tom Peters (1989: 39–
41) exhorts managers to be 'enthralled about the product' and to
'laugh, cry and smile' in order to be effective. Similarly, an
executive or trade union official could be expected to reveal anger
or disappointment if he or she has just failed to reach a key agreement. But the simmer and flow of everyday emotions is not
revealed. Given that 'real' stage actors work hard at the nuances
of emotional performance throughout their acts, it is especially
curious that organizational dramaturgy has given emotion so little
attention. A notable exception is the work of Mangham (1986) and
Mangham and Overington (1987) who apply a social role framework to the emotions of organizational executives as they go about
their interpersonal business.

    In sum, social constructionist organization theory offers a bold
picture of actors creating organizational order and being created by
it – but the canvas is painted in monochrome. The emotional
colours are missing.

The Emotional Organizational Actor

A refocusing of the social constructionist lens can bring emotions
into view.

    Most generally, it will be emotional energy that mobilizes
conflict or determines a sense of belonging or solidarity in
organizations (Collins, 1990). Hence the different groupings in
organizations, and their relative hierarchical and status positions,
must be held in place by feelings – such as belonging, respect,

diffidence, fear, awe or love. As social glue, feelings will make or break organizational structures and gatherings. But the organization is also a product of a wider social constituency, a nation, where various ideologies prevail, ideologies which shape norms or scripts on the dos and don'ts of particular feelings (Grossberg, 1986). The rules are moulded and transmitted in our schools, families, ethnic groups and religions; film, television and other media also play their part (Denzin, 1990). Gender rules are especially prevalent, signalling the feelings that women and men ought to have and ought, or ought not, to display (Hochschild, 1975, 1990). The control of sexuality in public is often fine-tuned in organizations, lending the impression that organizations are peopled by asexual characters (Hearn and Parkin, 1987).

Wider social mores are not fixed. The emotional complexion of 'proper' emotions at work will reflect their times. For example, Frederick Winslow Taylor and Elton Mayo were influential in the design of industrial organizations at the turn of the century. They were both from middle-class families where a nineteenth-century form of anger-control was dominant. They were appalled by the level of open anger they witnessed among workers, but failed in their early efforts to curb it (Stearns, 1989). By the 1940s, though, human relations training was well in place, aimed at assisting 'well-controlled' managers and professionals to hear, diffuse and smooth the angers and anxieties of workers. Today the rhetoric of emotional control is still in place, but it has shifted in emphasis: negative feelings are understandable and to be expected – because work can be stressful for anyone. However we all have responsibility for managing our stresses, and training (usually organized by management) can help (Newton et al., 1993). Additionally, continues the theme, some regard for the skilful display of certain emotions is an essential feature of many interpersonal exchanges in organizational life, so the management of impressions should be on the personnel training agenda (Giacalone and Rosenfeld 1991; Wouters, 1992).

Feelings and Work Meanings
The social norms of feeling provide a context for individual experience – where emotions are vital, both as means to ends and as ends in themselves. The experience *of* working can be felt as sense of involvement, goodness, tedium, gloom, excitement or surge, a peripheral awareness and meaning which, at first glance, does not seem to rely on interpretive processes (Sandelands, 1988). Feelings of work are a form of acquaintance-knowledge not

typically found in social science. Perhaps the closest we get are the 'insider' accounts of working from literary researchers such as Studs Terkel (1975) and Gunter Wallraff (1985). Importantly, such a sense *of* working is well contrasted with the surgical manner in which supposed feelings have been commonly tapped – as attitudes *about* work. This is normally a distant appraisal of one's job satisfaction – on investigator-prescribed scales (Locke, 1976).

The phenomenology of working has the appeal of exposing 'pure' emotions. But it is arguable whether even an almost subliminal awareness of working would be possible without the ability to use the discourse of language – in the head (Bedford, 1986). Furthermore, the feeling labels we use, and the logics we apply, will necessarily be cultural or subcultural. We would expect emotion-thoughts to mirror the value and language system to which the individual belongs. The Chinese, for example, will talk far less than Americans about emotions in accounting for their psychological problems – focusing more on the body (Lutz and White, 1986). Subculturally, we might expect emotion accounts from car assembly workers to have different syntax and emphasis from those of, say, consultant physicians – both in public display and in private thought.

Feelings and Organizational Order

There are subtle codes of emotion which connect all interpersonal encounters. Learned facial movements, body postures and voice intonations offer a constant stream of messages about feeling, which makes human interaction possible. Our judgements of these are key to the quality or continuation of our relationships – work or otherwise. They also test our skills at disguising private feeling with a public face (Ekman, 1985), key to many a commercial exchange. Cognitions and emotions intertwine; ideas are laden with feelings, feelings contain ideas. The unique reflexivity of human beings means that they can 'work over', alone or with others, consciously or unconsciously, some of their internal states. They can observe their own experiences, and add meaning to them from a cultural armoury which contains, as already suggested, emotion scripts – stocks of knowledge which provide socially acceptable guidelines for feeling (Rosenberg, 1990; Fischer and Frijda, 1992; Hochschild, 1983). Thus, there is a social consciousness about what feelings to show in what circumstances. This is clear in situations such as funerals, parties, courts of law and road accidents. Indeed, those who transgress the social rules of emotion – laughing joyfully at a fatal road accident, crying with misery at a celebratory dinner party – risk being judged as sick, even mentally ill. The emotional/behavioural expectations in these situations are rooted deeply in the social order – which also defines the psychiatric order (Averill, 1988).

Whether or not we conform to expected emotional performance itself depends on our feelings about failure to conform. The risk of rejection from others can be painful. Crucially, the socially connected emotions of embarrassment, shame and guilt are central to many aspects of organizational order. They are the motivational springs to self-control – without which most organizations could not function (Scheff, 1988; Shott, 1979). They are emotions which relate to how we think others are seeing us, or how our performances are judged. The discomfort of personal embarrassment can itself ensure that most people will do more or less the right (i.e. 'organizational') thing with clients, customers, colleagues and bosses. The force of embarrassment avoidance can sometimes take on an institutionalized quality. For example, deep in the unwritten rules of British party politics is the expectation that a party, especially the ruling one, should not be publicly embarrassed (Flam, 1990). Embarrassment reduces public credibility, so it is to be avoided at all costs. Consequently opposing parties are constantly trying to embarrass one another. At the same time, through a variety of means (being 'economical with the truth', skilful rationalization and internal censorship) they strive to smooth or duck publicly embarrassing moments.

The social-control function of emotions is particularly important in moral conduct. If we cannot feel, or anticipate feeling, love or guilt or shame, moral functioning is crushed. Such feelings are the personal, inner, emotional force that check behaviours that may do harm to others (Callahan, 1988). Some work organizations offer a cultural value system with feeling rules which compromise, conflict with, or even negate, moral principle. People's lives and livelihoods can be devastated by intentional acts to deceive and cheat. Executives have taken actions which they know can destroy parts of the natural environment on which others depend, dupe customers, lose a colleague his or her job, or renege on an agreement. If health-damaging products cannot be sold in one market, they are promoted in another (Smith, 1990). What happens in these cases is that a strong and secretive organizational culture, or a subculture of strong, secretive people, becomes so defined as to render moral considerations irrelevant to organizational survival: 'it's a dog eat dog world' 'if we don't do it, someone else will' go the rationalizations. Such values determine the feelings that are

OK, acceptable, to indulge (Harré, 1986). The pleasure, even joy, of gaining power, position or wealth, whatever, are self-defining and organizationally sufficient. Wariness and fear hold potential dissidents in their place – as is revealed in the experiences of whistleblowers, and the decisive way they are handled by the organizations they 'betray' (Jackall, 1988; Marcia and Near, 1991).

The Drama of Emotions
Dramaturgy in work settings can, in developed form, reveal some provocative insights into the tensions of emotional performance. Hochschild's (1983) seminal work with flight attendants suggests that the wearing of the company-prescribed 'mask' – to smile and enjoy all encounters in the turmoil of flight-deck service – constitutes, for some, real work; it is 'emotional labour'. She found that compliance to organizational feeling rules, as clearly laid out in recruitment and training, can be more than skin deep. Some flight attendants perform the desired emotions in accord with their private feelings; they acquire a naive zealousness about their work, and find it hard to conceptualize themselves and their feelings apart from their job. Others, however, define for themselves an emotional role which is 'all about good acting': they convincingly switch on the smile, laughter and look of concern as and when appropriate – skilled impression management. But over time, and under pressure, the emotional labour takes a toll; the act can go stale, and the private feelings leak through the mask – in irritation, anger or sheer rebellion.

In effect, the airline buys the flight attendant's emotional performance – in a very obvious way. Hochschild emphasizes particularly the personal costs of this sort of business, and the self-estrangement that can occur. Maintaining a mask that is required for no other reason than 'the company demands it and if I don't do it I'm sacked' is a pernicious feature of 'personality market' (Mills, 1956). A shop assistant's smile without warmth, or a waiter's glum or disdainful expression the instant he turns away from his customer, reminds us that emotional performance can be a fragile affair. As hierarchical control and surveillance bears down more firmly on the *detail* of emotional performance, emotional labour becomes more demanding. We can but wonder at the Tayloresque scheme devised by an American supermarket chain which promises gifts ranging from $25 to a new car for clerks 'caught' being friendly to mystery shoppers. Additionally, large bonuses are awarded to regional managers when a high percentage of sales clerks in the stores they manage are observed thanking, greeting and smiling at customers (Rafaeli and Sutton, 1987, 1989).

The negative picture of corporate control over emotions is a seductive one, but somewhat overstated. Stepping into the limelight of the aircraft cabin, restaurant lounge, shop floor or a client's office, can be a performance-game of mutual winners – and fun to play (Wouters, 1989). Like a scene from the *commedia dellárte*, we can witness a play, a tease, of emotional masks between server and served, customer and client. Neither party quite believes the 'genuineness' of feeling that the other is portraying, but each needs the other to play out their role. The pleasure is in pulling off a good performance, doing the 'right things' well. The difficulties occur when work-laboured performances stick; they become situationally unspecific. The 'handle 'em tough' executive carries the mask home. The 'sincere' salesman cannot switch off his patter when with his friends. The limelight never fades; work demeanour and self merge.

Emotional labour has been presented as a feature of routinized, face-to-face service jobs. In such circumstances the bureaucratization of feeling rules is at its most obvious. But many professional workers – counsellors, doctors, nurses, social workers and the like – are also, in effect, paid for their skill in emotion management. They are to look serious, understanding, controlled, cool, empathetic and so forth with their clients or patients. The feeling rules are implicit in their professional 'discipline' (an apt term) – 'rational', 'scientific', 'caring', 'objective'. Benign detachment disguises, and defends against, any private feelings of pain, despair, fear, attraction, revulsion or love; feelings which would otherwise interfere with the professional relationship. There are costs if the mask slips – perhaps a feeling of unease between professional and client or, more seriously, expulsion from the professional community for revealing 'inappropriate' emotions (Fineman, 1985a; Hosking and Fineman, 1990).

There is an intricate order of permissible emotional display attached to different categories of jobs and situations. For instance while a waitress in an informal restaurant may playfully 'flirt' with a male customer, a dentist would not do so with a patient. A nurse may slightly sexualize some of his or her interactions with a patient in order to 'build rapport'; a doctor would be on dangerous ground if he or she did the same. A local shopkeeper might tell a regular customer about some work worries; a counter clerk in a bank would be less likely to reveal such news. And a finance director can get openly angry with peers who challenge his professionalism, while his junior staff have to swallow their pride when he criticizes them (Mangham, 1986). Emotions, as social currency, vary in their rates of exchange and validity. The relative status of participants, their work role, sex, type of job and previous familiarity, all make a difference. This territory has yet to be extensively explored (Rafaeli and Sutton, 1989; Fineman, 1985b).

The Emotion of Culture and Politics

The organization of dramatic appearance, and the intrinsic emotionality of organizational order and meaning, means that organizational culture, in its swirls, sectors or solidity, is of emotion. The more or less consensual structures reflect what people feel, what they ought to feel, and what feelings should be displayed. This can occur gradually as people find ways of organizing themselves, or it can be prescribed by skilful and persuasive 'emotion managers' – such as top executives.

In some of the major attempts at cultural manipulation, corporate leaders have crafted their words and arranged the physical setting to create emotional images intended to capture the imagination of their audience – to move minds *and* hearts. In 1978 Jan Carlzon, president of Sweden's domestic airline, made a stirring speech in a huge aircraft hangar to his assembled staff, an oration which signalled a turning point in his company's fortunes. Standing on a tall ladder he opened, 'This company is not doing well. . .', and closed: 'I have some ideas of my own, and we'll probably be able to use them. But most important, *you* are the ones who must help *me*, not the other way round' (Carlzon, 1987: 11). The evocation of feelings of family, belonging, and everyone sharing the same worry, marked the emotional tone of the company's culture in the early years of its growth. It also proved hard to recover in such, or any other, unifying spirit when the common enemy– oblivion for all – faded.

Other companies specializing in 'strong cultures' mobilize emotion in their own particular fashion. The much-quoted IBM, for example, offers an elaborate social calendar and extensive training to impress the company spirit on its new recruits. So successful has this been that some employees report greater pride in seeing the IBM flag fluttering over corporate offices than when seeing their national flag (Seidenberg, 1975). Home-sales organizations, like Tupperware, create a cosy, warm and cheery party feeling for their domestic sales teams. Regular sales meetings and reward ceremonies have a distinct evangelical tone – to keep spirits high (Peven, 1968; Van Maanen and Kunda, 1989).

The stage-managed events which ritually 'handle' emotion are more than cultural add-ons. They function in important ways to keep alive a managerially inspired vision of collective feeling. Organizations so invigorated are easier to move in a single direction than are those split by affective loyalties. Company breakfasts, dinners, dances, jamborees and intensive weekend 'motivating' sessions, symbolize to participants a special form of company membership. They provide channels for reinforcing company values and bonds, and for orchestrating the desired mood. Significantly, because many of them occur outside normal working hours, they blur the boundaries between work and non-work. Such a process is usually potent enough to ensure that a critical mass of people believe the company's message and feel the company feelings. Those who do not will feign what is required of them, or leave.

Ritualized expression of emotion can also be part of the informal culture of the enterprise. For example, there may be strong (unwritten) obligations on organization members to participate in events such as drinking sessions, parties, pub crawls, sports and shared meals. Apart from their manifest purpose, these are activities where people are expected to share 'real feelings' safely with a receptive audience of peers (Van Maanen, 1986; Van Maanen and Kunda, 1989).

Emotion Space and Place
The emotion architecture of organizational culture contains spaces where different feeling rules may apply; where the public courtesies of emotional control can be relaxed. The school staff room, the restaurant kitchen, the nurses' rest area, the works canteen, the galley on an aircraft, are places where the pupil, customer, patient, manager or passenger safely can be chided, cursed or reviled (Goffman, 1956, 1959; Gabriel, 1988; Hochschild, 1983). Apart from being individually cathartic, the social sharing of normally hidden feelings creates a subculture through which organizational members can emotionally bond, feel at one. They are out of reach – literally or symbolically – of the performance expectations of those who supervise them and those they serve.

Such off-stage settings are not emotion free-ports. They are normally circumscribed by their own implicit emotion rules – determining just how much, and what, colleagues can reveal to one another to keep the organizational order intact. For example, field social workers in a study of stress would regularly seek solace from one another in informal gatherings at work – and they were pleased to do so (Fineman, 1985a). One worker who felt this way confided to the researcher her considerable difficulties in coping with the demands of a particular client, on top of her home pressures. Asked if she had shared the problem with her colleagues, she quickly retorted: 'Oh no! I wouldn't want to be social worked by them' (1985a: 100). Here we have a mark of the frailty of professional identity. Anxiety about personal competence is hidden from colleagues whose support is both desired and feared. Off-stage moans are directed firstly, and safely, outwards – towards the client, customer or 'management'.

Stories and field observations, beloved of organizational cultural researchers, reveal how the emotional balance of organizational life is often checked and nudged through a political weave of symbolic processes, of which the grander rituals are just a part (Martin, 1982; Gabriel, 1991; Van Maanen and Kunda, 1989). For example, the circulation of tales against the boss provides, in lightly coded form, a way of venting anger and frustration. It symbolizes a gathering of power and voice which cannot be achieved within the normal constraints of hierarchy; likewise, the way the secretary or janitor is 'unfortunately just too busy' to deal with a manager's urgent request. Such political processes are strategic renegotiations of 'social place' (Clark, 1990). In small but significant ways, they reverse the conventional expectations of who should be in awe of whom.

The play of, and quest for, status and power can be regarded as key dimensions of organizational social relationships (Kemper, 1978, 1981; Mangham and Overington, 1987), and what cannot be attained by right of formal position can be sought in the micro-politics of daily encounter. Knowing one's status and power is a feeling as much as anything else. Its meaning and motivational force accrue from the anxiety, shame, pride or happiness that follow contests for position and influence. Companies that reward strictly according to hierarchical position are likely to provoke the greatest degree of emotion work in this area. People who cannot obtain the formal positions they desire will create their own distinctions between themselves and their neighbours – to help them look, and feel, better.

The social construction of organizational emotion adds substantial colour to the skeletal constructionist theory of organization. Pushed to its limits, the emotionalized framework suggests that the social constitution of organization simply cannot be without human feeling. The experience of work, and the thinking and doing that establish the politics, leadership and culture of organizations, are directed and shaped by emotional actors and factors.

However, social constructionism rarely asks where the emotions come from. Why are people driven to 'make meaning' through constructing often remarkable organizational forms? Is it, as hinted by Berger and Luckmann (1966), to avoid an existential hell? What is there in the psychosocial history of human beings which suggests that work organizations will, perhaps, inevitably and profoundly reflect the emotional needs, difficulties and conflicts of their members? To address these questions we need to turn to the ideas of psychodynamic theorists.

Beneath the Mask, Beyond the Acts

The responses of organizational actors reflect their biographies and being. Our personal histories are not simply placed on hold, but are activated by, or in, the daily encounters of working. Leadership, group behaviour, interpersonal style, quarrels and manoeuvrings are, in part, manifestations of an invisible psychic world. From this perspective, our 'rational' work on the organization's 'primary task' is a rationalization of our anxieties, fears, hates, sexual desires and yearnings – which normally have no official status in the business of the organization. It is an emotional substructure imported from our experiences in becoming, and continuing to become, a person.

This psychodynamic formulation offers the central notion that our personal past, expectations of the future, and organizational present will all interact. Exactly how is shown, or at least implied, in different ways by different psychodynamic theorists. My purpose here is to summarize some of the key organizational/emotional connections rather than attempt a review of the voluminous literature on psychodynamics.

A Deep Fear of Nothingness?

Social constructionists talk much, and sometimes blithely, of 'meaning' and its making in terms of more or less transient understandings between people – their actions and symbols. Meaning, though, has a different significance when we ask why, in existential terms, organizational actors should do as they do in the first place. Or, to turn it around, where would they be if they did not work and organize?

Some clues to this second question can be found in studies which detail the experiences of the forcibly unemployed. In losing their immediate social framework of meaning – their colleagues, a daily task, a workplace, time-markers to pace the day – some report a devastating, and fearful, loss of identity and reason for living (Fineman, 1983a, 1983b, 1987). The job, the work organization had, de facto, provided that reason for being. Or, as Schwartz (1985) suggests, it had conferred a myth of immortality, a continuity into the future, on people otherwise lost for a sense of where to go in the face of their own mortality. When the organization dies, so do they – at least spiritually, sometimes literally.

Organizations and culture can be regarded as vital self-deceptions to help us avoid the 'truth of own powerlessness and finitude' (Schwartz, 1985: 35). The shadow of desperation that enfolds this process provides the emotional vitality to maintain and protect the organization. In this way we create an illusion of realness and permanence in the face of an unconscious fear that everything is fleeting, fragile and meaningless (Becker, 1973, 1975). Resistance to change in organizations replete, typically, with feelings of fear, anxiety and anger, can be regarded as microcosm of this phenomenon. When our solid, taken-for-granted world is being threatened, we move a step closer to the edge of the abyss. Therefore we need desperately to ensure the survival of the organization and our place in it, in so doing preserving a semblance of personal freedom (Fromm, 1942).

These existential arguments capture emotions which underpin organizations at their most fundamental level. Our ingenious efforts to organize will create purpose out of rootlessness – but chaos, the void, is always just round the corner. To appreciate this point we have to accept a central premise – the unconscious: we do not always know, or want to know, why we do what we do; it is just too painful. We need to look beyond the roles we play in order to appreciate the full context of the emotional meanings we attach to events and activities. The meanings are displaced and distorted products of our elemental fears and anxieties (Whyte, 1979; Wollheim, 1971).

Working with our Past
The details of psychodynamic approaches vary considerably (e.g. Wollheim, 1971; Stevens, 1990; Klein, 1981). However, they share certain common elements: firstly that we are all prisoners of our personal history, and rarely as free in our choices and movements as we would like to believe; secondly, we are unaware of some of our most basic motivations and feelings: they are repressed, pushed from consciousness, because of the anxiety, guilt or shame arising

from the events with which they are associated. Often these are childhood experiences related to sexual identity, or the expression and control of strong feelings towards siblings or parents. Some of these events may have been particularly traumatic – such as the death of a family member, or the break-up of a marriage. Thirdly, repressed feelings do not disappear from the psyche, but are held in check through various mechanisms of defence which disguise the conscious presentation of the feelings. Defence mechanisms include the elaborate justification of one's intentions (rationalization), attributing one's own feelings to others (projection), adopting patterns of behaviour which were comforting in childhood (regression), channelling 'unacceptable' urges into socially acceptable forms (sublimation), and changing a feeling into its opposite (reaction formation).

If this psychic underworld be the case, organizations, will be shaped, in part, by the unconscious concerns of their members. People's actions will have an internal rationality which reflects their own personal, hidden, emotional dramas. Some of these will be in tension with the more formal agenda and structure of the organization; sometimes they will determine it. It is a process that may be observed in both individual and collective action.

Individual Action: the Shadow behind the Leader
Some psychodynamic writers have been particularly intrigued by organizational leaders and managers. To what extent do repressed, 'unresolved' early-life emotional struggles re-emerge in the organizational forms they create? Are work structures and processes a coded representation of the leader's unacknowledged psychic tensions?

The much pored over life of Frederick Taylor is a case in point. I mentioned earlier that Taylor came from a family which prided itself on its emotion control. We learn also, from his biographers (e.g. Kakar, 1970; Morgan, 1986), that Taylor's youthhood was one of obsessive preoccupation with order, control and parsimony, clearly rooted in the puritanical strictures of his family. This extended to his fastidious analyses of his sporting activities, country walks, sleeping position, and even the organization of his dancing. For the latter he would make an advanced list of the unattractive and attractive girls expected to attend, and then compute the time he would spend with each – on a precisely equal basis.

Taylor's highly influential 'scientific' approach to management mirrors his personality. His denial of feelings and concern with the minutiae of efficiency was well translated into the robotizing of the industrial worker, and to the meticulous programming of productive processes and methods. He was aggressive and authoritarian in style – and vilified for it by those he 'managed'. Yet consistently he claimed, with all sincerity, that he had their friendship – a 'reaction formation' *par excellence*. The link between Taylor's psychodynamics and his approach to organizational management is compelling. However, the determinism should not be overstated. He was able to do what he did because the organizations of his day – in an era of slump, high unemployment and poorly organized labour – needed the kind of 'fix' he was offering.

There are parallels with Taylor amongst other corporate leaders, people of puritan or Quaker background. For example, Henry Ford's extraordinary car production line, with its uniformity and control, can be seen as a product of his strongly conservative upbringing. He did not see the jobs he created as alienating – a representation, perhaps, of an emotional world he preferred not to perceive in himself (Jardin, 1970; Zaleznik and Kets de Vries, 1975).

The Taylor/Ford temperament is not unlike analyses of the 'authoritarian personality'. Anchored in Freudian theory, authoritarians are seen to be products of status-anxious parents who enforce a rigid set of rules of discipline on their offspring, based on conventional middle-class values (Adorno et al., 1950). The harsh discipline is apparently sufficient to elicit strong negative feelings, especially fear of failure, hostility and anxiety. When these feelings are repressed they reappear in a cluster of authoritarian traits – which include aggression, submissiveness in the face of higher authority, and strong conservatism.

The unfortunate mark of the authoritarian leader in military organizations has been noted by Dixon (1976). He examined military fiascos from the Crimean War to the Second World War and noted that the errors made were typical of authoritarians (who were most likely to be attracted to military organizations in the first place). These included an inability to admit mistakes, an underestimation of the capability of the enemy, a tendency to discount warning signals and to use perilous frontal assaults in battle. The link between military incompetence and authoritarianism is an intriguing one, as it raises the question of the extent to which essentially undemocratic organizations of all sorts can be driven – to ill, or good – by the emotional complex of their leaders. Probably not as strongly as Dixon claims (Hosking and Morley, 1991), but stories abound about the stifling effect of working for authoritarians (Jackall, 1988). Lee Iacocca, reflecting on his executive career in the Ford Motor Company, tells us:

> Each time Henry [Ford II] walked into a meeting, the atmosphere changed abruptly. He held the power of life and death over all of us. He could suddenly say 'off with his head' – and he often did. Without fair hearing, one more promising career at Ford would bite the dust. (Iacocca, 1986: 103)

Kets de Vries and Miller (1984) pursue the notion that executives will seek to gratify their 'neurotic' needs in the organization. They contend that the predominant culture of the organization and its shared fantasies are configurations inseparable from the psychodynamics of the top executives. In other words, the anxieties and fears expressed by rank-and-file managers, and others, in the daily running of the business are a product of the deep-seated anxieties and fears of the chief executives. Paranoid executives will generate a suspicious, defensive, organization; depressive executives foster pessimism and indecision; staff will feel bewildered by the behaviour of a schizoid executive – and so forth. The emotional tone, so set, will also explain the success or failure of the organization, and Kets de Vries and Miller muster case studies to illustrate their point.

Their thesis is most convincing when applied to small, centrally controlled firms with a dominant chief executive (Miller and Toulouse, 1986). In larger operations the chief executive's personal influence will be less direct; diluted and redefined by factional interests (although the psychodynamic rationale could be applied to each department and its head). We need also to consider that the executive's anxieties can be a response to a work group's inability to cope, rather than a cause of their difficulties. Neurotic behaviour in work teams may be a necessary reaction to bleak working conditions – which offer little hope, or scope, for personal growth or achievement. Finally, history teaches us that a spot, or indeed large measure, of neuroticism is not necessarily the enemy of 'successful' leadership – as in the cases of Napoleon, Stalin or Hitler.

Collective Action

A psychodynamic perspective suggests that 'behind' the work behaviours of interacting individuals and groups are biographically based, often unconscious, emotional subtexts. Because of this, working socially can raise feelings of vulnerability, threat, embarrassment or fear which come to intermingle with, or dominate, task activities. The difficulties may be traced to the tensions and dramas of early family life: the roles and plots, tragedies and despair, are rekindled and re-enacted at work (Weinberg and Mauksch, 1991). For example, Sievers (1992) shows how a group of professional carers working with foster families come to feel the anguish, loss and privation of their own childhood experiences – to the extent that they lose their ability to help the foster families. They handle their feelings defensively, projecting them on to the 'inadequacies' of the foster families. Childhood suffering and suffering at work intermix (Gabriel, 1984).

The politics of organizational life takes on a distinctive dimension. Strategic action towards desired ends can be seen as having an unacknowledged defensive role. Unconscious fears, insecurity and envy may lead to the resentment of rivalry or competition, where formal and informal power is mobilized to shut people out, build protective and collusive coalitions, or block or diminish another's success (Zaleznik, 1970). Other people or groups are defined as having 'the problem' – which essentially resides within one's own group or work relationships (Eagle and Newton, 1981). Wrangling within troubled work groups can intensely focus people's defensive energies where anxiety about the dynamics of the situation can swamp the original task agenda. Managing this anxiety, and self-protection, become, de facto, the tasks in hand. Bion (1959) points to common symptoms of this, such as proclaimed helplessness and idealizing the present, or some future, leader as a saviour. In all of these cases people are constructing realities in response to unconscious concerns, and building those realities into a protective way of working.

Social defences are likely to be part and parcel of the life, or death, force of any organization. Key corporate decisions can be made in ways such that people avoid facing one another and confronting their mutual fears. The boss takes unilateral action on resource allocation rather than face the anxieties of all involved; the policy group decides to divide the annual budget by departmental size – rather than voice their feelings of envy or anger to one another. If social defences prevail, the organization can resemble a mini-society where personal risk is minimized, and creativity is near zero. The extreme is a form of corporate madness, where people are motivated to ignore warning signs that something is going wrong (De Board, 1978).

Hirschhorn (1988) develops this theme in suggesting that the complex post-industrial technologies are increasingly more demanding and less forgiving. In other words, their failure can have dramatic, if not catastrophic, consequences. As the risks of working grow, so does anxiety – and so do social defences. For example, the 'impossible' has happened when a nuclear power reactor has failed, or an aircraft or space rocket has dropped from the skies. The important point is that in some instances there grows a corporate belief in the invulnerability of the machine, based on past successes and feelings of pride and arrogance. This helps to shelter organizational members from the anxiety that something terrible *could* go wrong, while also increasing that very probability. It has been proposed that the fatal explosion of the American space shuttle *Challenger* was far from a bit of bad luck (Hirschhorn, 1988; Schwartz, 1988). The stresses of confronting the full technical and political realities of the launch were simply too great, so wishful thinking (a transformation of meaning) obscured the warning signs that the shuttle's booster seals might fail: a post-industrial manifestation of the sin of pride.

There is a fine line between social defences that erode the viability of the organization to produce whatever it is supposed to produce, and those which help people function and survive in circumstances that regularly touch fundamental anxieties. Hospitals are a case in point. Following Melanie Klein's (1959) work on ego defences, Menzies-Lythe (1988) suggests that a complex of early-life anxieties concerning death and sexuality are triggered in the nurse's daily work:

> Nurses are confronted with the threat and the reality of suffering and death as few lay people are. Their work involves carrying out tasks which, by ordinary standards, are distasteful, disgusting and frightening. Intimate physical contact with patients arouses strong libidinal and erotic wishes and impulses which may be difficult to control. The work situation arouses very strong and mixed feelings in the nurse: pity, compassion and love; guilt and anxiety; hatred and resentment of patients who arouse these strong feelings; envy of the care given to the patient. (Menzies-Lythe, 1988: 46)

It is these powerful emotions which determine, ultimately, the culture and shape of the organization of nursing work, she argues, limited by the technology of medical care and the nature of the primary task. Nurses create a social defence system in which they can practise, relatively protected from the anxieties which threaten to overwhelm them. These include (1) keeping the nurse and patient apart as far as possible: the core of anxiety lies in the close relationship with the patient, so patient rotas, and specific tasks carried out on a large number of patients, help to reduce familiarity; (2) depersonalization – patients are known by their bed number or disease type; 'the pneumonia in bed 15'; (3) a rhetoric of coping and detachment – 'a good nurse doesn't get too involved and doesn't mind moving'; (4) checks and counterchecks – to dissipate the burden of anxiety about a final decision on a patient; and (5) rituals – precise task-lists, regularly repeated, which induce thoughtlessness and help nurses avoid anxiety. Nurses would regularly wake patients to give them drugs, even when it was better for patient care to let them sleep.

Menzies-Lythe's original study was conducted in 1959. It can be read as an unusual account of the role of bureaucracy in the containment of anxiety. The tidiness and routinization of the bureaucratic process helps people to depersonalize anxieties triggered in relations with patients (as well as with colleagues and external agencies). There is little reason to believe that the psychodynamics of nursing work have changed some thirty years on, and many of the routines and rituals described by Menzies-Lythe are still in place. However, the tight discipline and formality has relaxed, and in its place are new drugs and more sophisticated technologies – which widen the separation between nurse and patient. The new technology offers an additional mechanism by which anxiety can be contained – and also created:

> A doctor-patient said recently how much it had disturbed her that whenever the nurses came to see her they looked first at her monitor, and only then at her. (Markillie, 1990: 326)

In Conclusion

Social constructionism and psychodynamic theory each has a key role to play in the humanizing and emotionalizing of our understanding of organizational behaviour. Organizational theory needs them both, but in ways which are currently ignored or underworked. The interpretive frame shows how emotions both determine, and are determined by, organizational order; strictly cognitive categories are insufficient. Traditional organizational concepts such as culture, politics and roles are infused with issues of feeling, as is the phenomenology of working. Psychodynamic theory, while more restricted in the range of emotions it tackles, moves in where sociology stops. We get a picture of the fearful roots of the meaning-making process; we see organizations as key sites where early anxieties are replayed; and we see the very structures of organizations as reflections of the apprehensions and frustrations of their members. Organizations are emotional arenas.

Notes

1. The terms 'feeling' and 'emotion' are very often used interchangeably in the literature, so I have not attempted to draw a strict distinction between them. For example, Frijda et al. (1991), Van Maanen and Kunda (1989), and Hochschild (1983) speak of feelings as emotional states, of a self-referential sort. They signal something about one's position, performance or relationships in the world. Some writers present feelings as essentially private sensations which become 'emotions' when enacted in social situations – according to cultural rules of definition and display (Sandelands, 1988; Rosenberg, 1990). In the psychodynamic literature feelings dominate the discourse, especially feelings of anxiety and fear (Freud, 1953; Hirschhorn, 1988).
2. Max Weber, however, acknowledged the important role of emotionality in the functioning of some types of organization (Albrow, 1992).

References

Abelson, R. P. (1976) 'Script processing in attitude formation and decision making', in J. S. Carroll and J. W. Payne (eds), *Cognition and Social Behavior*. Hillsdale, NJ: Lawrence Erlbaum.

Adorno, T. W., Frenkel-Brunswick, E., Levinson, D. J. and Sanford, R. N. (1950) *The Authoritarian Personality*. New York: W. W. Norton.

Albrow, M. (1992) 'Sine ira studio – or do organizations have feelings?', *Organization Studies*, 13(3): 313–29.

Aldrich, H. E. (1992) 'Incommensurable paradigms? Vital signs from three perspectives', in M. Reed and M. Hughes (eds), *Rethinking Organization*. London: Sage.

Argyris, C. (1964) *Integrating the Individual and the Organization*. New York: Wiley.

Averill, J. R. (1988) 'Disorders of emotion', *Journal of Social and Clinical Psychology*, 3(4): 247–68.

Becker, E. (1973) *The Denial of Death*. New York: Free Press.

Becker, E. (1975) *Escape from Evil*. New York: Free Press.

Bedford, E. (1986) 'Emotions, and statements about them', in R. Harré and R. Finlay Jones (eds),*The Social Construction of Emotions*. Oxford: Blackwell.

Berger, P. and Luckmann, T. (1966) *The Social Construction of Reality*. New York: Doubleday.

Bion, W. R. (1959) *Experiences in Groups*. New York: Basic Books.

Callahan, E. (1988) 'The role of emotion in ethical decision making', *Hastings Center Report*, June/July: 9–14.

Carlzon, J. (1987) *Moments of Truth*. New York: Harper & Row.

Clark, C. (1990) 'Emotions and micropolitics in everyday life: some patterns and paradoxes of "place"', in T. D. Kemper (ed.), *Research Agendas in the Sociology of Emotions*. Albany: State University of New York Press.

Clegg, S. (1983) 'Phenomenology and formal organizations: a critique', *Research in the Sociology of Organizations*, 2: 109–52.

Collins, R. (1990) 'Stratification, emotional energy, and the transient emotions', in

T. D. Kemper (ed.), *Research Agendas in the Sociology of Emotions*. Albany: State University of New York Press.

Czarniawski-Joerges, B. (1992) *Exploring Complex Organizations*. London: Sage.

De Board, R. (1978) *The Psychoanalysis of Organisations: A Psychoanalytic Approach to Behaviour of Groups and Organisations*. London: Tavistock.

Denzin, N. (1990) 'On understanding emotion: the interpretive–cultural agenda', in T. D. Kemper (ed.), *Research Agendas in the Sociology of Emotions*. Albany: State University of New York Press.

Dixon, N. F. (1976) *On the Psychology of Military Incompetence*. London: Jonathan Cape.

Eagle, J. and Newton, P. M. (1981) 'Scapegoating in small groups', *Human Relations*, 34: 283–301.

Ekman, P. (1985) *Telling Lies*. New York: W. W. Norton.

Fine, G. (1984) 'Negotiated order and organizational cultures', *Annual Review of Sociology*, 10: 239–62.

Fineman, S. (1983a) *White Collar Unemployment*. Chichester: Wiley.

Fineman, S. (1983b) 'Work meanings, non-work, and the taken-for-granted', *Journal of Management Studies*, 20: 143–57.

Fineman, S. (1985a) *Social Work Stress and Intervention*. Aldershot: Gower.

Fineman, S. (1985b) 'The skills of getting by', in A. Strati (ed.), *The Symbolics of Skill*. Trento: Dipartimento di Politca Sociale.

Fineman, S. (1987) *Unemployment: Personal and Social Consequences*. London: Tavistock.

Fischer, A. H. and Frijda, N. H. (1992) 'The emotion process as a whole: a response to Greenwood', *New Ideas in Psychology*, 10(1): 23–7.

Flam, H. (1990) 'Emotional "man"': II. Corporate actors as emotion-motivated emotion managers', *International Sociology*, 5(2): 225–34.

Fontana, A. (1980) 'The mask and beyond: the enigmatic sociology of Erving Goffman', in J. Douglas (ed.), *The Sociologies of Everyday Life*. Boston: Allyn & Bacon.

Freud, S. (1953) *The Complete Works of Sigmund Freud* (tr. and ed. James Strachey). London: Hogarth Press.

Frijda, N., Mesquita, B., Sonnemans, J. and Van Goosen, S. (1991) 'The duration of affective phenomena, or Emotions, sentiments and passions', in K. T. Strongman (ed.), *International Review of Studies on Emotion*. Vol. I. New York: Wiley.

Fromm, E. (1942) *Escape from Freedom*. New York: Farrar & Rinehard.

Frost, P. J., Moore, L. F., Louis, M. R., Lundberg, C. C. and Martin, J. (1985) *Organizational Culture*. Beverly Hills: Sage.

Gabriel, Y. (1984) 'A psychoanalytic contribution to the sociology of suffering', *International Review of Psycho-Analysis*, 11: 467–80.

Gabriel, Y. (1988) *Working Lives in Catering*. London: Routledge.

Gabriel, Y. (1991) 'Turning facts into stories and stories into facts: a hermeneutic exploration of organizational folklore', *Human Relations*, 44(8): 857–75.

Gerth, H. H. and Mills, C. W. (1958) *From Max Weber: Essays in Sociology*. New York: Oxford University Press.

Giacalone, R. A. and Rosenfeld, P. R. (1991) *Applied Impression Management*. Newbury Park: Sage.

Giddens, A. (1977) *Studies in Social and Political Theory*. New York: Basic Books.

Goffman, E. (1956) 'Embarrassment and social organization', *American Journal of Sociology*, 62: 264–71.

Goffman, E. (1959) *The Presentation of Self in Everyday Life*. New York: Double-day/Anchor.

Goffman, E. (1971) *Relations in Public*. New York: Basic Books.

Grossberg, L. (1986) 'History, politics and postmodernism: Stuart Hall and cultural studies', *Journal of Communication Inquiry*, 10: 61–77.

Harré, R (1986) 'The social construction of emotions', in R. Harré and R. Finlay Jones, *The Social Construction of Emotions*. Oxford: Blackwell.

Hearn, J. and Parkin, P. W. (1987) *'Sex' at Work: The Power and Paradox of Organisation Sexuality*. Brighton: Wheatsheaf.

Hellriegel, D., Slocum, J. W. and Woodman, R. W. (1988) *Organizational Behavior*. St Paul: West Publishing Company.

Hirschhorn, L. (1988) *The Workplace Within: Psychodynamics of Organizational Life*. Cambridge, MA: MIT Press.

Hochschild, A. R. (1975) 'The sociology of feelings and emotions: selected possibilities', in M. Millman and R. Kanter (eds), *Another Voice*. Garden City, NY: Anchor.

Hochschild, A. R. (1983) *The Managed Heart*. Berkeley: University of California Press.

Hochschild, A. R. (1990) 'Ideology and emotion management: a perspective and path for future research', in T. D. Kemper (ed.), *Research Agendas in the Sociology of Emotions*. Albany: State University of New York Press.

Hosking, D. and Fineman, S. (1990) 'Organizing processes', *Journal of Management Studies*, 27(6): 583–604.

Hosking, D. and Morley, I. E. (1991) *A Social Psychology of Organizing*. Hemel Hempstead: Harvester Wheatsheaf.

Iacocca, L. (1986) *Iacocca*. Toronto: Bantam.

Jackall, R. (1988) *Moral Mazes: The World of Corporate Managers*. New York: Oxford University Press.

Jardin, A. (1970) *The First Henry Ford: A Study of Personality and Business Leadership*. Cambridge, MA: MIT Press.

Kakar, S. (1970) *Frederick Taylor: A Study of Personality and Innovation*. Cambridge, MA: MIT Press.

Kemper, T. D. (1978) 'Toward a sociology of emotions: some problems and some solutions', *The American Sociologist*, 13 (Feb.): 30–41.

Kemper, T. D. (1981) 'Social constructionist and positivist approaches to the sociology of emotions', *American Journal of Sociology*, 87: 336–62.

Kets de Vries, M. F. R. and Miller, D. (1984) *The Neurotic Organization*. San Francisco: Jossey-Bass.

Klein, M. (1959) 'Our adult world and its roots in infancy', *Human Relations*, 12: 291–303.

Klein, M. (1981) *Love, Guilt and Reparation and Other Works*. London: Hogarth Press.

Langer, E. J. (1978) 'Rethinking the role of thought in social interaction', in J. Harvey, W. Ickes and R. Kidd (eds), *New Directions in Attribution Research*. Hillsdale, NJ: Lawrence Erlbaum.

Lawler, E. J. and Bacharach, S. B. (1983) 'Political action and alignments in sociology', *Research in the Sociology of Organizations*, 2: 83–107.

Likert, R. (1961) *New Patterns of Management*. New York: McGraw-Hill.

Locke, E. A. (1976) 'Job Satisfaction', in M. Dunnette (ed.), *Handbook of Industrial and Organizational Psychology*. Chicago: Rand McNally.

Lutz, C. and White, G. (1986) 'The anthropology of emotions', *Annual Review of Anthropology*, 15: 405–36.

Mangham I. L. (1986) *Power and Performance in Organizations*. Oxford: Blackwell.

Mangham, I. L. and Overington, M. A. (1987) *Organizations as Theatre*. Chichester: Wiley.

Marcia, P. M. and Near, J. P. (1991) 'Whistleblowing as an organizational process', *Research in the Sociology of Organizations*, 9: 139–200.

Markillie, R. (1990) 'Review of I. Menzies-Lythe, *Containing Anxiety in Institutions. Selected Essays*' (London: Free Association Books, 1988), *Journal of Management Studies* 27(2): 235–7.

Martin, J. (1982) 'Stories and scripts in organizational settings', in A. Hastorf and I. Isen (eds), *Cognitive Social Psychology*. New York: Elsevier-North Holland.

Martin, J. and Siehl, C. (1983) 'Organizational culture and counterculture', *Organizational Dynamics*, 12: 52–64.

Menzies-Lythe, I. (1988) *Containing Anxiety in Institutions. Selected Essays*. London: Free Association Books.

Miller, D. and Toulouse, J. M. (1986) 'Chief executive personality and corporate strategy and structure in small firms', *Management Science*, 32: 1389–409.

Mills, C. W. (1956) *White Collar*. New York: Oxford University Press.

Mintzberg, H. (1985) 'The organization as a political arena', *Journal of Management Studies*, 22: 133–54.

Morgan, G. (1986) *Images of Organization*. Beverly Hills: Sage.

Newton, T., Handy, J. and Fineman, S. (1993) *Stress at Work: Alternative Perspectives*. London: Sage.

Parsons, T. (1951) *The Social System*. Glencoe, IL: Free Press.

Peters, T. J. (1989) *Leadership and Emotion*. California: TPG Communications.

Peters, T. and Austin, N. (1985) *A Passion for Excellence*. New York: Random House.

Peters, T. J. and Waterman, R. H. (1982) *In Search of Excellence*. New York: Harper & Row.

Pettigrew, A. (1979) 'On studying organizational cultures', *Administrative Science Quarterly*, 24(4): 570–81.

Peven, D. (1968) 'The use of religious revival techniques to indoctrinate personnel', *Sociological Quarterly*, 9(1): 97–106.

Pfeffer, J. (1978) 'The micropolitics of organizations', in M. W. Meyer and Associates (eds), *Environments and Organizations*. San Francisco: Jossey-Bass.

Pfeffer, J. (1981) *Power in Organizations*. Marshfield, MA: Pitman.

Pfeffer, J. (1982) *Organizations and Organization Theory*. Marshfield, MA: Pitman.

Rafaeli, A. and Sutton, R. I. (1987) 'Expression of emotion as part of the work role', *Academy of Management Review*, 12(1): 23–37.

Rafaeli, A. and Sutton, R. I. (1989) 'The expression of emotion in organizational life', *Research in Organizational Behavior*, 11: 1–42.

Rosenberg, M. (1990) 'Reflexivity and emotions', *Social Psychology Quarterly*, 53(1): 3–12.

Sandelands, L. E. (1988) 'The concept of work feeling', *Journal for the Theory of Social Behavior*, 18(4): 437–57.

Scheff, T. J. (1988) 'Shame and conformity: the deference-emotion system', *American Sociological Review*, 53: 395–406.

Schwartz, H. (1985) 'The usefulness of myth and the myth of usefulness: a dilemma for the applied organizational scientist', *Journal of Management*, 11(1): 31–42.

Schwartz, H. (1988) 'The symbol of the space shuttle and the degeneration of the American dream', *Journal of Organizational Change Management*, 1(2): 5–20.

Seidenberg, R. (1975) *Corporate Wives – Corporate Casualties?* New York: Double-day/Anchor.

Shott, S. (1979) 'Emotion and social life: a symbolic interactionist analysis', *American Journal of Sociology*, 84(6): 1317–35.

Sievers, B. (1992) 'Characters in search of theatre'. Paper presented at SCOS Conference, 'Organization and Theatre', Lancaster University, 30 June–3 July.

Smith, N. C. (1990) *Morality and the Market*. London: Routledge.

Stearns, P. N. (1989) 'Suppressing unpleasant emotions: the development of a twentieth-century American', in A. E. Barnes and P. N. Stearns (eds), *Social History and Issues in Human Consciousness*. New York and London: New York University Press.

Stevens, A. (1990) *On Jung*. London: Routledge.

Strauss, A. (1978) *Negotiations*. San Francisco: Jossey-Bass.

Terkel, S. (1975) *Working*. Harmondsworth: Penguin.

Turner, B. (ed.) (1990) *Organizational Symbolism*. Berlin: De Gruyter.

Van Maanen, J. (1986) 'Power in the bottle', in S. Srivasta (ed.), *Executive Power*. San Francisco: Jossey-Bass.

Van Maanen, J. and Barley, S. R. (1984) 'Occupational communities', *Research in Organizational Behavior*. 6: 287–365.

Van Maanen, J. and Kunda, G. (1989) '"Real feelings": emotional expression and organizational culture', *Research in Organizational Behavior*, 11: 43–103.

Wallraff, G. (1985) *Lowest of the Low*. London: Methuen.

Weick, K. E. (1969) *The Social Psychology of Organizing*. Reading, MA: Addison-Wesley.

Weick, K. E. (1979) *The Social Psychology of Organizing*. Reading, MA: Addison-Wesley.

Weinberg, R. B. and Mauksch, L. B. (1991) 'Examining family-of-origin influences in life at work', *Journal of Marital and Family Therapy*, 17: 233–42.

Whyte, L. L. (1979) *The Unconscious before Freud*. London: Freedman.

Wollheim, R. (1971) *Freud*. Glasgow: Fontana.

Wouters, C. (1989) 'The sociology of emotions and flight attendants: Hochschild's "Managed Heart"', *Theory, Culture & Society*, 6(1): 95–123.

Wouters, C. (1991) 'On status competition and emotion management', *Journal of Social History*, 24(4): 699–717.

Wouters, C. (1992) 'On status competition and emotion management: the study of emotions as a new field', *Theory, Culture & Society*, 9:229–52.

Zaleznik, A. (1970) 'Power and politics in organizational life', *Harvard Business Review*, 48: 47–60.

Zaleznik, A. and Kets de Vries, M. (1975) *Power and the Corporate Mind*. Boston: Houghton Mifflin.

Zucker, L. G. (1987) 'Institutional theories of organization', *Annual Review of Sociology*, 13: 443–64.

2

Organizations, Emotion and the Myth of Rationality

Linda L. Putnam and Dennis K. Mumby

One construct which has only recently entered the research on culture and organization is the study of emotions. Since emotions are embodied in the language and symbols of organizational members, it is surprising that cultural studies in organizations have not focused more directly on this important phenomenon. This reticence to undertake studies of emotion in organizations may stem from the belief that emotion is a physiological construct, relevant only to those who are interested in either the cognitive or the psychophysical states of individuals. Hence people often think that the phenomenon of emotion is not accessible or relevant to studies of social collectives.

In addition to treating emotion as a physiological state, people regard emotion as a value-laden concept which is often treated as 'inappropriate' for organizational life. In particular, emotional reactions are often seen as 'disruptive', 'illogical', 'biased' and 'weak'. Emotion, then, becomes a deviation from what is seen as sensible or intelligent (Lutz, 1988: 62). Emotion is also linked to the expressive arenas of life, not to the instrumental goal orientation that drives organizations.

This chapter critiques the prevailing view of emotion in organizations by showing how it is rooted in a 'myth of rationality'. Adopting a feminist approach, the chapter sets forth a way to position emotion as central to the process of organizing and as integral to participation in organizational life. Emotion, then, is not simply an adjunct to work; rather, it is the process through which members constitute their work environment by negotiating a shared reality.

To this end, we examine the current literature on the role of emotional labour in organizations. To ascertain why emotional labour in organizations seems inevitable and immutable, we show how it is tied to the myth of rationality that pervades Western culture and underlies bureaucratic structures. Then we employ feminist theory to critique the use of emotional labour in organizations and to show how it marginalizes the personal and relational nature of emotions. We illustrate this critique through two case examples that demonstrate how simultaneously defining and negating emotions creates a contradiction that exposes the myth of rationality and makes emotional labour problematic.

Finally we provide alternatives that treat emotion as central to organizational experiences. We show how these alternatives might function in an organization through a case study in which emotions are treated as central to the participatory process of organizational members.

Emotional Labour in Organizations

Inspired by Hochschild's (1979, 1983) writings on the 'managed heart', recent research in organizational behaviour centres on the way individuals change or manage their emotions to make them appropriate or consistent with a situation, a role, or an expected job function. *Emotional labour* is the term used to typify the way roles and tasks exert overt and covert control over emotional displays. Through recruitment, selection, socialization and performance evaluations, organizations develop a social reality in which feelings become a commodity for achieving instrumental goals (Mumby and Putnam, 1992; Van Maanen and Kunda, 1989).

Research on emotions in organizations has centred on norms or display rules for expressing emotions (Rafaeli and Sutton, 1987, 1989, 1990), ways employees deviate from prescribed norms or roles (Sutton, 1991), links between expressed and felt emotions (Rafaeli and Sutton, 1989, 1990; Waldron and Krone, 1991), the use of contrasting emotions to induce compliance (Rafaeli and Sutton, 1991), and the role of targets and interaction encounters in shaping emotional displays (Rafaeli, 1989; Rafaeli and Sutton, 1990; Waldron and Krone, 1991). The evolution of research on emotion in organizations reveals a shift from studying normative practices to uncovering differences in employee use of emotional displays (Rafaeli and Sutton, 1990). That is, initial work on emotion in organizations centred on display rules for specific occupational roles. More recent research recognizes that display rules extend beyond occupational roles. Target, setting and interaction patterns contribute to both the development and the enforcement of display rules.

Although this research reveals that contextual factors account for differences in emotional displays, organizations continue to manage hearts by calling on employees to exhibit forced niceness, phoney smiles and suppressed anger. For example, Hochschild (1979) notes how the expressed feelings of flight attendants are set by management to evoke passenger contentment. Employee training manuals urge clerks to express concern for customers, to make their voices warm and friendly, and to prevent emotional leakage of frustration and impatience (Sutton and Rafaeli, 1988).

Management even prescribes combinations of positive and negative feelings to help police officers and debt collectors adjust social interaction to organizational aims (Rafaeli and Sutton, 1991). Specifically, training sessions show debt collectors how to adapt their display rules to the emotional reactions of debtors. Through the use of scenarios and role-playing sessions, debt collectors are taught to express warmth with anxious debtors, neutrality or calmness with angry respondents, and urgency and disapproval with reluctant customers. These rules surface in company training sessions, in informal socialization experiences, and even in performance evaluations to get employees to obtain specific dollar amounts for payment. New collectors also rely on experienced employees to learn which emotions should be expressed. In fact, both co-workers and supervisors reinforce the norms and urge collectors to 'talk like you mean business with your clients'. Finally, raises, promotions, cash prizes, criticisms, warnings, demotions and firings are used to sanction those who deviate from appropriate emotional displays. Managers may also use a spy-and-tell computer system to monitor collectors and to provide them with written feedback (Sutton, 1991).

Emotional labour is experienced most strongly when employees are asked to express emotions that contradict their inner feelings. Managers also exert extra effort to enforce organizational norms when expressed emotions clash with inner feelings. These inner feelings or intrapsychic states are felt emotions that differ from the verbal and nonverbal cues that employees exhibit (Sutton and Rafaeli, 1988; Waldron and Krone, 1991). Specifically, the prescribed norm of expressing irritation or anger with friendly debtors goes against the inner feelings of warmth and kindness to affable people. In contrast, rude, loud and insulting debtors generate anger as a felt emotion, but collectors are required to express calm and neutral tones to get debtors to focus attention on payment (Sutton, 1991). Employees typically cope with emotional dissonance by pounding on desks, using obscene gestures or joking, and even hanging up and calling back later. Experienced debt collectors rely on detachment, cognitive appraisals, and co-worker social support to reduce the dissonance between their inner feelings and the prescribed norms for emotional displays.

The amount of stress employees experience through the gap between emotions felt and feigned differs across organizations and among employees. In studies of police detectives (Stenross and Kleinman, 1989) and Disney employees (Van Maanen and Kunda, 1989), workers rarely complain of emotional dissonance. Rafaeli and Sutton (1987) contend that disagreeing with the norm for expressed emotion creates more dissonance than does faking an acceptable emotional display. Significance of the felt emotion and status of the target also influence the amount of stress employees feel in complying with organizational norms.

Individuals, then, differ in the stress they feel when expressed emotions differ from felt ones. Despite varied reactions, the prevalence of display rules and the existence of normative practices for reducing emotional stress constitute a form of corporate control aimed at welding individuals to managerial interests. Employees rarely question whether the display rules are necessary and who reaps the benefits of enforcing emotional displays. Thus, emotional expressions become 'objectified as part of an organizational system that members treat as inevitable and immutable' (Mumby and Putnam, 1992: 473).

Dualism and Rationality as Sources of Emotional Labour

Two dominant traditions in organizational life contribute to the presumption that emotional labour is immutable and inevitable. The first tradition stems from the dualities that surround the use of emotion in Western culture. These dualities are evident in the language we use, our system of morality, and our beliefs about knowledge. Our perceptions and experiences are typically black or white, good or bad, happy or sad. Our language draws from the use of spatial metaphors that depict experiences as up or down, in or out, and front or back (Lakoff and Johnson, 1980). In Western society, rational is up and emotional is down. The dualities are evident in such phrases as 'The discussion fell to the emotional level, but I raised it back up to the rational plane' (Lakoff & Johnson, 1980: 17). Rooted in this system of dualities, rationality surfaces as positive while emotionality is viewed as negative. The prevalence of these dualities contributes to treating emotion as a form of labour or as a tool for exerting influence in organizational settings. In organizations, emotions are consistently devalued and marginalized while rationality is privileged as an ideal for effective organizational life. Moreover, the devaluing of emotions and the elevating of rationality results in a particular type of moral order, one that reflects the politics of social interaction rather than a universal norm for behaviour.

The second dominant tradition that contributes to the presumption that emotional labour is inevitable is the myth of rationality in Western culture. This system begins with a set of values and beliefs which split thought from emotion and align certain concepts with rationality and others with emotionality. Specifically, reason/passion, cognition/affect and thinking/feeling are bipolar opposites that set up descriptors for rationality and emotionality. Reason, cognition and thinking become processes linked to rationality while passion, affect, and feeling become indices of emotionality. Moreover, irrationality, a concept that connotes the absence of reason and understanding, is often treated as the opposite of rationality. A rational person is calm and deliberate. In organizations, rationality is revered while emotions are illegitimate or inappropriate.

Other dichotomies are linked to the system of values that bifurcates rationality and emotionality. Rationality is typically seen as objective, orderly, and mental while emotionality reflects the subjective, chaotic, and bodily drives. Feelings are physical and chaotic as evident in such phrases as 'her stomach was tied in knots' and 'he's falling apart'. Data acquired experientially or through personal interest are suspect and potentially distorted. This system of dualities also treats certain concepts as masculine and others as feminine. Hence, rationality, cognition and order are descriptors of masculinity while emotionality, affect and chaos depict the feminine (Lutz, 1988; Mumby and Putnam, 1992). Thus, rationality evokes a positive, masculine image while emotionality is linked to a negative, feminine world view.

Even though Western culture privileges rationality, emotions serve essential relational needs. Emotions ignite creativity and form the foundation for moral and spiritual development (D'Andrade, 1987). Emotions contribute to the development of community, commitment, and collective morality. These values suggest that an inability to experience any emotion is negative: an unemotional person is alienated and amoral. Hence, a contradiction exists in devaluing emotions. On the one hand, emotions are subjective, chaotic and weak, but on the other hand, they ignite creative energy and involvement. To understand the nature of this incongruity, we need to explore the links between rationality and bureaucracy.

Bureaucracy and Rationality as Sources of Emotional Labour

Bureaucracy is intertwined with the system of dualisms that privileges rationality and marginalizes emotional experience. That is, emotion is normally juxtaposed against rationality as a marginal mode of experience to be minimized in routine organizational life. Bureaucracy perpetuates this emphasis on rationality through its aim to undermine authority based on tradition, birthright or social status. The rational character of bureaucracy frees it from the arbitrary rule of monarchies by positioning authority in the chain of command and standard operating procedures. Positions within the hierarchy are determined by technical competence rather than by family ties or friendship. Rules and regulations are recorded in written code and are treated as objective and impersonal. Bureaucracy also becomes a form of technical authority by constituting the knowledge base for decisions, by serving as a vehicle for task accomplishment, and by determining what is productive and efficient.

Rationality, however, not only governs organizational tasks, but also encroaches into the private realm of emotion and intimacy. Emotional labour typifies this encroachment. As Ferguson (1984) notes in recounting Hochschild's (1979) example of a flight attendant:

> The flight attendant's smile is like her makeup; it is on her, not of her. The rules about how to feel and how to express feelings are set by management, with the goals of producing passenger contentment. . . Emotional laborers are required to take the arts of emotional management and control that characterize the intimate relations of family and friends . . . and package them according to the feeling rules laid down by the organization. (Ferguson, 1984: 53)

Even though individuals ultimately manage their own emotions, rationality appropriates this private sphere into the public domain. Bureaucracy perpetuates the belief that rationality and the control of emotions are not only inseparable but also necessary for effective organizational life.

Bureaucratic rationality also constructs a particular gender relationship, one that favours patriarchal forms and reproduces organizational power along gender lines. To explore the consequences of emotional control, we employ feminist theory to critique bureaucracy and emotional labour.

**Feminist Theory, Postmodernism and Organizational
Studies**

Researchers rarely question how organizations would look if they
were not shaped by bureaucracy. Feminist theory provides possibilities for reconceptualizing the nature of organizations. This
approach treats gender as a critical factor that shapes the routine
practices of contemporary organizations. Thus, feminist theorizing
is not simply the study of equal opportunities for women or the
adding of gender as a variable to extant research. Nor does this
critique centre on sex differences in rationality or emotionality.

In this chapter we adopt a particular type of feminist approach,
postmodern feminism, to critique the role of bureaucracy and
emotional labour in organizations. This critique centres on the way
bureaucracy elevates rational forms of knowing while simultaneously marginalizing emotional and intuitive experiences. Postmodern feminism treats gender as a form of power-knowledge
relationship that underlies bureaucratic rationality. Gender is
conceptualized as a culturally constituted category or as the
product of social and institutional relations. Treating the individual
as a product of a particular power-knowledge relationship provides
us with the opportunity to uncover the links between patriarchy,
bureaucratic rationality, and emotional labour.

We draw from Derrida's (1976) notion of *différance* by showing
how the meaning of a particular term is dependent on its connection to an opposite concept, even though that opposite term is
absent from a text. Meaning, then, resides in the system of bipolar
opposites that stem from the myth of rationality in Western
culture. Specifically, the meaning of rationality depends on both
the existence of and the absence of emotionality. A postmodern
feminist approach examines the way the oppositional pair
masculinity/femininity functions within the dualities of rational-
ity/emotionality to constitute specific power relations (Martin,
1990; Pringle, 1988). This system of meaning has become
naturalized within Western culture, thus contributing to the belief
that bureaucratic rationality and emotional labour are fixed social
relationships.

*Feminist Critique of Bureaucracy and Emotional
Labour*
From a postmodern feminist perspective, bureaucracy is a particular kind of patriarchal form that reproduces power relations
along gender lines. Even though the bureaucratic rules and

structures appear neutral, they actually favour masculinity. As Pringle notes:

> Weber's account of 'rationality' can be interpreted as a commentary on the construction of a particular kind of masculinity based on the exclusion of the personal, the sexual and the feminine from any definition of 'rationality.' The values of instrumental rationality are strongly associated with the masculine individual, while feminine is associated with that 'other' world of chaos and disorder. (1988: 88)

Instrumental rationality, in turn, is defined by its opposition to emotionality as an alternative mode of experience. Bureaucracy draws from and reconstitutes the previously mentioned dualities that exist in Western culture. Bureaucracy imbues the first term in each pair (for example rational/emotional, mind/body and objective/subjective) with a positive value while situating its opposite as marginalized or as inappropriate to organizational life.

The oppositional terms in these pairs are marginalized by denying their relevance to organizational life. For example, until recently issues such as child care were typically excluded from organizational concerns for productivity and profit margins. They were regarded as feminine matters that resided outside the work situation. As a whole, organizations continue to ignore or devalue the personal (feminine) needs of employees. On-site day-care facilities, flex-time and employee support programmes are just beginning to surface as agenda items in corporations.

When emotions are incorporated into organizations, they are treated as commodities. Feelings are appropriated by the organization for instrumental ends. For example, the instrumental goals of getting promises to pay debts determine which display rules debt collectors must learn. To elicit confessions from suspects, police interrogators employ combinations of positive and negative emotions. Through treating emotion as a commodity with a particular exchange value, feelings become public performances.

Stripped away from the spontaneity of human interaction, emotional labour can lead to negative consequences for an employee and for his or her work relationships. Hochschild (1983) identifies self-estrangement as a harmful side effect that results from emotional labour. In particular, the gap between felt and expressed emotions marginalizes individual experience and the intimacy that typically accompanies personal feelings.

The process that reduces emotion to a form of labour treats the body and the mind as separate entities. This mind–body split alienates and fragments an individual. As Ferguson (1984: 54) notes, 'Like prostitutes, flight attendants often estrange themselves from their work as a defense against being swallowed by it, only to suffer from a sense of being false, mechanical, no longer a whole integrated self.' Van Maanen and Kunda (1989) note that emotional numbness and burnout frequently accompany the incongruence of felt and displayed emotions.

In addition, organizational control of emotions often leads to suppressing disagreements, eliminating employee voice, and reducing upward information flow (Waldron and Krone, 1991). Employees are less likely to protest against perceived unjust actions for fear of experiencing negative consequences. In cultures with a high degree of emotional control, respondents may fail to provide adequate justifications for company actions. For example, supervisors may withhold such messages as, 'I wanted to tell him that everything isn't as simple as it seems' (Waldron and Krone, 1991: 302).

Norms for emotional control also affect co-worker relationships. In particular, suppression of feelings during interactions with colleagues may result in altered relational perceptions and changed communication patterns. Changes in the degree of liking or closeness toward a person may lead to demoting an intense friendship to the status of casual co-working. These changes may preserve short-term work relationships while jeopardizing long-term friendships. Emotional labour, then, may incur significant personal and relational side effects. However, expression of emotions that defy cultural conventions may also lead to negative side effects. That is, the expression of highly intense negative emotions may result in perceptions of distrust and disrespect between employees.

Rationality is sustained only because bureaucrats continue to devalue the marginal terms in these signifying pairs. The presence of contradictions within bureaucracy and Western culture points to potential ruptures in the system of dualities that elevates patriarchy and marginalizes the feminine experience. Specifically, the term 'emotional labour' functions as an oxymoron by linking 'emotion', a negatively valued experience, to 'labour', a positively valued means of production. In like manner, Western culture derogates emotion while simultaneously valuing it as a protection against nihilism and amorality.

The existence of these contradictions signifies that the rationality/emotionality dualism is socially constructed and, consequently, open to change. A contradiction is 'a necessary feature of any dualism whose simplicities cannot hold in the face of the demands [that] social processes . . . put on it' (Lutz, 1988: 56). The complexities of time, place, purpose and context lead us to challenge the inevitability of emotional labour in organizational life. The myth of rationality is exposed at those times when employees cannot obscure the contradiction between defining and negating emotionality. Two case examples illustrate how this contradiction surfaces. From these cases emerge alternatives for positioning emotion as a central phenomenon in organizational life.

Case Examples: Exposing Patriarchy and Emotional Labour

The Boss–Secretary Relationship

The first case highlights a work relationship in which both defining and negating emotionality are central to the organizational task. Pringle (1988) and Ann Game conducted a study of secretaries in a variety of large and small organizations based in Sydney, Adelaide, and New South Wales, Australia between 1985 and 1987. Pringle interviewed approximately 400 people, including pairs of bosses and secretaries as well as managers, clerical workers, and administrators with whom secretaries work. She also employed historical and statistical information from 1890 to 1987 and studied media representations of secretaries. Her study reveals the power relations linked to the secretary role. Although the research was carried out in Australia, Pringle's discussions with representatives from international associations suggest similarities in boss–secretary relationships across different countries.

This relationship represents a rupture or a point of disjuncture in the seemingly coherent nature of rationality and bureaucracy (Pringle, 1989). It is organized around the private realm of family and sexual imagery. The secretary employs empathy and supportiveness in her roles as office wife, slave, or nanny who takes care of her boss's formal institutional needs as well as his informal emotional needs. Bosses break down the separation of work and home by asking their secretaries to purchase gifts for them, to make medical appointments, to do grocery shopping, and even to go home and take washing off the line (Pringle, 1989: 169). Bosses and secretaries spend time talking about personal problems and chatting about their families.

Secretaries are bonded to their bosses through feelings of pride and gratitude that evoke a sense of protective loyalty. Bosses often capitalize on this loyalty by requesting overtime work at short notice for no additional pay. This control through 'caring' becomes a gentle version of the master–slave relationship, even for secretaries who claim they are equal to their bosses. For instance, in the relationship of Richard and Stephanie, both talk the language of reciprocity, but Richard sees Stephanie as his emotional support: she is expected to anticipate his needs, to provide encouragement, and to mind his activities. Although he depends on her, neither of them would admit that she is subordinated, almost like a nanny, in minding Richard's affairs. Richard has the power in the relationship while Stephanie gleans the pleasure of being needed, feeling useful, and being a woman (Pringle, 1988).

Even though bureaucracy ostensibly banishes sexuality from the workplace, organizations rely on sexuality to reproduce existing power relationships. Rather than being alien to the workplace, sexuality and emotional bonding are basic to the practices that constitute secretaries as objects. A contradiction exists in valuing loyalty and emotional allegiance to the workplace while simultaneously devaluing sexuality and the secretarial role.

Pringle (1988) argues that by insisting on the presence and defining quality of sexuality, secretaries can challenge and subvert bureaucratic rationality. First, secretaries can exaggerate and ridicule existing stereotypes of themselves and their bosses, employing parody to assert their rights to be subjects rather than objects. A second way that secretaries can form a gender identity that challenges bureaucratic rationality is through the discourse of bitching. 'Bitching' is a social construction that encompasses complaining, gossiping, joking, and friendly conversation (Pringle, 1988: 232). The discourse of bitching entails sharing feelings, listening to others' problems, and making someone feel better by putting others down. Although this activity may reinforce self-pity and powerlessness, it can also form a strong emotional bond with other secretaries that serves as a foundation for female power. Pringle (1988: 238) provides an example of this type of discourse: 'I resigned last August because they gave me another boss. I had four bosses and there was one girl sitting there with one boss doing her nails all day . . . and I thought, that is it, and I wrote out my resignation and that was it.'

Humour, play, and childish behaviour can also serve as acts of resistance to submissiveness and emotional allegiance. For example, when a boss was absent from his office, the secretaries debunked the company's rigid hierarchy by eating their packed lunches on his posh carpet. In another instance, a secretary who was aggravated because she was doing the work of two employees released her frustrations by drying her shoes on her boss's elegant cream-coloured curtains (Golding, 1986). These examples show how secretaries are aware of the contradictions inherent in emotional labour and can challenge bureaucratic rationality through parody, the discourse of bitching, and acts of resistance. In the second case example, contradictions between the scientific model of emotional labour and the ethic of care create space to expose the myth of rationality.

Medical Social Workers
The second case example focuses on sources of ambiguity in hospital social work. Meyerson (1989, 1991a, 1991b) employed in-depth interviewing and 14 months of participant observation to study 59 social workers in two private and three public hospitals in a large metropolitan area. Four of the five hospitals were acute care facilities, while one hospital focused on rehabilitation. Most of the social workers held Master's degrees and professional certification. Meyerson collected her data by following social workers as they conducted their daily routines; by attending workshops, staff meetings, parties, and lunches; and by asking social workers to provide a sketch or diagram that would depict their experiences of ambiguity and burnout. Although Meyerson (1989) set out to examine how ambiguity, stress, and burnout were socially constructed, she uncovered contradictions in her data that led her to re-examine sources of ambiguity.

Contradictions surfaced in the ideology of medical social workers from two different hospitals. Medical social workers typically 'adopted the scientific language of objectivity, rationality, and control' to talk about health-related problems (Meyerson, 1991a: 19). For example, the use of technical terminology, specialized knowledge base, professional dress and emotional detachment were indices of scientific language and medical professionalism. Medical problems were pathologies in that they deviated from a set statistical norm. An ideology of cure characterized the medical model. Staff aimed to 'fix what was broken, treat the disease, [and] focus on outcomes' (Meyerson, 1991a: 5). Meyerson's study of stress and burnout uncovered contradictions in emotional expression and in the medical model of social work.

The contradictions arose from the ways that social workers in different groups reacted to stress and burnout in formal versus informal settings. The social workers in hospitals dominated by medical/scientific values denied the existence of stress and burnout in informal settings but indicated in formal questionnaire data that these conditions were acute. In settings dominated by scientific and patriarchal values, stress and burnout surfaced as diseases or pathologies that had to be treated or controlled. They believed that professionals should not let their emotions interfere with their objectivity.

However, social workers in one hospital, Chronic, used these contradictions to challenge the authority of the traditional medical model. They espoused an ethic of care that fitted a psychosocial model characterized by ambiguities in technology, idiosyncrasies in tasks, and emotionality. Their jobs entailed focusing on tasks that were difficult to measure (like coping with AIDS), attending to the emotional needs of medical care (family reactions to a patient's illness), and centring on problems that cannot be controlled (like old age) (Meyerson, 1991a).

For these social workers, stress and burnout were inevitable conditions that resulted from dealing with the ambiguities and inconsistencies of patient care. As one social worker commented, 'It sounds like you're trying to find a place to stand in the middle of a kaleidoscope' (Meyerson, 1991b: 137). Rather than being pathologies, these conditions allowed social workers to adapt their care to their clients' needs. As another social worker observed:

> Let's say there's one gentleman (the client) and Gene goes to see him and does an intervention and I go to see him and do another intervention. Because of who we are they are going to be different. The client's experience is going to be different. (Meyerson, 1991b: 137)

Obviously, the 'non-scientific' and feminine values of emotionality, empathy, and subjectivity were relevant to the needs of health care. But in settings dominated by the medical/scientific model, they were marginalized and considered illegitimate. The expression of emotion and the ethic of care were consequences of cultural and political processes mediated by gender (Meyerson, 1991a: 23).

In the first case example, the contradiction between treating sexuality, family, and emotional bonding as simultaneously foreign to the workplace and yet essential to the boss–secretary relationship exposes rationality as a myth that is socially constructed. A secretary engages in emotional labour to serve the informal and emotional needs of her boss and to maintain allegiance through servitude.

In the second example, the contradictions between acknowledging and denying the emotional states of stress and burnout stem from inconsistencies between the medical/scientific model and the ethic of care. Social workers, whose cultural norms adhere to the dominant model, treat stress and burnout as pathologies or as personal and professional failures. Emotional labour occurs through the necessity to remain in control and to deny the presence of stress and ambiguity.

Newton et al. (1993) refer to this type of emotional labour as implicit feeling rules that people employ to negotiate their professional and organizational lives. Thus, the medical/scientific model inculcates the implicit display rule: 'never show that you can't cope'. Feelings of uncertainty and stress must be handled in ways that preserve the professional persona. Implicit feeling rules, then, are habitual and automatic – a by-product of the complex process of occupational training, client relationships, and organizational constraints.

Both cases offer opportunities to challenge the myth of rationality. In the first case, secretaries can engage in parody, the discourse of bitching, or resistance to assert their rights to be subjects rather than objects. These actions may change the way a secretary negotiates her role and her relationship with her boss. These approaches, however, are reactive rather than proactive. They work primarily to expose and resist emotional labour and are not necessarily effective in redressing the politics of emotion.

In the second example, the social workers at Chronic talk freely about ambiguity and stress in both formal and informal settings. They alter the occupational and cultural meanings of stress and burnout through linking them to freedom, flexibility, and adaptability. By valuing these conditions, they remove burnout from its pathological state and treat it as a collective rather than an individual phenomenon. Social workers at Chronic treat emotional expression as both central to patient care and as necessary for participation in the work process. These social workers, however, function in a particular culture that supports this ideology. Social workers who espouse the medical ideology, or who are indoctrinated to control their emotional displays, may be unable to alter their display rules, especially those that preserve managerial prerogatives (Newton et al., 1993).

Work Feelings: An Alternative to Emotional Labour

As an alternative to emotional labour, organizations might strive to make work feelings central to participation in the work environment. Work feelings are those emotions that emerge from human interaction rather than being imposed by instrumental goals and bureaucratic rationality (Mumby and Putnam, 1992). Human interaction in this case is concerned with developing mutual understanding through messages that emerge from the co-construction of meaning. That is, work feelings aid in negotiating meanings about roles and relationships rather than in conforming to predetermined display rules or to prescribed norms. So in opposition to overt or covert control over emotional displays, work feelings are *emergent*.

This plea for emphasizing work feelings acknowledges that people often mask their feelings to manage social impressions, to avoid embarrassment, and to save face. Felt and expressed emotions are not necessarily consistent. Individual goals and cultural etiquette necessitate some degree of emotional control in which people alter expressed feelings to create a public image or to avoid hurting another person. This effort to control facial expressions, tone of voice, and demeanour may be stressful. But when emotional labour becomes institutionalized with deliberate, ascribed feeling rules aimed at serving an organization's commercial or strategic ends, the tension between felt and feigned emotions is often great and the potential for employees to lose touch with their own feelings is heightened.

Rather than aiming to control emotional expression, training programmes might help employees analyse task and social interactions, understand how meanings are constructed through discourse, and describe and interpret verbal and nonverbal cues. By providing employees with diverse situations and relationships, training sessions could help employees understand the complexity of emotional displays and introduce alternatives for handling situations. 'Having employees develop skills in listening, negotiating, and understanding feelings is more liberating than turning them into emotional robots' (Mumby and Putnam, 1992: 478). Although this type of training would be difficult to sell to a McDonald's or a Disneyland, an emphasis on work feelings could reduce the cynicism and alienation that many employees experience in organizations.

Norms that define work feelings should emerge from *adapting to the social context* and personal relationships. Feeling rules should be fluid rather than static prescriptions like the flight attendant's instructions to provide a modest but friendly smile. Rules such as 'employees should control their emotions at work' should be replaced with guidelines for understanding the link between emotional expression and human interaction.

For example, the first author of this chapter noticed that a ticket agent at an airline counter seemed disoriented and upset. I explained that my day had been exhausting and frustrating. I had missed a connection because of a delayed flight and then I was misrouted when another agent misread the destination on my ticket. The agent lamented that her day had been an emotional roller-coaster. A tear began to appear as she explained that she had agreed to substitute for one of her colleagues while he went to the hospital to visit his wife, but he had just called to say that she died. More tears rolled down her face. She turned her head and apologized for her 'loss of control'. She exclaimed, 'I know agents are supposed to control their emotions when they are at work.' I told her that I thought employees should express their emotions when the situation seemed appropriate.

Rather than viewing this interaction as a sign of incompetence, I saw it as personalizing a typically estranged situation. Her grief made my frustration and anger over delayed flights seem trivial. Although in this example we shared our emotional reactions, exchanging other confidences may seem awkward for either the customer or the agent. The interactional context must serve as a guide for disclosure of feelings.

Expression of feelings also serves a communicative role by developing a sense of *community*. Instead of functioning as a commodity with instrumental value, emotions should serve expressive functions that build interrelatedness. The sharing of emotional experiences develops mutual affect, connectedness, and cohesion that break down anonymity. Community forms by fusing individual experiences with co-constructed meanings to facilitate joint actions. The social workers at Chronic developed a sense of community through sharing their feelings about burnout and by forming a culture that accepted stress as an inevitable aspect of their work. Expression of emotions showed employees how ambiguity contributed interpretive slack to their work.

Interrelatedness and a sense of community produce *mutual understanding* and develop self-identity. Individuals rely on empathy to understand motives, purposes, and beliefs about action and to share in another person's experience. Employees develop a dialogic relationship in which each person sees the other as sharing meanings and cumulative experiences. These meanings surface through language and interaction patterns in particular social contexts. Emotions are key factors in forming mutual understanding by cueing empathy, gaining insights into expectations, building shared interpretations and understanding life histories.

In addition to facilitating mutual understanding, work feelings provide employees with *alternatives* for dealing with covert control in organizational life. For instance, a social worker at Chronic who openly expresses frustration and reveals her job stress participates in shaping an environment characterized by tolerance of ambiguity and a sense of community. Tolerance of ambiguity facilitates organizational practices that value divergent positions among members and open up possibilities for organizing. Expression of work feelings may also serve as a type of resistance, similar to the secretary who makes jokes about her situation.

In summary, work feelings are guidelines for appropriate expression of emotions. Work feelings are emergent rather than organizationally ascribed behaviour. They contribute to the building of community by forming a bond of interrelatedness. Rather than serving the needs of bureaucratic rationality, work feelings facilitate mutual understanding and open up alternatives for legitimizing marginal forms of organizational experience.

Since work feelings are not ascribed by corporate training manuals or occupational norms, most of us experience them in small group or dyadic work settings. The following case study differs from previous cases in focusing on the way group interaction constitutes a participatory context. It illustrates how work feelings are incorporated into an organizational setting through collaborative processes developed in work units.

Case Study: Work Feelings and Employee Participation
Nelson (1988) conducted case studies of five teacher–graduate student training teams in the Composition Tutorial Center (CTC) at George Mason University. The CTC is an instructional unit housed in the English Department to provide tutorial assistance to undergraduates who are having problems with writing. Students come to the centre twice a week for a semester to work with graduate teaching assistants on particular writing skills. Faculty administrators of the CTC are responsible for designing the tutorial programmes, training the teaching assistants to teach writing, and supervising their work.

One case study focuses on the training teams of faculty and graduate teaching assistants that met in daily seminars for two weeks before their work began and weekly during the first semester. The training teams were composed of 6 to 10 first-year tutors, several doctoral students and a faculty administrator. The tutors ranged in age from 22 to 50 years old.

The training sessions emphasised techniques for helping students understand and resolve writing problems blended with theories of composition. At one time the CTC provided teaching assistants with specific directives for managing their communication with students. These directives paralleled a modified form of emotional labour (e.g. avoid giving negative feedback), a hierarchical pattern of organization (e.g. clear distinctions between leaders and subordinates) and a linear pattern of decision making (e.g. follow agendas and sequential formats). Under new leadership of the CTC, the tutorial teams experienced flexibility in implementing their tasks and in developing collaborative processes.

In her study, Nelson (1988) uncovered two teams that functioned differently from most training groups. The interaction among team members showed how feelings played a pivotal role in developing a supportive atmosphere and in participating in the work process. These teams demonstrated collaborative decision making and effective conflict management by employing the four key elements of work feelings: emergent emotional expression, adaptation to the social context, community and interrelatedness, and mutual understanding.

In one team mutual support and community came from the lateral flow of information to and from all members. Experienced teaching assistants and faculty members functioned as coaches rather than as authority figures or leaders. With mutual support as a primary goal and leadership based in a lateral rather than a hierarchical structure, problems became field dependent and decisions were emergent and consensual rather than authoritative and imposed from above.

Open expression of emotions facilitated the formation of community and developed a 'sanctuary' atmosphere in which teammates provided emotional support and constructive criticism. Teams dealt with negative feelings and competitiveness through reducing defensive reactions. In one team, Lynn and Francie, two strong personalities, handled their competitiveness by openly expressing their emotions outside the group and exploring why they made each other feel uncomfortable. Within the group, members shared their anxieties about the tutorial experience, dealt good-naturedly with their frustrations, and shared honest but supportive criticism. Benyam, a male group member, saw the team as emotional, open, emergent, and happy. He remarked, 'I felt threatened by experienced tutors from previous years, but I was able to express my fears about teaching . . . so . . . I could see them as others did, could get distance on my anxiety, and learn from it' (Nelson, 1988: 215).

Not only were interactions rooted in supportiveness, but team members identified problems and collaborated on solutions through an intuitive, holistic pattern of reasoning. Transcripts of group interaction revealed a logic that was associative and unfocused rather than linear and agenda specific. Members exchanged experiences as a way of understanding each other while they simultaneously engaged in problem solving. The following excerpt from group interaction illustrates this process.

> *Lynn:* I have students who aren't interested in learning. They just want their papers corrected.
> *Marie:* What if you told them we don't do that in this progam?
> *Fran:* Yeah. Once they try freewriting, they see that it works.
> *Lynn:* Most of mine have not had that insight.
> *Caroline:* I would hate to lay down an edict that we can't work on papers, because it has really, really worked for me. Maybe we just have to emphasize process when we let them do it.
> *Marie:* Yeah. Or you could say that 'Working on assignments isn't help-ing your writing at this point. You need to back up and practise writing about things you know about first.'
> *Caroline:* That's what I did with one student, and it worked too. (Nelson, 1988: 207)

This dialogue continued in the same holistic, nonlinear manner and concluded with a number of collaboratively developed memos from the CTC that would inform composition teachers of their purpose. In effect, a policy statement about the role of the CTC emerged from group interaction rooted in sharing experiences and discuss-ing problems with correcting student papers.

Group conflicts were managed with the same collaborative approach. Rooted in emotional openness, conflicts were addressed through direct confrontation aimed at a win–win outcome that would benefit the group and protect each individual's self-esteem. Freedom to confront Marie, the director, and fellow graduate students aided in building interrelatedness and mutual affect. Members of the group noted how rare it was in academia. Indeed the group became an alternative mode of organizing, one that legitimized spontaneity, equality, and community.

This example of work feelings stands in direct contrast to many groups that root team interactions in emotional labour, individual competition, hierarchy, and negative evaluation. Although an organization may stress team playing, rewards typically stem from individual achievement and a principle of exclusion and emotional isolation. This emphasis on individual achievement breaks down the collaborative goal and the safe environment that promotes emotional risk. An emphasis on work feelings affirms the structures and values that reconstitute organizations within networks of relationships rather than bureaucratic rationality.

Conclusion

Emotions play a vital role in organizational life, not simply as forms of labour or the means to instrumental ends but as ways to enhance community and interrelatedness. Work feelings, in contrast to emotional labour, emerge from human interaction, aid in co-constructing meaning, build mutual understanding, and provide options for alternative forms of organizing. Unlike emotional labour, work feelings are not aimed at organizational control through adhering to managerially governed display rules.

Work feelings expose the myth of rationality and signal a rupture in bureaucratic efforts to define and negate emotion. When bureaucracy can no longer obscure or marginalize the devalued terms in the rationality/emotionality dualism, emotion can surface as central to a participatory work context. As a way of knowing that differs from rationality, emotion produces information grounded in personal experience, mutual understanding, and community. Emotion comprises sentiments about what is good, right, and possible. Sensitivity to other people's feelings is essential for understanding diversity in the workplace and may form the foundation for organizational change.

Organizations do not need to abandon instrumental goals, productivity, or rationality to develop alternative modes of discourse. Emphasizing work feelings calls for including what is currently ignored or marginalized in organizational life. Rationality is not an objective, immutable state. Rather, it is socially constructed and cast as the dominant mode of organizing. Rationality and technical efficiency, however, should be embedded in a larger system of community and interrelatedness. Perhaps organizations of the future could offer society a new alternative, one shaped by emotionally-connected creativity and mutual understanding as necessary elements for human growth.

References

D'Andrade, R. G. (1987) 'A folk model of the mind', in D. Holland and N. Quinn (eds), *Cultural Models in Language and Thought*. Cambridge: Cambridge University Press. pp. 112–48.
Derrida, J. (1976) *Of Grammatology*, trans. G. Spivak. Baltimore: Johns Hopkins University Press.

Ferguson, K. (1984) *The Feminist Case against Bureaucracy*. Philadelphia: Temple University Press.

Golding, J. (1986) 'Some problems in the concept of secretary', *International Studies of Management and Organization*, 16: 94–111.

Hochschild, A. R. (1979) 'Emotion work, feeling rules and social structure', *American Journal of Sociology*, 85: 551–75.

Hochschild, A. R. (1983) *The Managed Heart*. Berkeley: University of California Press.

Lakoff, G. and Johnson, M. (1980) *Metaphors We Live By*. Chicago: University of Chicago Press.

Lutz, C. A. (1988) *Unnatural Emotions: Everyday Sentiments on a Micronesian Atoll and Their Challenges to Western Theory*. Chicago: University of Chicago Press.

Martin, J. (1990) 'Deconstructing organizational taboos: the suppression of gender conflict in organizations', *Organizational Science*, 1: 339–59.

Meyerson, D. E. (1989) 'The social construction of ambiguity and burnout: a study of hospital social workers', doctoral dissertation, Stanford University, Stanford, CA.

Meyerson, D. E. (1991a) 'Nested blindspots: a feminist critique and re-vision of stress talk'. Paper presented at the Conference on Narrative Approaches to Organizational Theory, Boulder, Colorado (September).

Meyerson, D. E. (1991b) '"Normal" ambiguity? A glimpse of an occupational culture', in P. J. Frost, L. F. Moore, C. C. Lundberg and J. Martin (eds), *Reframing Organizational Culture*. Newbury Park, CA: Sage. pp. 131–44.

Mumby, D. K. and Putnam, L. L. (1992) 'The politics of emotion: a feminist reading of bounded rationality', *Academy of Management Review*, 17: 465–86.

Nelson, M. W. (1988) 'Women's ways: interactive patterns in predominantly female research teams', in B. Bate and A. Taylor (eds), *Women Communicating: Studies of Women's Talk*. Norwood, NJ: Ablex. pp. 199–232.

Newton, T., Handy, J. and Fineman, S. (1993) *Alternative Perspectives on Occupational Stress*. London: Sage.

Pringle, R. (1988) *Secretaries Talk*. London: Verso.

Pringle, R. (1989) 'Bureaucracy, rationality, and sexuality: the case of secretaries', in J. Hearn, D. L. Sheppard, P. Tancred-Sheriff and G. Burrell (eds), *The Sexuality of Organization*. London: Sage, pp. 158–77.

Rafaeli, A. (1989) 'When cashiers meet customers: an analysis of the role of supermarket cashiers', *Academy of Management Journal*, 32: 245–73.

Rafaeli, A. and Sutton, R. I. (1987) 'Expression of emotion as part of the work role', *Academy of Management Review*, 12: 23–37.

Rafaeli, A. and Sutton, R. I. (1989) 'The expression of emotion in organizational life', in L. L. Cummings and B. M. Staw (eds), *Research in Organizational Behavior*, Vol. 11. Greenwich, CT: JAI Press. pp. 1–42.

Rafaeli, A. and Sutton, R. I. (1990) 'Busy stores and demanding customers: how do they affect the display of positive emotion?', *Academy of Management Journal*, 33: 623–37.

Rafaeli, A. and Sutton, R. I. (1991) 'Emotional contrast strategies as means of social influence: lessons from criminal interrogators and bill collectors', *Academy of Management Journal*, 34: 749–75.

Stenross, B. and Kleinman, S. (1989) 'The highs and lows of emotional labor: detectives' encounters with criminals and victims', *Journal of Contemporary Ethnography*, 17: 435–52.

Sutton, R. I. (1991) 'Maintaining norms about expressed emotions: the case of bill collectors', *Administrative Science Quarterly*, 11: 322–36.

Sutton, R. I. and Rafaeli, A. (1988) 'Untangling the relationship between displayed emotions and organizational sales: the case of convenience stores', *Academy of Management Journal*, 31: 461–87.

Van Maanen, J. and Kunda, G. (1989) '"Real feelings": emotional expression and organizational culture', in L. L. Cummings and B. M. Staw (eds), *Research in Organizational Behavior*, Vol. 11. Greenwich, CT: JAI Press. pp. 43–104.

Waldron, V. R. and Krone, K. J. (1991) 'The experience and expression of emotion in the workplace: a study of a corrections organization', *Management Communication Quarterly*, 4: 287–309.

PART II

EMOTION WORK

3

Fear, Loyalty and Greedy Organizations

Helena Flam

Organizations are usually studied from either rationalistic or normative perspectives, suggesting that they are immune to emotion (Flam, 1990a).[1] Similarly, in studies of work and organizational life, emotions are usually either completely ignored or very narrowly conceived.[2] Studies that do deal with emotions tend to focus on work satisfaction, work enthusiasm, or self-actualization. The negative emotions, such as fear, guilt or embarrassment, do not receive the attention they deserve although they play a key role in the shaping of the organizational order.

My previous work on emotions (Flam, 1990a, 1990b) largely overlooked the private feelings of individuals who act within organizations. It did not pay any attention to how such feelings drive personal choices and actions, in particular the choice between normative and rational action. Yet it is important to understand feeling-informed individual choice for it results in entry, membership and exit[3] from an organization, affecting its very effectiveness and viability. In this chapter I will focus on fears which compel individuals to delay their decision to take the exit option. I will explore the argument that three distinct selves – emotional, normative and rational – are at work within an individual, and that an emotional self – experiencing a specific organization-induced feeling: fear – helps the rational self to suppress and/or engage in a battle with the normative self. Finally, I wish to pinpoint the circumstances – the presence of the 'defiant peers' (Milgram, 1974) – under which the normative self again reasserts itself.

Fear and the Multiple Selves

In his path-breaking work, Etzioni (1988) argues that normative-emotional 'action logic' profoundly transforms rational decision making. He merges norms and emotions to show how they interact with reason. In contrast, I propose that the emotional self is separate and distinct from both the normative and the rational self. However, it has a capacity to affect the choice between the rational and the normative action courses. When imbued with fear it mixes with reason to produce a rational-emotional action.

Frank (1988: 53–4) points out that feelings, such as anger, guilt and love, successfully compete with those derived from rational calculations. He argues that in changing the subjective payoffs, they help sustain moral behaviour and, once communicated, establish lasting commitments. For Frank the core problem is how feelings help to create moral individuals.[4] Here the basic premise is that feelings have a capacity to both moralize and demoralize – it depends on the feeling and the context. What power holders define as moral may be subjectively amoral.

A 'feeling' can be seen as a warning signal, an expectation or reality check (Hochschild, 1983: 201–22). It is an interactive product. Here I am only interested in one feeling – fear. As with Hochschild, I see it as a subjectively felt product of power relations in the broadest sense.

The 'irrational' feeling of fear signals that a specific desire is associated with danger, and therefore cannot be easily satisfied. This particular feeling does not weaken or alternate with reason (as Schelling, 1984 argues about the irrational). Nor does it derive from rational calculations. On the contrary, it is at the very base of 'reason'. Fear compels an individual to construct a cost-and-benefit argument demonstrating why the spontaneously desired action should not be pursued. In this sense, fear, in prompting rational calculations, helps to narrow the range of subjectively available action options, and even transforms the rank-ordering of desires. Its further specific contribution to these calculations is to inflate the costs and deflate the benefits of the desired, yet threat-bringing courses of action. In this sense, a 'preference' or 'interest' – a cherished rationalistic concept – is not a purely cognitive concept. Instead, it has an emotional foundation and a feeling-prompted bias.

Let me now put it in a language which reflects my own image of the multiple selves, understood as heuristic devices (cf. Flam, 1990a: 42). By definition, a rational self is cost-conscious. Because it is resource-constrained, a rational self always calculates whether a given course of action is such that the benefits will exceed the costs. If the costs are higher than the benefits, no action will be undertaken, unless the individual is coerced or receives cost-reducing benefits. In contrast, a normative self is norm-conscious. Because it is value-constrained, a normative self always considers a given course of action in terms of what is socially proper. If the course of action deviates from the social norms, no action will be undertaken, unless the individual is resocialized to change his or her values. Finally, a 'pure' emotional self is oblivious to the cost. Always other-oriented, it generates a positive, indifferent or negative relational charge for which it seeks expression. It urges the other selves to deal with the relational charge it generates.

My thesis is that fear – as a warning signal and a negative relational charge – forces the individual to reconsider his or her normative preferences. A considered course of action which as a matter of principle should not be subject to a calculus, becomes subject to a cost-benefit analysis under the influence of fear. The value-informed preferences are no longer measured by a normative yardstick, but by a rational one.

Here fear is a reality check in two senses. First, because it signals the (present or impending) threat to one's self stemming from a violation of the power relations. Secondly, because in signalling that a pursuit of a specific preference invites danger, it begs the question whether it should remain a preference. It also begs the question whether the cost of upholding certain values is not too high. By questioning, it opens up the door for a 'battle of the selves', wherein the value argument confronts the cost argument. The rational self calculates whether indeed a normative course of action will not be too costly. If it is too costly, and fear presses towards such a conclusion, the battle of the selves ends with the defeat of the normative self. Under fear's unrelenting pressure, the rational self takes charge. The subjectively normative course of action is abandoned. As I will show, the duration of such a retreat from, or bracketing of, one's norms varies – it can last a few minutes or for ever.

To illustrate my overall argument, I would like to cite an extraordinary autobiographic account. It deals with the terror-ridden Polish city of Lwów during the Second World War. As an extreme case this highlights the dynamics that more conventional organization settings – about which more later – only sketch out. The narrative sequence which follows supports a twofold thesis: that it indeed makes sense to speak of three-dimensional selves (emotional, normative and calculating-rational) and that an emotion – fear – is a selector of a self to be in charge.

Fear – Poland 1939

Alexander Wat (born in 1900), a prominent Polish poet, acquired a status of a communist party sympathizer before the Second World War (Wat, 1990). Here he tells of his short stay in Soviet-occupied Lwów in 1939–40. On occasion, he refers to his wife Ola and his son Andrzej. He first indicates his anguish and loss of self-esteem as he learns to act a part in fear for his own life, and for the safety of his family:

> Those three months in Lwów . . . three months of fear, play-acting, clumsy lies. Clumsy because I was betraying myself, because I could not stand up to it all . . . I was afraid. I knew that everyone connected to *The Literary Monthly* had been killed in Russia, so I didn't have the slightest doubt that the same thing was in store for me. I could imagine what Soviet prisons and camps were like – I knew – and I knew what Ola's and Andrzej's fate would be. (Wat, 1990: 97)

> I would say that those few weeks in Lwów were the most disgusting period in my life. I acted like a coward . . . I was trembling in my boots. I didn't harm anyone. On the contrary. And I wrote no poetry about Stalin . . . But of course I told lies. (Wat, 1990: 101)

A friend convinced Wat that to join the staff of the publication *The Red Banner* would be the safest for him. As a member of its staff Wat went through his 'worst' Lwów experience – a staff purge:

> One day a group came to the editorial offices. . . They were professionals who had come to question the staff. Everyone was there. They asked the questions, and everyone had to speak about himself, tell his life story . . . the room [was] full of inquisitors and eyes. (Wat, 1990: 103)

Now comes the key point – Wat's description of his decision to kill his normative self on the spot in order to successfully play a life-saving role. He also describes the demand for an 'inner surgery' that fear-motivated play-acting requires:

> That was the only time that I engaged in any self-criticism. I played it like an actor, knowing that I was playing for my life and Ola's. There had already been a purge. One ex-Trotskyite had been thrown off the editorial board and had been immediately arrested afterwards. I played it like an actor, splitting myself in two. You're here, it's your turn in five minutes, and during those five minutes you have to split yourself into two distinct entities. Like a guillotine. You have to sever one part from the other. And you have to feel that split within yourself because otherwise it doesn't work and you foul up.

The inquisitors have excellent eyes and sharp ears. I remember glancing at my watch and saying to myself: I'm going to have to talk in five minutes. And during those five minutes I had to perform inner surgery. I really could feel something tearing apart inside me. The actor, Alexander Wat, was there, and I was also there in the wings, an eye that watched that actor move, speak – his gestures, intonations, everything. Later, when I went back home to Ola, I was covered in sweat; the sweat was still pouring off me. Apparently, I had played the part brilliantly. I admitted that I had said that there was a dictatorship, terror, and fear in the Soviet Union, that everyone lived in fear, but now I had come to see the error of my ways. Terror – why the very idea! And I said that now I understood the wisdom of the policy that had anticipated the current situation with scientific accuracy. (Wat, 1990: 103)

Of key interest to us here is that a particular emotion – fear – served as a switch, a sort of selector of the self to be put in charge. The normative, regime-opposing self was completely suppressed. The rational self, in its turn, dictated the specific role to be played in public. A 'faithful breast-beating, sin-confessing communist' presented itself to the inquisitors.

In a nutshell, Wat's account shows that fear is, at times, a source of an extremely disturbing, 'preference falsification' – a failure to express and act upon private (normative) preferences in public (Kuran, 1991). Later on I will show that fear compels individuals to stay within organizations which, otherwise, they would like to leave.

Greedy Institutions

A real-life laboratory which I selected for testing purposes is a 'greedy institution'. Greedy institutions, loosely following Coser (1974), are organizations which attempt to secure complete loyalty and voluntary compliance from their members. They also try to become the sole basis for their members' social identity. In this sense, they set up extraordinarily demanding requests on the individuals. They do not use coercion, but instead rely on voluntary recruitment.

The Polish communist party, from 1956, was one such greedy institution. During this period entry to the party was constrained but non-coercive. In this respect it could be compared to many Western organizations. On the other hand, this communist party extended much more control over the individual life than any single comparable Western organization. It controlled permits for work and residence. It tried to control all work assignments and appointments. It also set up an official power and status hierarchy. Many feared its vast decision-making powers which threatened their livelihood and work aspirations. Most came to see an accommodation with the communist party as a necessary means towards a vocation. A small percentage saw it as a vocation. Either way 'the party line' intervened between the individuals and their work and career aspirations. On the job, few dared to criticize either the system as such, or the work conditions which affected their everyday life (Nowak, 1988).

The Polish communist party, therefore, constitutes a magnifying glass through which the dynamics of emotions, especially fear, can be observed. It also provides a parallel to fear-constrained behaviours in the corporate West, as I shall show in the final section.

Fear of Exit

Although many party members increasingly came to perceive the party as an 'unjust authority' on normative grounds (Fireman et al., 1979), they delayed, sometimes never took, the decision to leave it. They feared losing their jobs, and thereby their only source of income and/or professional identity. A feeling – fear – informed the decision not to quit. It was pivotal in putting the rational, cost-and-benefit conscious, self in charge.

A narrator, born in 1922, was at first a firm supporter of the Polish communist party and had joined it in 1948 for idealistic reasons: 'Well . . . properly speaking, I belong to those, who from the very beginning, accepted and supported this communist power. Hence my presence in the party from the very beginning.'[5]

He frequently hesitated and stumbled over his words, in what was evidently a painful story to tell. The following heavily edited excerpt focuses the feelings of 'anxiety' that, for six to eight years, kept him from leaving the party:

> I left the party in 1976. The thing started in 1968 practically speaking. Well, during the time I belonged to the party I was not passive; that is, I reflected upon my membership. In 1968 I finally cottoned on to the fact that the party would not change to non-repressiveness, so to speak. Repression and harassment of people was in the soul of the party. Thus, at that moment, the problem of leaving started. And, well, this phenomenon, which is in your field of interest, followed . . . the matter of, indeed, anxiety. I admit that until then, because I accepted the world in which I lived, I had not really experienced any anxiety; perhaps a certain adaptive apparatus ruled me. I imagined that there were certain principles, certain ideals, still in practice, ideals which enlightened my youth.

But in 1968 I already understood that I was living in a dream world, and it would be necessary for me to really leave the party. But I also felt, somewhere in my subconscious, a threat – the threat of revealing my new attitude. As long as I did not have this attitude, as long as I did not make the decision to leave, I had no reason to be afraid. But now, since suddenly I felt I had to show I had changed, I could expect repression; I feared for my own skin.

So, I did not make a clear-cut decision to leave the party in 1968. Something – perhaps the strength of my illusions – held me back. Nevertheless, the alternative was already quite clear. The decisive moment was 1970 when absolutely all the arguments were gathered. There were no doubts after the events [in the Gdansk dockyards]. At that moment I was determined to leave. Yet I did not. I can't hide that something was still holding me back from leaving the party. It was the feeling of anxiety about possible repression. In the later years I had to muster courage or strength to take this crucial step. Back in 1970 I felt very vulnerable as my leaving would have been a single-handed act.

Obedience as a Problematic Play-Act

The communist party members and sympathizers were all firmly locked into their basic positions as people who live in a forced-consequence situation (Goffman, 1961: 89–90). As such, they were committed to taking, responding to and possibly suffering the consequences of the party-dictated courses of action (Goffman, 1961: 88–9). However, in the Polish communist regime, it seems, the 'doubters', although fearful, created a broad array of doubt-expressing, distance-indicating public roles. The critical party members with whom I spoke qualified their overt display of obedience by turning into 'professional' and 'internal' party critics, or 'leisure time oppositionals'. The 'ritualists' maintained a role distance to protect their individual 'ego, self-esteem, personality, or integrity from the implications of the situation' (Goffman, 1961: 120).

In party-staged 'as if' play (Kusy, 1985: 163–6) there were very many roles which doubting individuals who feared leaving the party could perform. There were also many niches which they could occupy. Here I only want to turn attention to the fact that, in search of a compromise between what they felt and what they had to express, the doubting individuals not only jumped into, but also creatively constructed ever new roles and role-distancing models. Ultimately, their private and distance-indicating public roles helped them to sustain their wavering self-respect while also assuring a modicum of social respect.

The Final Exit-Act as a Process of Disobedience

Given the fact that they managed to shape and find respect-maintaining public roles, it is worthwhile asking why so many joined the opposition even before the regime crumbled in 1989. Here I focus on those who, taking the repression risk, actually handed in their party cards. My core concern here is with the process of conversion from obedience to disobedience.

Weber's definition of obedience as a product of fear and loyalty, which in turn is based on either ideal or material interests or a mixture of both, is a good starting point for understanding the phenomenon of disobedience – provided that we take seriously the notion that even the material or ideal interests that are at the base of loyalty are underwritten by fear. The control of an organization over specific individual life chances has to combine with a corresponding set of individual aspirations (material or ideal values) in order to produce an organizational ability to exact obedience. In other words, it is the fear of very specific ideal or material loss(es) and of the consequences of forfeiting particular life chances which attaches an individual to the life-chance-controlling authority. When this fear is managed, a crucial – subjective – pillar of obedience crumbles. This type of emotion management is focal in this section.

What is interesting is that although the first acts of distancing and disobedience can often be dated, a considerable time distance (see p. 63) separates these first acts of disobedience from a complete rejection of an authority. A final act of disobedience – exit – presupposes a complex mental and a painful emotional process.

Disobedience entails a time-requiring crucial step: the gradual overcoming of the fear of the ideal or material loss(es) which disobedience, in all probability, will bring about. The fear of the ensuing highly probable loss of work, position, career or beloved profession is self-explanatory and needs no additional comment. In overcoming this fear, an individual slowly deflates, or completely renounces, his or her aspirations. The fear of ideal losses, in its turn, is best understood when (according to Arendt, 1973; Fromm, 1963; and Neumann, 1978) we recall how anxiety provoking is the prospect of an existential void. Many individuals, when confronting such a void, joined the ranks of Nazis and Communists (see also Wat, 1990). This fear is the easiest to manage when a symbolic alternative becomes available.

Although writers such as Hirschman (1970) and Pizzorno (1986) elucidate the cognitive processes that combine to prevent exit, they both miss the importance of emotions involved in decision making about exit. Hirschman points to the rational calculus which is at the base of an opportunistic self-deception preventing exit. In his view, organizational exit is very costly for an individual, in particular for the 'high-loyalty members', even when they are already aware that 'their' organization has deteriorated beyond any hope. Most such critical high-loyalty members never leave. They learn to live with the shame of being a member for the sake of the individual benefits they derive from staying. Their self-conscious motive for staying, however, is not these benefits but 'the avoidance of a hypothetical damage' inflicted on the public were they to leave (Hirschman, 1970: 103). Pizzorno also argues that the high-loyalty members stay put much longer than the low-loyalty ones. But his explanation focuses on the question of identity. In his view, for the high-loyalty members exit means a process of confronting, rejecting, and parting with both the organization which they helped to create/run/sustain and with their 'until-now' selves. This twofold rejection, which implies both social isolation and the necessity to construct a completely new identity, most individuals are unable to handle.

In contrast to Milgram, neither Hirschman nor Pizzorno recognize the emotion-laden process of turning disloyal. In Milgram's experiments those who make the exit decision very clearly refuse to identify any longer or at all with the authority figures leading the experiments supposedly inflicting pain on others (Milgram, 1974). A precondition of this refusal is that they manage to overcome their fear of authority and their anxiety about breaking the internalized norms (Milgram, 1974: 152). Exit means a personal rupture which is not only cognitive but also extremely emotional in its very nature. In real life, many different fears combine to block for a while a self-conscious, clear-cut self-redefinition. One narrator, whose preparations for exit lasted twelve years, recalls his fears, and their consequences:

> Should I leave or not? The situation compels you to take a stand, but you are still not ready. Fear means hiding away, occupying yourself with your professional work.
>   The fear of separateness, fear of being identified, fear stemming from hesitation, from a lack of decision, fear of one's own self, of self-defining oneself. . . Fear of being crossed, of being defined. When I started working on a critical theory, the work gave a feeling of relief – that you already know who you are, that I am not a Marxist. 'You are an opponent of this system.'

If different fears combine to postpone, even to completely preclude, the decision to exit, the key question that arises is under what conditions is the final 'exit' step most likely? In virtually all narrated cases the same cause of disobedience is more or less explicitly noted by the narrator him/herself. Milgram named this cause 'defiant peers' (Milgram, 1974: 118). Inspired by Milgram's experiments, several social scientists (in particular the students of social movements) have confirmed in their laboratory, case-study, and historical analyses that disobedience emerges with peer and community support (Cole, 1969; Cole, 1980: 12; Fireman et al., 1979; McAdam, 1988; Moore, 1978; Rüdig, 1990). Only a few of these analyses, however, mention or amplify the emotions involved in (dis)obedience. None assigns them a key role equal to that played by norms or rational calculus.

Acting from fear causes a profound loss of self-respect. Wat's account, for example, leaves no doubt just how humiliating and exacting his fear-based play-acting in Lwów was. The stuttering manner in which another male narrator tells of how 'anxiety' kept him in the party indicates how difficult living in terms dictated by this feeling was. His female counterpart recalled how painful and costly, in terms of lost self-respect, was her decision to stay in the party: 'From shame and humiliation, I cried through several nights. . . The most humiliating fear was this one with the party card . . . that I did not do something from fear.'

It is arguable that joining 'defiant peers'[6] constitutes a resolution of a long-lasting struggle for self-respect. If the fear of the complete loss of self- and social respect counterbalances to some extent the fear of repression, self-love and the internalized desire for self- and social respect press for a public affirmation and disclosure of the normative self. The defiant peers intensify both.

My research also suggests that very close contacts with defiant peers have to combine with blocked opportunities which prevent individuals from realizing in full their identity-sustaining aspirations. In such situations individuals are much more likely to explore alternative identities and to redefine the ideal or material interests which tie them to the life-chance-controlling authority. The parallel process – of fear management and aspiration renouncing – is a key to their tie-severing and risk-taking act of final disobedience.

Fear in the Corporate West

Fear as a response to life and body threats, and its role in producing overt obedience to organizations, has long been recognized as existing in the totalitarian regimes. What is lacking is a widespread recognition that the fear of forfeited life chances and/or of an existential void is also important. It plays a similar role in totalitarian and in non-totalitarian regimes and organizations. Even in the liberal Western regimes, no matter how low their unemployment rates and how good their unemployment and social benefits, the fundamental threat of unemployment exists. In these work-ethic-based societies, individuals fear both unemployment and a loss of their work identity. This fear exercises a powerful influence on the way we act. For fear of remaining unemployed/living in an existential void, many of us play-act in job interviews and, a far more serious matter, feel compelled to accept jobs we abhor. Once employed, we continue our play-acting (compromising our normative selves and becoming estranged from our feelings) in the presence of our colleagues, superiors and clients, while striving to follow organizational and career-path rules (see Hochschild, 1983). Citizen and worker rights notwithstanding, a decision to strike becomes a major fear-overcoming feat (Cole, 1969).

In Studs Terkel's *Working* (1972) the narrators make numerous references to the spiritually demanding and devastating play-acting in which they feel compelled to engage in their work life. They link such performance to the fear of losing their jobs or of incurring the disfavour of the bosses. An individual who is not afraid and, therefore, either refuses to play-act or plays unconvincingly, displays an undesired 'insubordination through manner' (Terkel, 1972: 82–3). Just like their Polish counterpart (Nowak, 1988), he or she acquires a 'reputation' and is labelled a 'trouble-maker', which undermines the efforts to get and hold on to a job. Terkel's book suggests that our allegedly rational work organizations just could not function without a core emotional ingredient – fear.

Since the celebrated Mayo studies of the 1930s (Roethlisberger and Dickson, 1939) it has been recognized that work-related emotions are of central importance to work performance. However, a serious analytic interest in emotion in general, and in the negative emotions in particular, is almost entirely missing in recent study of work and organizational life. The only exception is the study of stress. Indeed, rather than digging into the work-related feelings and paying attention to the play-acting that organizations enforce, most research has emphasized the importance of displayed work satisfaction and enthusiasm for the job. For example, Peters and Waterman (1982) have argued that a strict, bureaucratic authority and rational organizational models breed rigid and unnecessarily complex work organization while ensuring no business success. They also create change-resistant, dissatisfied and – allow me to say what Peters and Waterman only imply – fearful individual bureaucrats. In contrast, the most successful firms, on which Peters and Waterman focused, exhibit organizational and individual flexibility, enthusiastic employees and product innovation. They achieve these qualities by producing organizational norms and myths encouraging spontaneity, risk taking and experimentation. They also provide their employees with long-term job security, material and symbolic rewards for risk taking, respectful treatment, peer support and support networks.

At least two critical arguments could be advanced about Peters and Waterman's book. The first is that they failed to note the link between the organizational values and structures, individual feelings, and the employee propensity to take risk and innovate. The second argument is that all they observed was an anxiety-driven enthusiastic play-acting.

The risk-taking argument is based on the conviction that Peters and Waterman, although in principle correct, failed to connect risk taking to underlying feelings and their structural causes. They failed to acknowledge that the seven main factors which they identified as encouraging innovation and risk taking among the employees are also the very factors which help these employees to overcome their fear of change, authority questioning and initiative taking. These factors – innovation-encouraging organizational values, authorized peer support, material and symbolic rewards for risk taking, support in failure, a broad margin for mistakes, long-term job security – counteract fear, help to convert a fearful and isolated organization 'man' into a self-confident and enthusiastic initiative- and risk-taker. Because Peters and Waterman failed to deal with feelings in their structural context, their organizational '7-S' (structure, strategy, systems, shared values, skills, staff, style) model left out the eighth crucial, 'S' – the sentiments of the *homo sentiens* (Peters and Waterman, 1982: 10).

The 'play-acted' work enthusiasm argument is based on the conviction that Peters and Waterman noted only the 'representative emotions' which the employees are compelled to construct and display in response to the authoritative demands (Flam, 1990b: 227). They remained insensitive to, and failed to uncover, the play-acting rules and the real feelings of the employees in the successful firms. Such firms cultivate 'strong cultures' which demand a definite set of play-acting skills and 'representative emotions' from their employees. A failure to engage these skills and to display such emotions is read as an act of insubordination or a sign of incompetence. The individuals working in such firms are very likely to feel both entrapped and fearful. They may feel anxious not only about breaking the conduct rules but also about leaving.

The 'strong culture' organizations in particular provide their employees with a sense of belonging and with a social identity neatly placed in a symbolic universe of meaning and action. They make every effort to deny 'the irrelevance of persons' in the organizational structure which in fact is at the base of every organization (Coleman, 1982: 26–7). They prevent the threatening individual encounter with the existential void of which I spoke earlier. The mere thought of leaving can easily inspire anxiety or fear when associated with the prospect of losing identity, a place in the world, a sense of belonging and long-term job security, not to mention the fringe benefits. It is this very anxiety that Peters and Waterman entirely missed.[7] This anxiety, arguably, becomes converted into work enthusiasm among the Westerners working for the 'strong-culture' organizations, just as it was converted into enthusiasm for the communist party among some of the East European party members.

Jackall's thorough excursion into the world of the corporate managers supports the second argument. It reveals an anxiety-laden, but enthusiasm-displaying corporate world (Jackall, 1988). The very nature of their work organizations makes managers 'the great actors of our time' who, in order to remain upwardly mobile, have to follow the rules of the game and display 'iron self-control' to mask all emotions and intentions (Jackall, 1988: 47, 51, 56–62). In the first two-thirds of the book, almost every second page refers to such feelings as anxiety, fear, and panic which hide behind the amiable appearances and the plush interiors. The most often named fears are those of authority, loss of career chances and instant career termination. These fears are hidden behind the fears of recession, reorganization, being landed with responsibility for others' faulty decision-making, making mistakes, having mistakes uncovered, and peer, subordinate or 'whistleblower' indiscretion about such mistakes (Jackall, 1988: 12, 21, 22, 26–7, 31, 71–2, 146). They are also hidden behind the most often named anxieties caused by the indiscreet peers, 'blame time', being on constant probation, contingency-dependent evaluative criteria, and being in the wrong place at the wrong time (Jackall, 1988: 40, 42, 63, 65, 70, 73, 85). A special note is also made of the lower class, incomer anxiety, managerial mobility panic, and managerial and executive anxiety (Jackall, 1988: 14, 21, 70–9, 141–2).

Jackall convincingly argues that corporate managers live with the foreboding sense of organizational contingency and capriciousness. They cope with the uncertainty created by the constant potential for social reversal, absence of fixed loyalties, and insufficient and unreliable information about people on whom their life chances depend. Facing constant social and economic uncertainty, corporate managers feel endemic anxiety, but display work enthusiasm (Jackall, 1988: 35, 69, 79). This core finding is certainly applicable to all firms which offer no long-term job security to their employees. Only emotion-sensitive research can show whether it is also applicable to those protective of their employees which Peters and Waterman studied.

Peters and Waterman argue that the rigid, 'rational' organizations are less authority oriented than the flexible, 'irrational' ones. I believe, and Schein and Jackall show, that this is a wrong conclusion. In both 'rational' and 'irrational' organizations, the employee respects and fears authority. But the authority in the 'irrational' organization uses the vast resources at its disposal to decentralize and spread power (Jackall, 1988: 12, 36). In one such prototypical firm, its 'leaders . . . believed strongly that good decisions could be made only if one was encouraged to challenge authority and if peers were encouraged to debate every issue. The consequence of this belief was that passive and/or dependent behaviour by a subordinate was always severely punished' (Schein, 1989: 75–6). And, to cite some more in the same vein: 'the chairman got angry with a member who was not contributing and began to draw conclusions about the competence of that member. The chairman assumed . . . that the silence meant ignorance, incompetence or lack of motivation' (Schein, 1989: 67).

The 'irrational' organization also clearly encourages a different set of emotional and work habits than the 'rational' one. In particular, its leaders try to minimize the display and the innovation-killing effects of the 'fear hierarchy',[8] although they never completely relinquish it for the sake of the 'peer fear' system. Peers provide support and encouragement at the same time that they take over some of the control functions (Jackall, 1988: 34, 40). As a control device, 'peer fear' is probably a good equivalent of the fear hierarchy.

As important as work-related positive emotions and norms are for ensuring the desired work performance, they should not overshadow the importance of the negative 'controlling emotions' which a workplace generates, such as fear, embarrassment, shame or guilt. These negative 'controlling emotions' buttress whatever other (normative or instrumental) means of control organizations have at their disposal to ensure employee compliance (cf. Flam, 1990b: 228). It has to be explicitly recognized that different work settings and organizations vary in the emotional habits they want to instil, who instils and monitors these habits, what measure of play-acting they demand and how much tolerance there is for unconvincing acting. In all these respects, factory, bureaucratic and professional 'emotional' regimes differ. Each is also subject to internal stratification.

Conclusion

More than once it has been observed that the Western societies are organization prone:

> a very large part of the action that is carried out in society, and by far most of the economically productive action, is action carried out by one person to accomplish the ends of another – the corporate actor whose agent he is. (Coleman, 1982: 29, 10–12)

If one wants to accomplish anything, one is 'sentenced' to organizations and organizing. True, these societies supply many choices: not a choice between the individual and the organized action, however, but between different types of organized action. To be effective, one has a choice of initiating a new organization or joining one that is already established. A variety of fears, I suspect, stand behind such a choice. Rephrasing Pizzorno (1986), one can argue that one such fear is the fear of losing one's social identity. Out of this fear, individuals initiate new or join old organizations. This fear also lowers the cost of their participation in collective action.

Once a member of an organization, many an individual becomes vulnerable. He or she develops interests in the organizational survival. Some individuals turn into 'high-loyalty members' (Hirschman, 1970; Pizzorno, 1986). For fear of organizational deterioration or death, such an individual pushes for or accepts a variety of measures, such as discipline modifications, goal shifts and replacement, internal and external ungodly alliances, which violate to a greater or lesser degree his/her normative standards. A profound split between the corporate and individual morality is as commonplace today as the individual's unquestioning acceptance of its dominance over his or her decisions (Coleman, 1982: 28, 41).

This is a particularly disturbing statement of fact when combined with a finding that corporations breed individuals who, moved by a constant mobility anxiety and their fear of both peers and authority, are only capable of situational and organizational morality (Jackall, 1988). In politics, as well as in the anxiety-pervaded corporate world, potential 'whistleblowers', who may criticize their own organizations in public, are generally feared and punished (Jackall, 1988: 109, 111, 146, 206). The organizations try to weed them out and so they are rare. Moreover, corporate employees are under heavy pressure to renounce their original moral standards. Their life chances depend on their capacity to ignore or keep secret corporate failures and transgressions. Therefore, their emotional, fear-driven selves help the rational, organization-loyal selves to take over. Just like their Polish counterparts, they are unlikely to show concern for the public good, the affected third parties or their own normative selves.

In their turn, potential whistleblowers, just like their Polish counterparts, fear losing self-respect by not living up to their own moral standards. For a potential whistleblower, usually well aware of the consequences of expressing dissent or of calling attention to mistakes, this fear may, but does not have to, become more important than that of the authority, peers or forfeited life chances. As this text has tried to show, because of the emotions involved, there is a long step from a private to a public criticism or exit. Fear installs a – rationally argued – weakness of will in most critical individuals. It prevents specifying the criteria identifying the condition 'beyond any hope'. Wavering self-respect (or fear of losing one's self-respect) points towards exit as the only face-saving way out, but fear prevents fixing the exit point.

Rather than quitting, single, critical individuals engage in self-deception (Hirschman, 1970: 103, 115). The self-deception helps to maintain self-respect while preventing the actual taking of the 'no return' exit option. With no external stimulus or support, it can last for ever. This is why, in the absence of the 'defiant peers', forced exit is necessary to convert a single internal dissenter in an organization into its public critic.

Notes

I would like to thank Stephen Fineman, Brigitte Jessen, Timur Kuran, Ilja Srubar and Uwe Schimank for their contributions to this chapter.
1. First in the 1980s, a small group of scientists began to expand the rational choice paradigm to include norms and emotions. See Etzioni (1988), Frank (1988), and Schelling (1984) and footnote in Frank, 1988: 14.
2. For a review, see Hosking and Fineman (1990: 594–5, 598–602).
3. Hirschman (1970) introduced and Pizzorno (1986) adopted this term. Following

their reasoning, I use it in this chapter to emphasize the dramatic nature of an individual decision to leave an organization.

4. Elster (1989) makes a similar argument: 'norms are sustained by the feelings of embarrassment, anxiety, guilt and shame that a person suffers at the prospect of violating them' (1989: 99).

5. The narrative excerpts derive from my research project, 'Mosaic of Fear in a Communist Regime', funded by the University of Konstanz, for which I and the two volunteers (Marek Czunkiewicz and Tadeusz Lebioda) conducted about 80 tape-recorded interviews in Poland in 1991–2.

6. Milgram's defiant peers as catalysts for collective protest are the equivalents of Elster's everyday Kantians – the catalysts for cooperative action (Elster, 1989: 205). The contrasting case analysis which shows the impact of defiant peers on the exit decision had to be omitted for reasons of space.

7. Schein missed this, but spoke of another type of anxiety – that caused by cognitive uncertainty or overload (Schein, 1989: 82) – which is more readily recognized but not investigated.

8. For this useful term, see Hochschild (1983: 102, 116–17). In her view, job scarcity and the fear of hierarchy on the job are the two preconditions for obedient play-acting.

References

Arendt, H. (1973) *The Origins of Totalitarianism*. New York: Harcourt Brace Jovanovich.

Cole, S. (1969) *The Unionization of Teachers: A Case Study of the UFT*. New York: Praeger.

Cole, S. (1980) *The Sociological Method: An Introduction to the Science of Sociology*. Chicago: Rand McNally.

Coleman, J. S. (1982) *The Asymmetric Society*. Syracuse, NY: Syracuse University Press.

Coser, L. (1974) *Greedy Institutions: Patterns of Undivided Commitment*. New York: Free Press.

Elster, J. (1989) *The Cement of Society: A Study of Social Order*. Cambridge: Cambridge University Press.

Etzioni, A. (1988) *The Moral Dimension. Toward a New Economics*. New York: Free Press.

Fireman, B., Gamson, W. W., Rytina, S. and Taylor, B. (1979) 'Encounters with unjust authority', in L. Kriesberg (ed.), *Research in Social Movements, Conflicts and Change*, Vol. 2. Greenwich, CT: JAI Press. pp. 1–33.

Flam, H. (1990a) 'Emotional "Man": the emotional "man" and the problem of collective action', *International Sociology*, 5 (1): 39–56.

Flam, H. (1990b) 'Emotional "Man": corporate actors as emotion-motivated emotion managers', *International Sociology*, 5 (2): 225–34.

Frank, R. H. (1988) *Passions within Reason: The Strategic Role of the Emotions*. New York: W. W. Norton.

Fromm, E. (1963) *Fear of Freedom*. London: Routledge & Kegan Paul.

Goffman, E. (1961) *Encounters*. Indianapolis: Bobbs-Merrill.

Hirschman, A. O. (1970) *Exit, Voice and Loyalty*. Cambridge, MA: Harvard University Press.

Hochschild, A. R. (1983) *The Managed Heart: Commercialization of Human Feeling*. Berkeley: University of California Press.

Hosking, D. and Fineman, S. (1990) 'Organizing processes', *Journal of Management Studies*, 27 (6): 583–604.

Jackall, R. (1988) *Moral Mazes: The World of Corporate Managers*. New York: Oxford University Press.

Kuran, T. (1991) 'Now out of never: the element of surprise in the East European revolution of 1989', *World Politics*, 44 (1): 7–48.

Kusy, M. (1985) 'Chartism and real socialism', in J. Keane (ed.), *The Power and the Powerless: Citizens against the State in Eastern Europe*. London: Hutchinson.

McAdam, D. (1988) 'Micromobilization contexts and recruitment to activism', in B. Klandermans, H. Kriesi and S. Tarrow (eds), *International Social Movement Research*, Vol. 1. Greenwich, CT: JAI Press. pp. 125–54.

Milgram, S. (1974) *Obedience to Authority: An Experimental View*. London: Tavistock.

Moore, B. Jr (1978) *Injustice: The Social Bases of Obedience and Revolt*. White Plains, NY: M. E. Sharpe.

Neumann, F. L. (1978) 'Angst und Politik', in A. Söllner (ed.), *Wirtschaft, Staat, Demokratie. Aufsätze 1930–1945*. Frankfurt am Main: Suhrkamp. pp. 424–59.

Nowak, K. (1988) 'Covert repressiveness and the stability of the political system: Poland at the end of the seventies', *Social Research*, 55 (1/2): 179–208.

Peters, T. J. and Waterman, R. H. Jr (1982) *In Search of Excellence: Lessons from America's Best-Run Companies*. New York: Harper & Row.

Pizzorno, A. (1986) 'Some other kind of otherness: a critique of "rational choice" theories', in A. Foxley et al. (eds), *Development, Democracy and the Art of Trespassing: Essays in Honor of Albert O. Hirschman*. Notre Dame: University of Notre Dame Press. pp. 355–73.

Roethlisberger, F. G. and Dickson, W. J. (1939) *Management and the Worker*. Cambridge, MA: Harvard University Press.

Rüdig, W. (1990) *Anti-Nuclear Movements: A World Survey of Opposition to Nuclear Energy*. Harlow, Essex: Longman.

Schein, E. H. (1989) *Organizational Culture and Leadership*. San Francisco: Jossey-Bass.

Schelling, T. C. (1984) *Choice and Consequence*. Cambridge, MA: Harvard University Press.

Terkel, S. (1972) *Working: People Talk About What They Do All Day and How They Feel About What They Do*. New York: Pantheon.

Wat, A. (1990) *My Century: The Odyssey of a Polish Intellectual*. New York: W. W. Norton.

4

Passion and Performance: Suffering and the Carrying of Organizational Roles

Heather Höpfl and Steve Linstead

'I can't carry on', 'I hope he can carry it off', 'I can't bear it any longer', 'His actions were insupportable', 'It was unbearable', 'She's weary', 'I'm worn out'. When people use these expressions to describe how they feel about their lives and work they are describing experiences which must be 'carried', 'borne', 'worn'; experiences which are likened to some burden, pressure, weight or stress; experiences that weigh heavily on the individual's sense of self.

The discussion which follows attempts to identify the nature of the burden, to understand what is experienced as being carried, by considering data from two organizations which make not dissimilar emotional demands on their members. In particular, we draw upon theories of acting and a dramaturgical perspective to explore how the passions, performance and suffering (as something which must be borne) relate to people's emotional experience of involvement with organizations. Acting theory is used to throw light on certain aspects of contemporary organizational behaviour via the conceptual vehicles of *motion, movement* and *comportment*, and the implications of these for the relationship between the actor and audience. The skill of the actor is assessed in terms of the extent to which his/her performance communicates appropriate emotions to the audience; that is, the extent to which the audience is *moved* or *transported*.

Drama and Acting

The dramaturgical approach is founded upon the metaphor of social life as theatre (e.g. Brissett and Edgeley, 1975; Burke, 1965, 1968, 1969a, 1969b; Goffman, 1959, 1961, 1963; Mangham and Overington, 1983, 1987; Messinger et al., 1968; Turner, 1982). It emphasizes both the analysis of social action and the analysis of explanations of social action. Language is the most important, but it is not the only means of constituting meaningful action. Complete explanations have five elements, providing answers to what was done (act), when or where it was done (scene), who did it (agent), how it was done (agency) and why it was done (purpose) (Burke, 1969a).

When only one or two of these five elements are presented as the explanation of what did, is taking, or will take place, *mystification* occurs as 'participants in or observers of some activity are persuaded by the parsimonious lure of such explanations to formulate the other elements as consistent' (Mangham and Overington, 1983). The emotional dynamics involved in sustaining mystification will be one of the themes of this chapter. Although we use theories of acting, viewing acting as a professionalized form of social performance,[1] in order to throw a more intense light on that performance, we are aware that theatrical acting is not social acting. In particular, the stakes in social life are much higher, and the audience is likely to be both less committed to playing its part in sustaining a successful performance and highly committed to its own performances. Michael Caine, the British actor, recently likened theatre acting to an operation with a scalpel, whilst film acting was like laser micro-surgery. The skills involved in social acting are less sophisticated, but the patient is not anaesthetized and may well wish to perform an operation him/herself! As Mangham and Overington point out, following Burke, people are not mere performers but are actors who play characters, moving from character to character and audience to audience with a 'theatrical consciousness' which enables them to retain a concept of an acting self (1983: 221). Moving from one role to another and using it to take a perspective on the previous one is a form of self-reflection which can expose mystification and enable demystification to occur.

We are also interested in the points at which the burden of sustaining consistency, creating sufficiently convincing conditions to *enable* the audience to formulate missing or incomplete elements as consistent, becomes too great for the actor to bear. This alienation of actor from performance both demystifies the performance and calls for 'repair work' from other actors if the social or corporate show is to go on (Goffman, 1952). We should also add that several writers have sought to make specific links between dramaturgical approaches and the study of emotion (Averill, 1980; Hochschild, 1983; Sarbin, 1986). What follows is located within this tradition and takes its starting point from the exploration of performance and passion.

Passions and Perturbations

It is useful to bear in mind that the modern usage of the term emotion dates back little more than 300 years. The earliest references to the term describe states of meterological agitation or disturbance (Latin, *emovere*: to move out, to stir up) and this usage eventually came to be applied to psychological states. However, from the time of the ancient Greeks to the eighteenth century, what are now referred to as emotions were known as 'passions' (Averill, 1980). The word passion is derived from the Latin (*patior*) to bear, to suffer, to support, to undergo, to allow, permit, endure and, in an obscene sense, to submit to another's lust, to prostitute oneself. In other words, passion is passive. It is to be borne or suffered. Indeed, this understanding of emotional experience is present in everyday aspects of conversation when expressed as something which happens *to* a person so that people talk of being 'overcome' by grief or terror, 'possessed' by anger or jealousy, 'overwhelmed' by joy, 'consumed' with rage.

In 1604 Thomas Wright's treatise on the emotions, *The Passions of Minde* was published. The passions of the mind were generally supposed to be of two kinds. The concupiscible (Latin *concupiscere*, to desire) and the irascible (Latin *irasci*, to be angry). Both types of passion were concerned with the way people were drawn towards or repelled by an object that excited them. Concupiscible passions were thought to involve movement towards an object, the object which excited desire, the desire to have – greed, love, joy – whereas the irascible passions were viewed as movements away from the object which brought about the perturbation, as in fear or hate. In 1651, Hobbes described the passions as 'Appetites' and 'Aversions'.

There is any number of different taxonomies of the passions, but the simplicity of this view of the passions as *oppositional movements* provides a useful dynamic for considering ways in which skilled performance in organizations can invoke the aversions, such as fear and, at the same time, offer a vision of the satisfaction of the appetites, such as greed.

Roles, Rhetoric and Performance

Acting, and passions and performances of organizational life, are inextricably linked to the rhetorics employed – and the roles played. From the time of Quintilian (AD 35–95) up until the middle of the eighteenth century, the predominant method of achieving propriety in acting was through rhetoric. The prevailing view was that an actor should exhibit emotions *as if* they were his own, that is, to 'impersonate' emotion (Roach, 1985: 24). Such affective embodiments, which Quintilian refers to as 'visiones', *affect* the state of mind of the actor to the extent that they become indistinguishable from genuine feeling, particularly those which belong to the rhetorical category of pathos; that is, the strong passions of grief, fear, anger and loathing (Roach, 1985: 25). In other words, arousing emotion in others depends on the power of the actor to imitate the passions, that is, on a capacity for *impersonation*. The *visiones* are inspirational visions, fantastic dreams based on the association between inspiration of breath and states of consciousness and with the physiological understanding of bodily humours and disposition.

According to Roach, the rhetoric of the passions endowed the actor with three potencies: the power to act on the actor's own body, the power to act on the physical space around the actor and to act on the bodies of spectators. As Roach puts it, 'In short, he possessed the power to act.' The actor could, therefore *affect* the audience in a number of ways and by conveying passions could touch and change the experience of the audience. A great actor had the capacity to 'move' his or her audience. The skills of classical oratory involved the orator being energized by an image so powerful that it could be communicated to the spectators, that is, 'the spirit moves the actor, who, in the authenticity of his transport, moves the audience' (Roach, 1985: 44–5). Skilled exponents of this style are able to communicate a vision to their audiences and to do it with authority. The capabilities of actors to exercise such power over their audiences has always been viewed with suspicion.

In such dramatic work there is something which must be conveyed, the drama itself – the action. The relevance of this point is in the emphasis placed in acting on outward signification and its consequences for the actor. Passions were regarded as needing control, to be kept 'down', not to be worked 'up' and actors were regarded as in danger of being overcome by the passions they were required to portray. The writings of Edmund Gayton (1654) refer to the pathological aspects of acting, suggesting that medicine or liquor are the only remedies for 'those who have "counterfeited" the passions for any extended period of time' (Roach, 1985: 48). Yet actors were expected to be capable of skilled control over their emotional repertoire and to move readily between different passions in any performance. The actor was regarded as a Protean figure, but this was not without attendant dangers. Gayton, who

was by profession a physician, comments adversely on the consequences of 'habitual self-transformation' (Roach, 1985: 52).

In the twentieth century, innumerable examples of powerful
orators and actors spring to mind and, despite some unfortunate
juxtapositions, it is possible to see that figures such as Billy
Graham, Martin Luther King, Richard de Vos, Tom Peters,
Winston Churchill, Adolf Hitler and so on, possess common
characteristics in terms of their ability to inspire a vision, make
vivid a dream and exercise considerable personal power. While
these qualities can be addressed via theories of charismatic leadership and traits, it is profitable to consider this type of behaviour
in terms of the passions it arouses and the agitations it creates as
oppositional forces. The skilled performer offers the audience
release from its 'burden' or transport from its effects. Skilled
rhetoricians offer freedom from persecution, threat, slavery, want
and oppression and in doing so they metaphorically *bear* the
suffering of others, that is, in what they seek to convey.

We can see this process in operation at the corporate level in a
way commercial enterprises manufacture 'dreams'. For instance,
the American direct marketing company Amway, which markets
household cleaning products and toiletries, produced a television
programme, *The Freedom Show*, which dealt with its audience's
'dreams and hopes for the future', and used the message: 'Who
can resist a dream?' Amway distributors, presumably inspired by
the vision rather than the household detergents they sell, frequently
describe their experiences of visiting the organization's headquarters as 'moving'. Similarly, Disney enterprises have produced
this effect by the realization of the vision in the various international Disney 'worlds'. 'When you wish upon a star . . . dreams
come true': many people visiting Disney pleasure parks comment
on how moved they are by the experience, by the intense emotional
response which is evoked: childhood satisfactions, carefree
pleasures, a deep sense of belonging. In other words, they are
transported from the day-to-day world with all its pressures and
stresses.

Cases and Contexts: Discovering Emotional Dramas

From the point of view of any investigation into the emotions, a
primary problem is how to gain access to this inner experience.
Clearly, while behaviour is observable, inner experience is more
difficult to explore. Consequently, the emotions are difficult to
investigate and define. For some methodologies, the inability to

measure emotions and their unreliability would preclude any meaningful research. Investigators into the emotions therefore must accept some sort of proxy as their manifestation. This entails either treating outward observable behaviour as expressive of inner emotional states, or trusting the verbal or textual reporting of the subjects to represent, or recollect, those states. Our investigation here contains elements of both, as both are cornerstones of the 'ethnographic' method.

Our methodology has serendipity as one of its key ingredients. In the course of our work as management developers we collaborated on parts of a culture-change programme for a recently privatized, large UK company, here referred to as British Carriers. As part of this programme, discussions with course participants on 'emotional labour' (Hochschild, 1983) produced some of the data we present here. We began by identifying a small group of those in jobs which had clear dimensions of 'emotional labour': high visibility, high contact with the public, the need to maintain a particular 'face', and the need to manage one's self. We then adopted a dramaturgical method, asking the core group to imagine that they were briefing an actor on how to get inside their role. Their responsibility was to present not just the visible, easily verbalized parts of that role, but the intangibles: the tensions, the strains, the moments of stress, the exhilarations of success which could only be effectively conveyed by examples and stories illustrating their lives. We asked them to consider what makes them tick in their job and to try to give the 'actor' everything necessary to achieve empathy, to don their uniform and 'feel' right in the role. We then subdivided the group and sent them into other groups who had the 'actor's' brief – to talk, question and converse with the core members, sufficient to feel that they were 'inside the skin' of the role.

The powerful recollections and recreations of emotional situations sensitized the group as a whole and released a great deal of energy which continued to produce discussion and insight outside the boundaries of the session. We realized that we were researching by stealth and that learning, as it often does, was creeping up on us immersed as we were in the flow of talk. Talk is an important element of social life, for the meaning of action is constituted both by the social act and by the way that act is described, explained and accounted for (Mangham and Overington, 1983: 219; Scott and Lyman, 1975). Conversation is a fruitful way of accessing 'a kind and quality of information unknown to interviewers' (Mangham and Overington, 1983: 232).

During the course of our own discussions of the ideas emerging from these sessions, we discovered parallel experiences from our work with a direct marketing organization, Parisienne – our second source of data. Parisienne is a network marketing organization selling perfume, and we offer direct accounts from some of its employees. We were also able directly to observe for ourselves the inner operations of the organization.

In sum, our data are partially ethnographic, drawn from two organizations, and gained by a combination of observed action and participants' own accounts of their actions.

Dreams and Motivations: inside Parisienne

Consider then the experiences of Julie Maddrell, a woman in her mid-thirties who had achieved high status, Group Director, in the direct marketing company, Parisienne. She described her feelings:

> They ended the presentation with the words, 'Tomorrow will be the same as today unless you do something about it now! Can you afford not to?' It was that that ensnared me into the positive thinker's nirvana. For a nominal fee I was soon on the road to building my dream and, whether I had a dream or not, I was soon to acquire one. After twelve years of working as a very committed teacher, I was drowning in despondency. Parisienne provided me with an ideal opportunity to build my own business with no financial risk [and] to feel valued, recognized and rewarded. For the next two and a half years I committed my every waking hour to network marketing and outwardly my dreams were realized – a personalized number plate on my new Mercedes, business trips to California and family holidays aboard luxury cruise liners. The kids were delighted with the perks of mum's new business. My husband was delighted to see me so fulfilled. The local newspaper ran a story under the headline, 'The Sweet Smell of Success' but for me it was all beginning to smell a little sour.

In short she was 'drowning' in her work. She was exposed to the persuasions of a skilled direct marketing operation – and she was simultaneously part of that circle of persuasion. She became committed to 'the dream'. The hype and razzmatazz is also wedded to a methodical and relatively gentle approach to the individual customer which makes it even more seductive – you can buy into the dream at your own pace. After two and a half years, in which she had achieved considerable success, she became disillusioned, that is, she could no longer sustain 'the dream'. The object of her excitement, the inspiration of her desire and appetites had become the source of dread, disgust, aversion.

Another of our respondents, Pepe, was a female graduate secretary. She joined Parisienne primarily to supplement her income, but had had experience in sales. She told us:

> Even the small meetings we have in the King's Head every fortnight are hyped up, they're all so bright and intense. There are a few sad, timid people who're just so unhappy or hard up they're desperate to do anything, and this won't help them. But most of them are so vulgar – all they want to know is how much commission you made last month so they can tell you how much they made, and they can't have a conversation without trying some smarmy sales technique on you. They show you some new idea for presenting or promoting the product (most of these come from the distributors themselves) and it doesn't seem to square with the fact that you're supposed to be supplying friends and acquaintances, not selling to strangers. They're all motivated by greed, and the more you get into it the less you see people as people but more as selling opportunities. You're using them for something rather shallow. In the end, I suppose that's what you've got to be like to make money, because that's all you do. If you don't have any other skills or value, than that, then I'll do without.

For those for whom the conversion experience had taken place, however, the burden of the day to day had been lifted. To continue, in Julie's own words,

> Once caught on the roundabout, many people become so involved that their whole life revolves around their team. Their friends are the people they recruit. Their social life revolves around company meetings. These are always fun events – bright lights, loud music, razzamatazz. For many people whose work life is routine, perhaps mundane, working in such an atmosphere of glitz becomes addictive. The alternatives cannot live up to this and even when their business is not succeeding they still pay out to go to company seminars and trainings because *their spirits are raised. They are transported out of their humdrum existence.*

This provides some clue to the way in which the direction of the emotions is changed. However, it goes further. The appetite having been stirred, recruits are encouraged to 'Live the Dream'. Great emphasis is placed on the fact that the opportunity is open to anyone. Everyone is a potential recruit and once recruited a new member is introduced to the idea of commitment at an early stage. New recruits are exposed to a series of personal testimonies which are reeled off night after night around the country. Such stories are of the type, 'Six months ago I was only a ——— but now . . .'. Julie continues,

> At this point people often *suffer* from the hot bath syndrome, i.e. they

are excited, hot and can envisage themselves in the place of the successful. Once reality dawns, however, very quickly they go cold and so it is very important to follow with step two. Painting and reinforcing the dream is done in many ways but several advocates of this theory encourage new recruits to experience their dream for a short period of time and the ultimate loss of it will spur them on to work harder to make the dream a reality again . . . sponsors should take their new found friend [the new recruit] to an appropriate garage (say), book a test drive in the dream machine, take sales literature and so on and then encourage their protégé to put pictures of the desired object in a prominent place in their home – the bed head perhaps.

Performing

In order to understand the performative aspects of this 'live the dream' philosophy, it is necessary to give attention to the framing of the performance, to the ways in which the situation is defined, since this, more than the techniques and devices available, is the foundation of the creation and fostering of illusion. The framing of the action in the Parisienne example is achieved by the use of transformational metaphors and patterns of association which move the subject from the drabness of their unworthy experience to a vision of experience in different domains.

The expressive events hosted by Parisienne, with their impressive stage management, function to convey three types of statement: states of adequacy, inadequacy, and transformation or transcendence of state (Fernandez, 1986: 43–4). The mass events serve to move the individual through a series of emotional experiences into a state of incorporation into the organization with a high level of personal commitment. Julie Maddrell described a Parisienne training rally in these terms:

It was held at the National Exhibition Centre in Birmingham and people had travelled from all over the country to be there. I took a mini-bus down with my distributors and I'd been briefed to get them 'worked up' before we arrived. We made several stops on the way and I had taken bottles of champagne which we opened – it gave a feeling of luxury. One woman hung back. I could tell she wasn't enjoying all the 'hype' but, honestly, by the time we got there she was the first to get up on her chair.

The description continues with details of the staging and setting for the event.

It was a magnificent set with two huge silver pyramids at the front. There was dry ice everywhere and then, suddenly, he [the founder] came out from between the pyramids and everyone went wild. He raised his arms and said, 'Manna from heaven' and hundreds of balloons were released onto the audience. It was amazing.

Julie had by this time become a group director and was responsible for disseminating the message, of creating and sustaining the dream for her own selling team. This involved a considerable amount of time and *patience* (also from the Latin, *patior*: to suffer). The fact that recruits came from different backgrounds and had different levels of intellectual and social skill placed a burden on the group director. In fact, the only real thing the recruits had in common was their desire to be free of their own particular personal burden. These ranged from financial worries to difficult personal relationships. By offering recruits a dream, the organization had established a complex network of emotional dependency in which the group director began to feel her role was to carry the burdens of her team. She commented that her kitchen was always full of people and that at any time of the day or night the team would contact her with all sorts of problems: 'The kettle was always on and the phone would ring in the middle of the night if one of them had a problem.'

At first this was fun and reinforced her personal sense of being wanted and worthy. However, as her own family began to be overwhelmed by the demands and problems of strangers, she began to take stock. Other aspects of the organization gave her pause to think. She says it was argued that for

> successful commitment the whole family should be involved. Family days are often organized and always include a rewards ceremony. The idea of your family taking pride in your achievements can unbalance your reason . . . I have actually heard two very successful people within the organization advocate to a conference of 3–4,000 people the benefits of committing the children.

The 15-year-old daughter of Tom, another very successful group director was doing her homework when we called at the house. Whilst waiting for Tom to complete a telephone call, a conversation began and she was asked what she wanted to do when she left school. 'That's easy,' she replied, 'I want to be the youngest Parisienne millionaire.'

In the theatrical demands of her role with Parisienne, Julie Maddrell found that she was required to work within specific training guidelines, to 'sell' a dream, that is, in the theatrical analogy to work within 'rules for delivery' in order to 'move' (motivate) her team. Motivational talks were scripted and rehearsed. Training manuals offered guidance on how to play the required role. She began to feel the burden of being all things to her team. An inner conflict began to open up between the need to 'work up' other people and yet 'hold down' her own emotions. Holding back her own feelings began to be an increasing burden and, as more and more demands were placed on her, she became disillusioned to the point at which she realized, 'I just couldn't carry on with it.'

Comportment

To explore why Julie Maddrell could not 'carry off' her performance, it is necessary to give some thought to the nature and meaning of *comportment* and its implications for behaviour and emotional restraint. The word comportment derives from the Latin *comportare* 'to carry together' and means 'to agree, accord, suit – to bear oneself, to behave, to conduct oneself'. In a theatrical performance, the actors comport themselves to the task of presenting the action of the play; to the skills they employ in 'carrying off' the performance. 'To carry it off' implies a successful outcome: a performance delivered with propriety. Hence, the role is always paramount and where the personality of the actor is used, it is to give emphasis to the action itself. Thus, if the performance is to be achieved with authority and propriety, any ambivalence towards the role needs to be concealed by a mask, in itself a paradoxical concept.

The actor's skill in the 'histrionic dissimulation of emotion used to create controlled illusions' (Roach, 1985: 138) led to the acting profession being regarded as a tawdry and somewhat degrading way of earning a living. It is only when the actor has learned and mastered every aspect of the role that he or she is able to create the grand illusion of impersonating the role without the threat of intrusion of personal emotion. Hence, the inner model directs the embodiment of the illusion. The actor is thus a *tabula rasa*, or empty vessel, lacking personal affections, friendships, family ties, identities. Like the beggar, the seducer, the prostitute and the unbelieving priest, the actor is a professional illusionist who trades in the dispassionate embodiment of the passions (Roach, 1985: 138).

Props and Propriety: inside British Carriers

Our second case study examines the emotional impact of sustaining the illusion, in particular the tension that exists when the audience vacillates between willing complicity with the 'show', and alienation.

In 1990 we attended a management development workshop held

for British Carriers' managers in Old Windsor. The hotel was comfortable and welcoming but, because it had grown by extending in all directions from its original frontage, finding the seminar rooms proved a task of orienteering. The workshop, the last in a series, focused on participants' futures with the company. Over three days the managers were presented with messages of hope and uplift from a series of outside consultants and senior managers. The whole event was organized with considerable stage management skills, culminating in the visit of the Chief Executive on the third day. Before his arrival there was a great deal of fluster and concern. Time was allowed after lunch for the course members to change into formal clothes, and the trainers rehearsed the participants in the timing and style of the event. The Chief Executive arrived punctual to the minute. He was well briefed and beneficent. The vetted questions were asked and the presentable course members presented. The Chief Executive gave his benediction and left. Course members and their trainers breathed a sigh of relief. Masks fell away, people changed back into comfortable clothing and made their way to the bar for a relaxed drink before dinner.

On another occasion at a hotel in Slough, the stage management proved even more impressive. The technical support for this particular workshop on 'Visioning the Future' was highly professional. At the appointed time, the managers were admitted to the darkness of the conference room to be greeted by a fanfare and the corporate logo on a huge screen at the front of the room.

Conceits and Counterfeits

Many of the managers had strong reactions to the way they felt the company attempted to influence and 'use' their emotions to motivate (Latin *movere*, to move) them. One commented, 'Does this remind you of the Live Aid concert? It's all Save the World togetherness – like Coca Cola.' The group morning session began with a series of images, sounds and light. It was a performance to raise the spirits and to inspire pride in the company. One man commented, 'You can't help it, you know, it definitely makes you feel proud to work for a company like this – it just gets you right there' and patted his chest for emphasis. It was not clear whether this was a sincere or cynical gesture. It was not unusual for managers to comment on their personal confusions about the repeated appeals to their emotions. However, these remarks were almost invariably made informally. In formal sessions and particularly when trainers were present, any suggestion of cynicism was masked by due propriety.

Once, over dinner, one of the managers told us the story of 'The Love Bath':

> It was dreadful. It was excruciating. Can you remember it? 'The Love Bath', is that what it was called? It was supposed to make you feel better about yourself. It was embarrassing. We all had to sit round in a circle – groups of us – and each of us in turn had to sit in the middle. It was really humiliating. Then everybody in turn had to say something nice about the person in the middle. It was dreadful, it makes me cringe just to think of it. You had to begin what you said with 'I like (him/her) because . . .', and it had to be genuine not just flattery. Sometimes the only thing you could think of saying was 'I like Jim because he wears nice jumpers.' It was unbelievable – so un-English. One day I got back to the office and I was telling an American woman who was working with us what had gone on. She just looked at me in amazement and said 'Say, why don't you just tell these guys to F—— off!'

Of course, not everyone found these experiences so excruciating. Some individuals thought they were among the best experiences of their lives. Some had experienced 'conversion' by the techniques of corporate evangelism. One woman said,

> When I came back from that programme I felt as if I'd seen the light. I knew the company was committed to change and would support managers who were prepared to take risks. It was a new approach. There's no place for cynicism if you want to bring about change and you've got to admit we needed change.

An alternative position was expressed thus:

> I've worked for this company now for nearly twelve years and I've seen the whole lot. I can't say it actually makes me feel more committed. You know, sometimes over the past few years, especially with 'visible management', I've felt quite the reverse. It's caused quite a few rows at home. My wife says she never sees me these days – into the office before seven in the morning sometimes not home until nine or ten in the evening.

Over coffee, another manager commented,

> I hated a lot of the 'touchy-feely' stuff and, if it achieved anything, it gave me the experience of shared humiliation rather than shared self-esteem but we all had that cosy feeling of having survived something together and there's something to be said for that. We know it's hype – they know it's hype. It's OK. It's reassuring. It makes you feel good. But do I believe in it – well that's a totally different question.

In effect, he is acknowledging that his experiences at work are like those of the theatre, they require the 'knowing' suspension of disbelief. Goffman (1959) observes that the 'willing suspension of disbelief' is to some degree required to sustain social performances if, as Mangham and Overington suggest, 'the very fabric of social life is not to be reduced to shreds' (1983: 223). The successful suspension of disbelief is achieved when processes which are 'in emergence' are brought together and given consensus in some frame of action. This is achieved by the mystificatory strategy of emphasizing coherent aspects so that other aspects are constructed by the audience to be consistent.

However, as in the example above, it is apparent that performance rests on the paradox of acceptance that things may indeed appear to be what they are not. In organizational life, what this means is that in order to play a role there must be a suspension of disbelief alongside the awareness of the illusion. The actor must play the appropriate organizational role with propriety within an intricate pattern of social complexity which seeks to achieve or 'carry' the appearance of cultural consensus. The organizational actor has the task of 'carrying' the action in performance. Organizational actors must comport themselves to the performing of their roles with propriety. Those who are unable to sustain the appearance of a coherent, enduring, authoritative self and commensurate commitment, pose a threat to the corporate definition of reality.

Corpsing

In modern theatre the term 'corpsing' is used for the occasions on which an actor becomes distracted in performance, is seized by an uncontrollable fit of laughter and cannot continue. Formerly, however, the term was used to refer to what happens when an actor loses his/her place in the script, dries, is unable to continue, no longer believes in the play, sees the audience watching and waiting, freezes to the spot, cannot sustain the illusion. When an actor 'corpses' the performance is put in jeopardy. Similarly, the presence of dissonant and ambivalent experience in the face of apparently consensual cultural conventions is treated as an offence against decorum; skilled actors need to find ways to improvise around the 'corpse'. When an actor 'corpses', the other actors falter, hesitate, strain to keep their place – sometimes fail – they are disconcerted by the 'corpse'. This is the precarious point at which the paradox is exposed. The corpsing actor sees the play for what it is and experiences the 'shock of recognition'.

An example of this occurred on a Management Development Workshop in British Carriers. The workshop, on the theme of

'Your Future with BC', was designed to focus on self-development activities and three senior managers were invited to address the course on the first morning. In the event, two of the three were, in effect, sacked the day before the course. Apart from the logistical problems it gave the course organizers, the contradictory messages this sent to the participants produced some evident 'corpsing' effects. Many found it difficult to sustain a coherent view of the company's attitude to them, or theirs to the company. The fact that the men who had been dismissed were both popular and not seen to be ineffective in their 'performance' caused confusion and cynicism. The course members could not sustain their reality definitions in the face of two conflicting versions of their corporate destinies.

In one tutorial session, a participant, clearly distressed, rehearsed two speeches, one corporate and one personal, in unresolved vacillations – to the obvious discomfort of the other group members. 'It's a good company,' he said. 'My wife and I both work for BC. We can live on her expenses alone.' Then he physically turned and began again, 'I'm only 29 now and I've got a £225,000 mortgage. We'd like to have children but I can't see when we could ever afford it.' Turning again, he continued, 'But it's a good life. We have marvellous opportunities. I was skiing in Alaska last week – staying in first-class hotels', then continued, 'All my friends work for BC – sometimes I think I don't know any non-BC people.' 'You know, I've set up my own business which I run as a sideline it's doing well.' 'Sometimes you get really fed up with all the corporate "hype" – you know you don't really matter.'

When 'corpsing' occurs the other actors are alerted to the nature of their craft and bring all their skills to bear to recover the performance by improvisation and ad libbing to cover the lapse. Extremely skilled actors may be able to gloss the failure so that the audience may be unaware that any disruption has occurred. These are the devices and deceits which are used to create and sustain illusion. The actors, as the embodiment of ambivalence, 'corpse'. Hence 'corpsing' is not a failure of technique but a failure of the mask. In the example above, when the particular individual corpsed and revealed to the others in the group the precariousness of his feelings, his appetites and aversions, his motivations and his perturbations, the rest of the group were profoundly uncomfortable. Sometimes there are situations where this type of corpse yields fresh insights into the feelings of a group that are normally hidden behind the mask of their work roles. However, the people in question were disconcerted. They averted their gaze and shifted in their seats. They were anxious for the speaker to finish or to comport himself to the task and to remain within the consensual frame of action. When the 'corpse' finished, they turned quickly to the security of their improvisations around the script in a consensual commitment to 'carry on'.

Precarious Passions

Any mystification is always vulnerable to its own incompleteness, although the persuasiveness and authority ceded to it by virtue of the careful manipulation of setting and content to mobilize the emotions make it less likely that such weakness will be exposed. However, as our examples show, the extent to which this illusion of control or of authorship in corporate performances can be sustained is perpetually at issue. There is always the threat of what is being suppressed by the action being revealed, that is, the dissimulation of emotion embodied by the actors. Threat is conciliated by the transformational metaphors of salvation and worthiness which create 'visions', uplift the heart, raise the spirit, and convey higher passions. Yet whilst organizational rhetoric may create visions of power, status and wealth; may meet needs for affiliation and belonging; may bolster self-esteem – at a fundamental level, the paradoxes of performance are never resolved.

From the actor's and the audience's point of view, comportment to the action means that contradictions are ignored or denied. This denial produces a burden which is the resistance of the demands of those things which excite aversion. In relation to organizational work, this means those experiences which are not under the control of the individual. The person is thus *subject* to powerful and conflictual inner movement and motivations but must 'carry' the role expectations required by the action. This becomes apparent only when the actor is no longer able to carry the role, becoming visibly and publicly alienated from it and exposing it to demystification, and the continuation of the performance is in doubt.

This is a social phenomenon which is not confined to experience in work organizations. However, in our examples it is obvious that organizations do adopt styles of presentation, motivation and cultural manipulation which are thoughtful, calculated, strategically planned and executed and depend almost entirely on effective agitation and channelling of the emotions for their success. This provides us with two research opportunities which we argue are in need of greater development.

The first is the opportunity to consider the costs to corporate actors of carrying their roles in support of organizational action, reflecting on what happens when people find their roles 'unbearable', become unable to 'carry on' and in theatrical terms, 'corpse'. This does have demystificatory potential although, as we have also seen, both performers and audience can become alienated from the 'hype' and yet continue comfortably to collude in the continuation of ritual.

The second is the need to counterbalance the overwhelmingly cognitive emphasis in the majority of studies of organizational culture, development and change. The recognition and study of emotion and its part in organizational life should give due regard to those implicit, suppressed yet powerfully shaping forces – joy, shame, fear, embarrassment, jealousy, love, friendship, guilt, revenge, compassion, reparation – which, given sustained empirical development, could transform our perceptions of significant aspects of the process of organization. At a theoretical level such development has potential links with postmodern approaches which emphasize that the nature of organization is more likely to be understood through examination of the flow of process rather than the abstractions of the specific forms which such organization takes.

Notes

1. This is specifically the case in theories of acting where the external, physical characterization expressed by the actor is the means by which the inner state is conveyed. Roman Jakobson, the semiotician and linguist, conducted a celebrated experiment with a Russian actor in which an audience of Muscovites successfully decoded the actor's emotional state delivered through tone of voice and expression alone in his pronunciation of the Russian phrase for 'This evening' (Hawkes, 1977).

References

Averill, J. R. (1980) 'Emotion and anxiety: sociocultural, biological, and psychological determinants' (1976) in A. O. Rorty (ed.), 1980, *Explaining Emotions*. Berkeley: University of California Press.

Benjamin, W. (1977) *The Origin of German Tragic Drama*. London: New Left Books.

Brissett, D. and Edgley, C. (eds) (1975) *Life as Theater*. Chicago: Aldine.

Burke, K. (1965) *Permanence and Change*. Indianapolis: Bobbs-Merrill.

Burke, K. (1968) *Counterstatement*. Berkeley: University of California Press.

Burke, K. (1969a) *A Grammar of Motives*. Berkeley: University of California Press.
Burke, K. (1969b) *A Rhetoric of Motives*. Berkeley: University of California Press.
Fernandez, J. W. (1986) *Persuasions and Performances: The Play of Tropes in Culture*. Bloomington: Indiana University Press.
Gayton, E. (1654) *Pleasant Notes on Don Quixot*. London: printed for W. Hunt.
Goffman, E. (1952) 'On cooling the mark out', *Psychiatry*, 15: 451–63.
Goffman, E. (1959) *The Presentation of Self in Everyday Life*. Harmondsworth: Penguin.
Goffman, E. (1961) *Encounters*. Indianapolis: Bobbs-Merrill.
Goffman, E. (1963) *Behavior in Public Places*. New York: Free Press.
Hawkes, T. (1977) *Structuralism and Semiotics*. London: Methuen New Accents.
Hobbes, T. (1949) *Leviathan*. (1651). Oxford: Blackwell.
Hochschild, A. (1983) *The Managed Heart*. Berkeley, CA: University of California Press.
Mangham, I. L. and Overington, M. (1983) 'Dramatism and the theatrical metaphor', in G. Morgan, (ed.), *Beyond Method*. London: Sage. pp. 219–33.
Mangham, I. L. and Overington, M. (1987) *Organizations as Theatre: A Sociology of Dramatic Appearances*. Chichester: Wiley.
Messinger, L., Sampson, H. and Towne, R. D. (1968) 'Life as theatre: some notes on the dramaturgic approach to social reality', in M. Truzzi (ed.), *Sociology and Everyday Life*. Englewood Cliffs, NJ: Prentice-Hall. pp. 7–20.
Roach, J. R. (1985) *The Player's Passion: Studies in the Science of Acting*. Newark: University of Delaware Press.
Sarbin, T. R. (1986) 'Emotion and act: roles and rhetoric', in R. Harré (ed.), *The Social Construction of Emotion*. Oxford: Blackwell.
Scott, M. B. and Lyman, S. (1975) 'Accounts', in D. Brissett and C. Edgley (eds), *Life as Theater*. Chicago: Aldine. pp. 162–70.
Turner, V. (1974) *Dramas, Fields and Metaphors: Symbolic Action in Human Society*. Ithaca, NY: Cornell University Press.
Turner, V. (1982) *From Ritual to Theater: The Human Seriousness of Play*. New York: Performing Arts Journal Publishers.
Wright, T. (1971) *The Passions of the Minde in Generall* (1604). Urbana: University of Illinois Press.

5

Divisions of Emotional Labour: Disclosure and Cancer

Nicky James

the nurses told me the night before not to get worried. Bill would be in intensive care and I'd see all these machines and everything. But not to worry that was normal. They warned Bill as well. Well when I went in in the afternoon . . . he was sitting in a chair. And I thought, that's odd. And I said to him, 'Have you had the operation?' 'Yes' he said . . . He said, 'Well I can tell you they found something, but don't say anything.' . . . Well me and my son went in [to see Sister] and sat down. And she said that she was very sorry to tell us there was nothing they could do for Bill. They had operated, they had put this tube in, and he'd think he was getting better for a while because the food will pass through. She said, 'I'm afraid we found a growth at an advanced stage.' She wasn't supposed to have told me. . . Anyway it didn't sink in what she was saying. I'd been told by all the doctors, no, no, no, no [i.e. it's not cancer]. And my son was cringing because he knew that she wasn't supposed to tell me.

I think he'd gone and had a word with one of the doctors without me and Bill knowing. And this particular doctor had said to my son Robert. . . 'Don't tell your mother. The surgeon has to see her himself.' And my son and I came out, and I didn't say anything to Bill, naturally, and he was all right.

When Sister finished with me a doctor walked in. And one of the staff nurses said, 'Did you do Bill Jenkins' operation? This is his wife and son.' And the doctor said, 'I can't tell you much about it because the surgeon will have a word with you, he'll explain better than I can. But I don't want you to think things are worse than they are.' You see, they're still telling me now that everything is all right, but meanwhile the Sister had already said . . . but I didn't say anything.

So I went back up but my son followed the doctor . . . and they went into his room. And my son said, 'You're holding something back and I want to know what it is.' 'Well, you see, I'm not supposed to tell you in front of your mother,' the doctor said . . . I just don't know why, I was his wife, I should have been told. Perhaps they thought I couldn't take it, I don't know. . . We came out of the hospital and my son said, 'Now look Mum, don't go thinking the worst, don't go thinking now there's cancer there.' He said, 'Dad's going to be all right.' Now he is saying this because of what the doctor had told him 'Well, anyway,' I said, 'whatever it is, the surgeon will tell us tomorrow.' We went in the following day. Fortunately Bill didn't see me. We went round to a little place to see the surgeon. He said he'd operated and fixed this tube in and that there was a huge growth by the side of it. And he said, 'I'm glad I've proved myself right, but I'm sorry that he's got cancer.' He said, 'I felt it all the time, but it wasn't showing up on the X-rays.' So of course when they operated they discovered it was more than there, it had risen right up, the cancer, gone right up. And never a pain but terrible discomfort. . . I still couldn't believe it. My mind was blank. And yet, looking back, I had a feeling there was something . . . (Mrs Jenkins, aged 67, widow. Report 1 – edited interview transcript)

Managing Emotion

Mrs Jenkins was one of 31 people I interviewed as part of a project on care of the terminally ill. The interviews, with unwaged carers, took place five to nine months after the death from cancer of the carer's close relative. The focus of this chapter is on one aspect of the project; that is the management of emotions during the disclosure of a diagnosis of cancer. Particular attention is paid to the divisions of emotional labour, where differences between lay and professional people are indicative of different roles, power and levels of personal involvement. I use interview data to identify *differential* divisions of emotional labour based on equal status work, and *deferential* divisions of emotional labour which are characterized by submissions to authority. I argue that these divisions shape the context of emotional labour in health (and other) organizations – but they are being challenged.

Emotion Labour and Cancer

The phrase 'emotional labour' is intended to highlight similarities as well as differences between emotional and physical labour, with both being hard, skilled, work requiring experience, affected by immediate conditions, external controls and subject to divisions of labour. Emotions can be regulated with varying sophistication and with various outcomes and, like other skills, emotional labour requires flexibility and adjustment. It involves anticipation, planning, pacing, timetabling and trouble-shooting. Emotions that are not acknowledged – whether our own or those of others – may be denied or suppressed, but full emotional labour involves working with feelings rather than denying them. At its most skilled emotional labour includes managing negative feelings in a way that results in a neutral or positive outcome.

Emotional labour is an integral yet often unrecognized part of employment that involves contact with people. It has been argued, and counter-argued, that emotional labour demands an individualized but trained response which exercises a degree of control over the emotional activities of the labourer, and thereby commodifies their feelings (Hochschild, 1983; James, 1989; Wouters, 1989). Hearn and Parkin (1987) have noted that although male-dominated professions, such as medicine, may define the limits and action of emotion for other workers and clients, the problems of dealing with emotional control are primarily located through others. However, emotional labour also underpins domestic care work. The skills of emotional regulation are learned at home, predominantly from women, and transferred to workplace carework where they have to fit in with workplace priorities (Hochschild, 1990; James, 1992).

Cancer is a particularly apt disease to review in order to analyse the management, control and 'labour' of emotions in health organizations. In *Illness as Metaphor* Sontag showed how the word cancer is used as a figure of speech to suggest a 'profound disequilibrium between individual and society' (1979: 73). Phrases such as 'it is like a cancer spreading amongst us' convey a sense of slow but relentless invasion, of a battle to be fought and won before the disease annihilates us. Sontag also observes how the use of cancer as a malign adjective for social ills has ramifications for those who have cancer. *Illness as Metaphor* was written as a tool of liberation from the social overtones of the disease, for 'conventions of treating cancer as no mere disease but a demonic enemy make cancer not just a lethal disease but a shameful one' (Sontag, 1979: 57).

Emotions are bound within a diagnosis of cancer in two ways. First, cancer was and still is explained as a disease resulting from certain emotions and experiences such as depression, lack of confidence, repression and past trauma. Second, there are the emotions evoked by a diagnosis of cancer – because of its physical implications and because of its social consequences. As Sontag notes:

> Since getting cancer can be a scandal that jeopardizes one's love life, one's chance of promotion, even one's job, patients who know what they have tend to be extremely prudish, if not outright secretive, about their disease. (Sontag, 1979: 8)

In a 1988 survey in Britain, carried out on behalf of the Cancer Relief Macmillan Fund, 40 per cent of respondents agreed with the statement that 'the fear of cancer is worse than the fear of death' (1988: 5). This sense of the intensity of emotions surrounding cancer is reflected in doctors' own attitudes to disclosure of cancer diagnosis. As an American doctor noted, of both the USA and Britain:

> doctors believed, and many still do, that for patients to have to face a cancer diagnosis is terrible, and by giving them the diagnosis, you can do nothing other than be destructive . . . the medical profession were representing the feeling of society in general about cancer, in keeping the secret from patients. (Kfir and Slevin, 1991: 5)

Yet cancer is hard to hide and, whether formally told or not, relatives, the person with cancer and professionals have to regulate their feelings. Even the diagnosis (or potential diagnosis) of cancer is surrounded by its own language – 'disclosure', 'communication' and 'insight' in health staff's terms; 'telling' and 'knowing' in lay terms. At a personal level cancer generates disbelief, fear, lies and chaos which are controlled through information, optimism, routine living and social expectation. One in three of us will get cancer at some time in our life and despite excellent survival rates for some cancers, one in four of us will, eventually die of it.

Those of us who are diagnosed as having cancer are likely to have sentiments ranging from informed pragmatism, fatalism and numbness, to total anguish and the feeling that an active death sentence has been imposed. Further, the social impact of a diagnosis of cancer is rapid with a powerful ripple effect, so it will always be people with cancer and their relatives and friends who have to manage the strongest emotions. They have to live with the disease and its consequences. Yet health staff have a role in shaping the division of emotional labour because they are involved in setting the context within which feelings are managed. Thus the symbolic nature of a diagnosis of cancer, and the physical and social consequences, mean that debates about 'disclosure' and 'telling' are not just a matter of passing on information, but are a surrogate means of talking about managing the emotions surrounding cancer. Whoever has knowledge of the cancer has some power to control, to fight and to protect.

Disclosure of cancer is governed by myriad formal and informal rules. In Britain those involved in this process meet through the network of the biggest formal organization in Europe, the National Health Service, while also relying on a network of informal health care systems. Yet lay and professional groups are heterogeneous, and people with cancer, staff, relatives and friends work to regulate their own and others' emotions – and express them in forms which are personally, privately, publicly and professionally acceptable.

Divisions of Emotional Labour and Disclosure

The division of emotional labour is particularly important when considering the wide range of people brought together by the formal and informal health system through which cancer is managed: the person with cancer, their family, friends and neighbours, nurses, porters, domestics, doctors, radiotherapists, the taxi driver that takes someone to the 'cancer hospital'. These systems also divide through a series of hierarchies, roles, negotiations and conflicting personal and professional needs. The interviewees' reports in this chapter indicate ways in which the process of diagnosing and disclosing cancer cut across the divide of lay and professional while also showing the significance of those roles. Similarly, other dichotomies become mixed in the process of disclosure, those of organization and individual, waged and unwaged, public and private, male and female, active and passive, with techno-scientific knowledge being challenged by 'personal' knowledge. The reports illustrate how people with cancer, the unwaged carers, the doctors and nurses are all active and reflective as the process of disclosure unfolds. All are more or less logical and skilled in the management of their own and others' emotions, though some manage by denying emotions rather than engaging them.

While rejecting the adequacy of any single dichotomy in explaining the division of emotional labour in disclosure, I suggest that the division of emotional labour can be understood by recognizing *different levels of involvement with the feelings* associated with cancer, but explained as resulting from *competing forms of status and knowledge*.

Divisions of emotional labour will be affected, first, by the depth of the feelings generated. In this respect, lay and professionals are likely to be differentially involved. A second element is the public context within which feelings are expressed and regulated. When cancer is being diagnosed and disclosed, despite the depth of involvement of the person with cancer and their relatives and friends, the context for the management of emotion is often dominated by staff in health service organizations, resulting in deferential divisions of emotional labour.

A third key element in the division of emotional labour associated with the disclosure of a diagnosis of cancer is separation brought about by active, day-to-day involvement in the regulation and management of emotions. As report 1 illustrates, although the context was set by the consultant surgeon, it was the patient, relatives, nurses and junior doctor who were doing the ongoing work of managing emotions. Thus, while there has been a rhetoric of hierarchical, male-dominated, information-giving disclosure which limits emotional expression, in practice information and feelings are mixed. In this system those who have been perceived as passive, deferential inheritors of 'given' roles (junior staff, patients, unwaged carers) play a key part in fulfilling or challenging the workplace, hierarchical norm. The result is that deferential divisions of emotional labour in the disclosure of cancer are currently subject to negotiation, change and 'de-differentiation'. Although the medical/organizational shaping of diagnosis and disclosure tends to dominate, permeable demarcations and expectations can be, and are, challenged.

In the following section additional interviewee reports and other research data are used to consider who or what is dominant during key aspects of disclosure, and also how the dominance is challenged.

Divisions of Emotional Labour: Methods of Control

The blank numbness of Mrs Jenkins in the report at the beginning of this chapter, the quietness of Bill, the patient; the urgency of the son; the controlled sorrow of the Sister; the embarrassment of the junior doctor at being put on the spot; and the self-congratulation of the surgeon, all attest to the range of sentiments generated by the disclosure of information about cancer. Two further insights that Mrs Jenkins' report highlights are, first, the number and range of people caught up in controlling the emotions and information, and secondly the effects of unwritten rules, status and organizational role in shaping who said what to whom – and how their feelings were expressed. Cumulatively these insights indicate that disclosure of a diagnosis of cancer is a complex process and not a single event, and interventions can be made at various stages in the process.

In the report the interplay of patient/client, family members, doctors and nurses is significant because it illustrates that concentration on any one or two of these groups gives a partial perspective. Further, not only did each family member in report 1 have different ways of handling their painful knowledge, 'don't say anything' (Bill), 'I didn't say anything, naturally' (Mrs Jenkins), 'Mum, don't go thinking the worst' (Robert), but they also all had different roles to play in relation to each other and to the hospital staff. Bill was patient/husband/father, Mrs Jenkins was wife/mother/formal next of kin and Robert was son and a key information route into and out of the formal health system, so that there was potential for a variety of demands and expectations of each person.

Mrs Jenkins' report also indicates how inter- and intra-professional hierarchies of junior and senior doctors and nurses have developed to control the disclosure of life-affecting information, with some resulting demarcation tensions. All those involved were in some way influenced by the view that the senior doctor, the consultant surgeon, was in charge of the diagnosis of cancer. It appeared that until he formally acknowledged the diagnosis of cancer, the emotional labour was carried out in secret or semi-secret. Mrs Jenkins indicated that doctors blocked any contemplation that the diagnosis might be cancer. They had thereby pre-empted any discussion of associated emotions. Yet the ward Sister appears to have subverted the acknowledged system of consultant disclosure, and ran the risk of incurring the consultant's disapproval. The Sister saved the family a thirty-hour wait for information from the time of the initial post-operative visit until the time when the consultant surgeon was available to see them. In doing so she also gave the family an opportunity to assimilate the information and compose themselves before they saw the surgeon – a factor of which he was probably completely unaware. In this instance, concern that the diagnosis might be cancer was initially unspoken but nevertheless actively managed by health staff, while each family member kept their thoughts to themselves.

The second report is of a mother, Mrs Downie, and her daughter, Mrs Sketty. In addition to the issues mentioned above, this report is an observation of the role of the unwaged carer in recognizing the significance of impending diagnosis of cancer and working to support her mother in the period leading up to and during the hospital consultation. It gave rise to the daughter asking a specific question about the consultant's communication skills – a key element in the control of emotions:

'Well, I've got an inverted nipple,' Mum said. So I said, 'Well in that case we'd better see about it. How long have you had it?' 'Oh about three weeks,' she said. And so I took her to the GP who immediately referred her to the hospital and they took her in, and she went to see the surgeon. Well my mum was most annoyed because for a woman of 78 she was very active and very alert. And she went to see the surgeon . . . I wasn't allowed in . . . My mum said, 'Oh come in with me,' and the nurse said, 'Oh you're not allowed . . . he likes to examine you on your own.'

So . . . Mum came out absolutely furious. And I said, 'What's the matter?' And she said – well she didn't actually come out – it was when we were coming home because I think I would probably have done something about it because, she said, 'I don't know whether he thought I was a complete imbecile,' she said, 'but I was sitting on the couch with nothing on, he was sitting the other side of the room with his houseman and said "*That'll* have to come off."'' And that was the first indication that my mother had that she . . . I mean she knew in her heart of hearts, having gone to the GP who said, oh we're a bit worried about this. . .

'Course when she said to the GP, oh I was ever so annoyed, he said, 'Oh well he's shy, and perhaps he can't . . .'. But he *should* be able to communicate with his patients, shouldn't he? (Mrs Sketty, aged 55, daughter of Mrs Downie. Report 2 – edited interview transcript)

Both the report from Mrs Jenkins and that from Mrs Sketty illustrate the degree to which, as reporters, they were able to reflect on their own role in the process of disclosure. They show how they and their relative were drawn into the bureaucracy of the hospital system where personnel have specific roles to play; and how they were invited into, or excluded from, the private spaces of the hospital. The reports also indicate how invisible their contribution as unwaged carers was to the regulation of emotion, and how they were absorbed into conformity with the hospital organization while remaining critical of it. For instance Mrs Sketty, herself a radiographer (but acting in the role of daughter and unwaged carer) concurred with the nurse's demand that she let her mother go in to see the consultant by herself because 'he likes to examine you on your own'.

The third report is something of a contrast with the first two, illustrating differential rather than deferential positions. Mr Evans was 79 years old and his account shows that he had less knowledge of cancer than the interviewees in reports 1 and 2. What was significant was his confidence in the control he was able to exert over a number of powerful professionals. He was nursing his wife at home after fifty-seven years of marriage and he was in charge. He asserted his personal knowledge of his wife as a means of controlling the professionals. When his wife was taken into hospital (he had sent the ambulance crew away once) he appeared to relinquish this control without concern, but he left no doubt during the interview that at home, despite considerable unacknowledged help from a niece, he was in charge:

> Last June she wasn't very well at all. So after a week I told her about going to the hospital. The doctor had been and advised her to have an X-ray. They found a shadow on her lung, so then she had to have the magic eye and took a little piece off her lung and sent it away for examination, and they found out she had a tumour right on the top of her lung here, which was working towards cancer, probably. She was getting weaker then, but still on her feet . . . and going to her meetings most days. In the end she was too weak and had to stay home, and got really ill then.
>
> The doctor was calling every week, occasional mornings. I went out with him down the path and I asked him straight. I had a shock. I thought my wife had TB you know. And I asked, 'What is wrong with my wife?' And he said, 'Oh she's got cancer.' And I had a shock with that. Because up until May of that year she had been well, and that was in June . . .
>
> She didn't know what she had, I kept it from her. I wouldn't show her. She always thought she had fluid on the lung, something like that. When she was a young woman she looked after her sister-in-law and she had cancer. She looked after her for a few weeks before she died. And she told me, I hope I never get that.
>
> Imagine, I was with her for a month . . . and I knew what she had. She didn't know. But she was getting a lot of drugs that was making her feel she couldn't care less. But the doctor told me and my niece, she might live two months. And I was sitting here, and it was exactly like sitting with someone in a condemned cell, waiting to be sent to be hanged. Because it was certain she was going to die.
>
> The doctor from Llanbeg came here and I had a good chat to him and I asked him, I asked the family doctor, I asked the head Sister, the nurse, I asked all of them would they please not say a word to my wife, as I had lived with her fifty-seven years and I know her nature. . . 'Well, why tell her?', I said. Everybody's of a different nature and some want to know. So the family doctor said, 'If she asks me, I'll tell her.' But she never asked. The last fortnight I think she guessed. I had that feeling. She never had the courage to ask, what have I got, what have I really got, what are they treating me for. She took it marvellous, mind. (Mr Evans, aged 79 widower. Report 3 – edited interview transcript)

Mrs. Evans' experience of nursing someone with cancer many years previously had influenced both her own feelings and knowledge about cancer, as well as those of her husband. Unlike Mrs Sketty, Mr Evans was not able to extrapolate the nature of the disease and its progress from the treatment that his wife received. What he did do though was to force the doctor into identifying the doctor's own rule over 'telling'. If Mrs Evans asked, the doctor would tell her. The implication was that he was not prepared to lie or prevaricate if asked a direct question, which contrasts with Mrs Jenkins' experience of evasion illustrated in report 1.

The three reports come from very different types of people: a widow of 69, a daughter of 55 who was a radiographer with her own family, and a widower of 79. Yet the differences in the interviewees' personal perspectives on the process of disclosure help illustrate the divisions of emotional labour. First, the issue of depth of involvement. It is worth noting that the management of emotion takes place day-in, day-out, from the time a diagnosis of cancer is suspected, throughout the actual diagnosis and disclosure. This means that, although the feelings may be denied and the emotional labour unrecognized, both the person with cancer and their unwaged carers may well be involved in the management of emotion before health service staff become dominant participants in the process. Secondly, it is also notable that, in the hospital, doctors are formally dominant in a way that is not necessarily matched when the 'patient' is at home. Thirdly, the reports illustrate that doctors and nurses do not agree about how open to be in discussing cancer, either on an intra-professional basis, or on an inter-professional basis. Nevertheless, their management of emotion affected lay people's willingness to talk about cancer.

Parameters of Disclosure: Prompt, Opportunity, Knowledge and Roles/Rules

The parameters of disclosure can be grouped under four inter-related headings: prompt, opportunity, knowledge, roles and rules. Each grouping reveals the extent to which the formal, organizational division of labour dominates the division of emotional labour between patient, relatives, nurses and doctors.

Prompt There has to be a prompt, a reason to discuss potential illness, for the process of disclosure to be initiated. In a (frequently) life-threatening disease such as cancer, there will be a series of prompts, often related to specific physical or technical events of diagnosis and treatment. These occasions are encircled by emotions as patients' hopes and fears are confirmed or denied and health service staff reflect their own feelings, knowledge and skills in the way in which they impart information and discuss the consequences of that information.

Report 2 illustrates a series of prompts. The first, private occasion was when Mrs Downie involved Mrs Sketty in concern about her breast. The second prompt was when Mrs Downie made her concern public by visiting the General Practitioner because both she and her daughter suspected something, probably cancer, was affecting her breast. Mrs Downie's appointment with the GP was associated with the uncertainty of what was wrong, with the expectation that the doctor would help her, and possibly with embarrassment at having to expose an intimate part of her body. Any woman who has felt a lump in her breast will be familiar with the anxiety of deciding whether or not it is serious enough to be revealed at a surgery. A third prompt occurred in the hospital where the physical examination and tests generated a brutally revealed diagnosis and method of treatment. On this occasion Mrs Sketty's feelings were managed by the egocentricity of doctors engrossed in their own medical interests, thereby denying her any chance of discussing her interests and instead generating anger at how she was treated. At one level the diagnosis itself was of more importance than the manner in which it was revealed – because of its long-term implications. But the encounter was also an indicator of Mrs Downie's relation with the consultant and of how she might continue to be demeaned by his denial of her feelings. It is interesting that under these circumstances the quality of the interaction was such that concern about the disease was displaced by concern about the failure to acknowledge Mrs Downie's feelings.

At each prompt in the process of disclosure the patient and/or relative is likely to take part in the encounter expecting information, either in the form of reassurance that nothing is wrong, or on the nature of the disease. Patients may expect to confirm or clarify their understanding to their own satisfaction, to explore available options, or to talk through their worries. If they are feeling a victim of the disease they may appear to be a passive recipient of professional interventions. Health staff's responses to a prompt will be similarly varied, and depend upon: their beliefs about, and interest in, patients and relatives; their own status and knowledge; and their skills in managing their own and others' emotions. Some staff will anticipate unspoken needs and encourage their discussion, as the Sister and staff nurse did in report 1, while others will evade them and control through denial as did the hospital staff in report 2. All staff attempt to 'keep the lid on' in the sense of avoiding emotional outbursts, but interpretations vary from those who consider crying to be an outburst, to those who can tolerate angry confrontation.

All the reports show that unwaged carers can bring about 'prompts' so that they do not necessarily depend on the dominant organizational hierarchy. Nevertheless the medical process of diagnosis and disclosure militates against lay initiatives and sets the context of emotional labour.

Opportunity – Place, Time and Circumstance Whatever the prompt to seek or reveal information, the opportunity has to be created in which to exchange or negotiate the passage of information, and this involves place, (public or private), time and circumstance. Opportunity is regulated by the bureaucratic nature of the health organization.

Place of disclosure has two key components which affect the emotions that can be expressed. The first is who has control of the space; the second is the type of space used, including its size, layout and privacy. Public health service space is controlled by staff who invite and exclude people from the space and who denote which particular part of the public space will be used. By default, and professional code, staff control the confidentiality of the encounter. However, the size and layout of the space also sets the tone of the interaction – so that we might expect a relative to feel more free to express strong emotions when invited into an office than he or she would in a corridor.

In reports 1 and 2 the 'place' for the revelation of specific diagnostic information was in the 'expert's' private domain in a public building. This meant that the family and patients were subject to the spoken and unspoken rules of the public arena, as well as being dependent on the availability of the person informing them and on access to the 'private' domain. In this sense opportunity is a linking of place and time. The mother and son in the first report had been to see the Sister earlier, but she had been talking to others. This meant that they had to manage their feelings so that Bill would not recognize their concerns. They had to wait, and secretly return, when the Sister was free. It was also notable that the son pursued the junior doctor to his room, making it difficult for the junior doctor to avoid permitting him access, and placing the power of timing in the son's control.

Report 3, from Mr Evans, is intriguing because, like the others, it was a matter of creating an opportunity for discussion. But, as is common of crucial health discussions at home, it was held on the semi-public space of the doorstep. Doorstep conversations help community health staff and unwaged carers because they facilitate secrecy; but since they are transitory they also facilitate a controlled response. In this instance the context for the feelings was differentially managed with a sense of shared control and exchange, rather than deferentially managed as in reports 1 and 2. From his later comments about 'sitting with someone in a condemned cell' it is clear that Mr Evans bore the burden of the revelation of cancer and would therefore bear the burden of controlling his feelings and 'protecting' his wife from them. Unlike Mrs Downie and Mrs Sketty in report 2, he did not have additional worries about being ignored by health staff.

Time is a key method of controlling what can be discussed. Report 1 illustrated an appointment system in which a time lapse of some kind occurred regardless of any sense of worry and urgency. A time-limited period can be used to ensure that only specific information is requested and disclosed thereby excluding open-ended discussion and negotiation, as reports 2 and 3 illustrate. In both instances those managing the 'opportunity', the consultant in report 2 and Mr Evans in report 3, ensure that the encounter will not be extended by broad-ranging conversation.

Davey (1990), in a study of communication about cancer in a general hospital, notes nurses' criticisms of doctors who disclose a diagnosis of cancer while conducting a ward round. In these circumstances the doctor is using a timetabled, routine event to control, not only place and time, but also participation in the event. It leaves patients in a highly public arena with minimal opportunities for either formal or informal response – regardless of the strength of their feelings. It takes a brave, desperate or skilled patient to demand deeper discussion under such conditions. After such an event nurses often deem it their task to 'pick up the pieces', making themselves available to the patient to explain the information, answer questions, and support the patient as they come to terms with the implications.

Under these conditions the doctor manages the emotion of the encounter by constraining its expression. The nurses, recognizing the depth of the feelings (and the need to talk about them) encourage patients to talk about their feelings. The deferential relationship between doctors and nurses is indicated by the doctor's ability to control the context of emotional labour without discussion with others. The day-to-day work is carried out by junior staff, often without any recognition of the work they are doing in managing emotions.

The second report also illustrates the significance of the circumstances surrounding disclosure. The opportunity and the time were appropriate, but the circumstances of the disclosure revealed the difference in status of those involved. Mrs Downie was physically exposed, with bare breasts, on the opposite side of the room to the consultant and junior doctor. The disclosure was made, not to the patient, but to the deferential junior doctor, although plainly enough to be heard by Mrs Downie. Mrs Downie, vulnerable from nakedness, was actively ignored, denoting no recognition of her feelings, her intelligence, her dignity, her interest or her knowledge. The senior doctor thereby limited the place, the time and the circumstances so effectively that the patient controlled her strong feelings for some time, only exposing her anger in the intimacy of the car with her trusted daughter. Later, in the GP's surgery, the patient was enabled to discuss the treatment and her feelings about the disclosure. Thus with two senior staff, the consultant and the GP, time and opportunity were right, but each of them controlled the circumstances to bring about quite different ends – the consultant to repress the expression of feelings, the GP to facilitate their expression.

Opportunity for disclosure, like prompt, is subject to organizational parameters. In turn the dominant figure in the organization sets the context of the division of emotional labour (the consultants in reports 1 and 2, Mr Evans in report 3), even though most of the active work of controlling the expression of emotions is carried out by others. The implication of reports 1 and 2 is that the low status of the person with cancer and the unwaged carers, dependants of the formal health system, can mean that their activity in controlling their own and others' emotions is not adequately recognized. Despite their much deeper feelings, it is more difficult for them to create the appropriate place, time and circumstances to discuss cancer than it is for health professionals.

Knowledge The most significant formal mechanism of organizational control in health services, dominating all the others, has been the assertion of a hierarchical, rational-scientific knowledge. By reference to this knowledge, as a society we have invested doctors not just with technical and clinical skills, but with the moral and organizational authority to control access to that knowledge. As the consultant surgeon's actions in report 1 illustrate, who discloses, how much, when and where, is shaped by the primacy accorded to this rational-scientific knowledge. It is this knowledge, rather than interpersonal, social or managerial knowledge, which shapes the medical curriculum, so that doctors are scientists first and practitioners second (Towle, 1991). Uncritical conformity to this influence is enhanced as junior staff observe senior staff at work. Kfir reflects on her experience, as a medical student, with a particular patient:

> Seeing this gentleman over a period of months, I often felt uneasy about continuing the lie when he so clearly wanted to know what was wrong with him, but the establishment and the norm were so strong that I never seriously doubted this was the right approach. (Kfir and Slevin, 1991: 5)

However, all the interviewees' reports suggest that the primacy of techno-scientific knowledge, and the breadth of the organizational authority it bestows, is being challenged. Mrs Sketty's outrage at the consultant's complete lack of skill in communication was emphatic, not least because it was he who set the context for the management of emotion and had her excluded from the consultation. In report 3 Mr Evans illustrated a different challenge by claiming his personal knowledge of his wife's 'nature' as the deciding factor over whether she should know or not. He implied that his knowledge was more important in these circumstances than that of all the health professionals who came to treat his wife. The division of emotional labour was different to that in reports 1 and 2 because the power to set the context for discussing the diagnosis was appropriated by Mr Evans.

Lemert (1992) has noted that raising the issue of competing knowledge bases does not necessarily undermine the value of one of them, but offers an opportunity to revalue the significance of others. It may be that current moves to empower consumers within the British health system (such as through the British government's 1991 *Patients' Charter*) will accelerate the process, and individuals' requirements will challenge the dominance of professional knowledge. Furthermore, a challenge to techno-scientific knowledge from management and nurses is likely to bring about a realignment in power structures. Mrs Jenkins' report indicates how tiny was the amount of techno-scientific knowledge required for the Sister to convey the result of the operation. In the second report the technical knowledge had no immediate relevance to Mrs Downie, the patient, who abstracted the implication of what was said by using her own knowledge. Yet while techno-scientific knowledge is predominant, the authority that ensues has wide-ranging effects on the division of emotional labour and the ability to harness this labour.

Basiro Davey notes how doctors can control nurses and patients through reference to assumed ownership of this technical information:

Even though she [the nurse] has seen the lab report she should say 'I don't know, I will ask the doctor' . . . It's not her job to read histology reports, she's seen it in passing. It's nothing to do with her really. Now *I'll* sometimes tell a white lie and say to the patient 'the result's not back'. (Junior House Officer, Davey, 1990: 8)

Here it is organizational hierarchy that affects disclosure, not the importance of the information, or patient need. However, once the information on cancer, technical or otherwise, is released, controlling the information clearly depends on others' sense of responsibility about the knowledge. It also means that the power of control becomes realigned or dispersed. The surgeon in the first report depended on the nurses and junior medical staff to refrain from passing information on to the patient or family. Yet, although they failed him, they worked to sustain emotional control. Even as they disclosed information to the family, and as soon as mother and son had the information, they extended the management of their own and each other's emotions. Again, though, it was the surgeon's knowledge-dependent status which set the context for the disclosure of information, and thereby set the context for the disclosure of emotions.

Roles and Rules The complexity of the negotiations surrounding disclosure is notable as the web of protection that staff and family attempt to weave around each other. The section above notes some of the systematic pressures to evade and lie to which doctors, nurses, patients and relatives are subject and to which they subject others. It is also clear that individuals within the system do have the power to challenge and alter the trajectory of disclosure and the alignment for the division of emotional labour. Reasons for altering systems of disclosure are likely to be affected by each person's perception of their role in relation to others, the strength of the incentive to challenge or comply, assertion skills, and their own needs.

The process of disclosure depends not just on lay and professional staff knowing the rules of what is required of them, but also on being prepared to comply with those rules – and with the division of labour they imply. The relatively new activity of consumers of cancer services organizing and writing for themselves is part of an assertion of different roles and different priorities. Ritchie (1992), writing to disseminate and explain the self-help group Cancerlink's 'Declaration of Rights for people with cancer', discusses declaration number 3, 'to know I have cancer, to be told in a sensitive manner and to share in all decision-making about my treatment and care in honest and informative discussions with relevant specialists and other health professionals'.

> A great deal of debate was given over to whether to include the right not to know you have cancer as well as the right to know. The conclusion was that the right to be told was considered essential for everyone as it was not appropriate for the medical profession to make judgements about who should be told. Once told, people can then decide if they really want to know and have the right not to hear or take in the information. (Ritchie, 1992: 71)

From Ritchie's observations it is clear that although there is dissension about how people with cancer want disclosure to be handled, there is a move away from the group 'victim' role of cancer sufferers described by Sontag (1990) in *Aids and its Metaphors*. The move is towards the assertion of individual rights to sensitive disclosure. This change in the patient's role will alter the dynamics of emotional labour.

While report 1 illustrated the hierarchical organizational rules surrounding disclosure, the precise roles of participants was a matter of each individual's own decision-making process. Report 1 showed that the Sister, the staff nurse and the junior doctor transgressed the unwritten rule of silence. But it is fascinating that, in conversation with the junior doctor, Mrs Jenkins deferentially conformed to his assumption that she did not know the outcome of the operation – thereby protecting the Sister. Further, the son in report 1 sought out information independently from his mother and also tried to assure her that 'Dad's going to be all right'. By pre-empting the surgeon's timing he asserted his right as the patient's son to know what was happening, but then attempted to reintroduce the rule of ignorance to protect his mother from the implications of the diagnosis. Thus it is that each of the participants in the process of disclosure creates their own role and breaks or conforms to the dominant position as they feel is appropriate.

In report 1 the incentives for the Sister to break silence may have been increased by current health service and nursing aspirations toward patient advocacy, delivering 'individual patient care', and considering the 'family as the unit of care'. Such influences run alongside pressures for greater professional accountability and identity (Salvage, 1985). Studies by Seale (1991) in Britain and Stein et al. (1990) in the United States suggest that there may be some realignment of inter-professional responsibilities. Yet staff and family and patients still act protectively toward their own group and others: misleading, denying and lying where it is thought appropriate, or facilitating 'open-awareness' (Glaser and Strauss, 1965) where that is thought preferable.

Like the other elements affecting disclosure, role is organizationally led, but can be subject to individual negotiation, particularly when there are social changes that facilitate this negotiation. Changes in roles that affect the way in which information about cancer is given will also affect the way in which the emotions associated with cancer are managed. Following Heller's speculation (1990) about the re-emergence of an emotional culture, it may be that the consensus will move away from the dominance of senior doctors in setting the context for disclosure. Dedifferentiation would mean that context setting would no longer be the sole prerogative of senior doctors. Broadening responsibility for it could result in a role realignment affecting the deferential division of emotional labour amongst professionals, and between lay and professional people.

Change and Potential Change: The Nature of Disclosure

Glaser and Strauss' key text on disclosure, *Awareness of Dying*, published in 1965, exposed some of the ways in which knowledge about diagnosis and prognosis were used to control the social and emotional contexts of dying. They identified stages of 'closed awareness', 'suspicion awareness' and 'open awareness'. They also noted the 'ritual drama of mutual pretence', and the effects of the different forms of awareness for family and nurses.

In Holland too, Wouters (1990) has described the control of emotions through non-disclosure drawing on old medical and nursing journals to show the mechanisms used to avoid discussion. He identifies three phases. The first, between 1930 and 1950, is the period of the 'sacred lie' when prognosis is not only not revealed, but must not be revealed. He explains this as being health care's part in the civilizing process, where feelings do not fit in with paternal/ hierarchical systems. As a symbolic means of enforcing this silence he notes the imposition of fines on patients heard discussing death in the ward. He observes the second phase from 1955 to 1965 as being one both of growing resistance to the codes and of hardening of views on both sides of the debate. In the last phase, which he identifies as being from 1970 onwards, he notes the sacred lie as being totally superseded by emancipation of dying *and* of emotions. He describes an opening up of the 'emotional world' in health care, legitimizing it as a matter of appropriate concern for health professionals.

Both these studies illustrate the dominance of health organizations, and of senior doctors within them, in setting the context within which emotional labour is carried out. There is considerable evidence of patterns of disclosure from Seale in Britain (1991), Peteet et al. (1991) in the US, Hattori et al. (1991) in Japan, Mosconi et al. (1991) from Italy, and Krause (1991) in Finland, suggesting that disclosure is doctor led. Yet, if change were proven, it might herald an alteration in the locus and means of regulating emotion. If doctors have 'represented the feeling of society in general about cancer' (Kfir and Slevin, 1991), they may be reflecting broader social change in views about cancer, as well as in lay and professional alignments. Patients and unwaged carers, despite having very different interests, may be beginning to exert greater influence on the organization and delivery of health services assisted by the extension of philosophies of individualism and a growing distrust of professionals (Perkin, 1989; Smart, 1992). Internal health service change, which emphasizes a rhetoric of 'holistic care' and assessment of consumer needs, may facilitate lay involvement in health organization. In such circumstances the division of emotional labour may be altered from the dominant, deferential, organizationally led 'context setting' management to a differential management negotiated by the lay people and professionals who regulate emotions day by day.

As the largest European employer, the British National Health Service is an intriguing indicator of Western changes in negotiations over the expression of emotion. While an emphasis on organizational change in the recognition and management of emotions may be an illusion, perhaps merely a form of millenium fever, it may genuinely herald a specifiable era of reflexivity which can accommodate different forms of knowledge, including knowledge and practice of the management of emotion (Giddens, 1991). A cynic may view the greater acceptance of 'consumer views' and plans for unwaged carers (Robinson and Yee, 1991) as reflecting a growing decentralization and realignment of accountability which is intended to ameliorate the political reality of limited health resources and an ageing population. As a nurse, though, it does seem to me that there is a cultural change in health services which encourages discussion and negotiation between doctors and nurses and patients and relatives. This is accompanied by medical and nursing curricula which increasingly encompass formalized 'communication skills' to complement techno-scientific knowledge (ENB, 1988; Towle, 1991). Yet, together, these trends denote a powerful tension between enabling lay people to voice their concerns and to have their knowledge and skills recognized, while equipping the friendly, emotion-conscious professionals with more subtle skills of emotional control.

However, regardless of sophistication of skills in the management of emotion, sociologically and ethically it is worth returning to the nature of the emotions being managed. No matter how precise our analyses of emotion may become, no matter how the nature of organizations may change, and no matter how involved lay individuals may be in the process of disclosure, the anguish of many emotions can never be ameliorated. Mr Henderson, the father of 7-year-old Alex, said he liked to talk about his son because it made it real. Alex's mother, his first wife, had died of cancer six months before Alex first became ill, aged 4. His second wife, Alex's stepmother, found out the week before our interview that her cancer had metastasized. The following report from Mr Henderson and Mrs Henderson is both an illustration of the exquisite emotional control exercised by a young child and his family, and a reminder to be wary of an over-refined sociology of emotion:

> *Mr Henderson*: We were going back and forth to the hospital for six months. He was continually ill and they kept saying they thought he was pining after his mother. And I can't explain what it was but I knew he wasn't right. You get a feeling about a child. And of course when they diagnosed cancer, it was shooting straight back to my wife. She kept going back and forth to hospital. And it was the . . . it was just the . . . being so alone. . .
> We never sat him down and said it is this and that. If he asked us any questions we would always answer him completely truthfully.
> *Mrs Henderson*: And we used to prepare him for what was going to happen. Because after a couple of treatments he started to feel better. And he couldn't understand why he had to go back and have them do it to him again and make him feel bad. So we had to explain to him why. This lump that was in his tummy. We didn't say, 'Oh it's cancer'. We said that he had a lump in his tummy and that was why he couldn't eat very well, and the treatment was to try and make the lump smaller so he would have more room for his food. But then as he got older we explained to him about cells.
> *Mr Henderson*: And he was terribly sensible. And he realized that at times when his blood count was low he wasn't able to mix with other people [because of infection]. And he would accept this, and if someone came to the door he would automatically go upstairs. . .
> And he was always very considerate to other people. If you walked in and asked him how he was, however ill he was feeling, he would say, 'Very well thank you. How are you?' (Mr Henderson, aged 39,

father of Alex, who was diagnosed with a childhood form of cancer, aged 4. Report 4 – edited interview transcript)

In Conclusion – Issues of Generality and Researcher Responsibility

While the disclosure of a diagnosis of cancer is an issue specific to health service organizations, the division of emotional labour and the mechanisms by which such labour is divided have broader organizational application. I would suggest that the concepts of differential and deferential divisions of emotional labour are robust to the extent that they reflect divisions of power and role in most organizations – and to the social ingredients of emotion highlighted in this book. While the management of emotion is necessary to all organizations (and domestic life) it is intriguing to note differences in the organizational circumstances in which emotions are expressed or restrained. Outbursts during the 'creative process' of designing advertising campaigns are tolerated because they bring benefit to the company, while emotions deemed negative are expected to be contained, such as in customer services and complaints departments.

Just as health service staff direct and control emotions for themselves and others, so do a variety of other staff such as clerical workers (Davies and Rosser, 1986), prison warders (Caudroy, 1987), and personnel managers (Coleman, 1976). Fineman (1983) tells of the female secretary, instructed by her male boss to deliver a redundancy notice into the hands of one of his staff at the person's home, in the very early hours of the morning. In each of these examples relatively low-status, often female, staff are expected, often without formal acknowledgement, to protect their superiors or their organization from the disruption of unmanaged 'negative' emotion.

The mechanisms through which emotion is controlled during the disclosure of cancer are applicable to a wide range of organizations. The mechanisms may be commonly observed: the use of particular kinds of space and time; more or less public encounters; denial of the emotion; limiting the information released; formal and informal disciplinary rules; gender-divided labour; and most, importantly, through senior staff setting the context, routines and rituals within which other staff and clients can express their emotions. These systems of controlling emotions may be challenged, as shown in the previous sections, although more explanation of the circumstances, mechanisms and power structures which facilitate this are required.

In the workplace we all have a sense of whom we can allow to see our stress, how we curtail anger, and the circumstances under which we must be seen to be enthusiastic. While structural hierarchical role relations and gender divisions shape these expectations, the possibility of negotiation exists between individuals, and broader social change may challenge received expectations. Sewell and Wilkinson (1992) argue that technology and changing management systems which emphasize teamwork actually increase the possibilities of organizational control of individuals in the manufacturing industry, but Hosking and Fineman (1990) note that emotion rules (who may disclose what to whom) can be redefined if the social actor is powerful enough. Yet hierarchical deference is not a complete explanation. The tantrums of a key skilled operator or valued staff member may be overlooked if she or he is difficult to replace.

The nature of the emotion work to be managed, how the emotional labour is divided, and the overt or covert nature of the work and the labour, will be specific to different organizational cultures. With flatter, more flexible, responsible management structures in manufacturing and service industries, and increased opportunities for clients to voice their interests, enhanced opportunities for negotiation may emerge – so altering divisions of emotional labour. Alternatively the status quo may be sustained by adapting current mechanisms for controlling emotion.

Listening again to interview tapes for this chapter left me aware of the contradictions between the way I was using the data and the painfully negotiated, often disordered, intensely personal process through which interviewees told me a story of a diagnosis of cancer and the subsequent death of their relative. There is a deliberate transgression of feelings in the very nature of the academic process. Data collection and analysis are planned to remove personal involvement, to be systematic and rigorous, to clarify, to refine, and to categorize. The tapes were a reminder of how I, as an interviewer, and the relatives I had interviewed, had controlled and managed our own and each other's emotions. Some relatives were matter of fact and untroubled. Others spoke with a calmness belied by eyes filled with tears while glancing at photographs of their loved one, and often accompanied by some busy activity such as making a cup of tea for me, or continuing the fervent pummelling of bread dough.

A reflexive examination of emotion research raises questions as to whether the academic process transgresses feelings, and is thereby exploitative. This is an issue which could take a separate chapter, and indeed is handled in more detail in the final part of this book. For now, it is not inappropriate to recall that sociologists and feminists have long questioned whether the depersonalized, natural science method is ethically conducive to generating an understanding of society. This message seems particularly pertinent to an empirically based sociology of emotion.

Note

1. All participants in the interviews are given pseudonyms.

References

Cancer Relief Macmillan Fund (1988) *Public Attitudes to and Knowledge of Cancer in the UK 1988*. London: Britten Street.

Caudroy, A. (1987) 'Children in prison', *Observer*, 4 October.

Coleman, C. (1976) 'Personnel: the changing function', in H. Chruden, and A. Sherman (eds), *Readings in Personnel Management*. Cincinnati, South Western Publishing.

Davey, B. (1990) 'The nurses' dilemma: truthtelling or big white lies', paper presented at the International Conference on Communication in Health Care, Oxford, June.

Davies, C. and Rosser, J. (1986) 'Gendered jobs in the health service: a problem for labour process analysis', in D. Knight and H. Wilmott (eds), *Gender and the Labour Process*. Aldershot: Gower.

ENB (1988) *Project 2000 - 'A New Preparation for Practice': Guidelines and Criteria for Course Development and the Formation of Collaborative Links between Approved Training Institutions within the National Health Service and Centres of Higher Education*. London: English National Board.

Fineman, S. (1983) *White Collar Unemployment*. Chichester: Wiley.

Giddens, A. (1991) *The Consequences of Modernity*. Cambridge: Polity.

Glaser, B. and Strauss, A. (1965) *Awareness of Dying*. Chicago: Aldine.

Hattori, H., Salzberg, S. M., Kiang, W. P., Fujimaya, T., Tegima, Y. and Furunao, J. (1991) 'The patient's right to information in Japan - legal rules and doctors' opinions', *Social Science and Medicine*, 32 (9): 1007–16.

Hearn, J. and Parkin, W. (1987) *'Sex' at 'Work': the Power and Paradox of Organisation Sexuality*. Brighton: Wheatsheaf.

Heller, A. (1990) *Can Modernity Survive?*. Cambridge: Polity.

Hochschild, A. R. (1983) *The Managed Heart*. Berkeley: University of California Press.

Hochschild, A. R. (1990) *The Second Shift*. London: Piaktus.

Hosking, D. and Fineman, S. (1990) 'Organizing processes', *Journal of Management Studies*, 27 (6): 583–604.

James, N. (1989) 'Emotional labour: skill and work in the social regulation of feeling', *Sociological Review*, 37 (1): 15–42.

James, N. (1992) 'Care = organisation + physical labour + emotional labour', *Sociology of Health and Illness*, 14 (4): 488–509.

Kfir, N. and Slevin, M. (1991) *Challenging Cancer: from Chaos to Control*. London: Routledge.

Krause, K. (1991) 'Contracting cancer and coping with it: patients' experiences', *Cancer Nursing*, 14 (5): 240–5.

Lemert, C. (1992) 'General social theory, irony, postmodernism', in Steven Seidman and David Wagner (eds), *Postmodernism and Social Theory*. Oxford: Blackwell.

Mosconi, P., Meyerowitz, B. E., Liberati, M. C. and Liberati, A. (1991) 'Disclosure of breast cancer diagnosis: patient and physician reports', *Annals of Oncology*, 2 (4): 273–80.

Perkin, H. (1989) *The Rise of Professional Society*. London: Routledge.

Peteet, J. R., Abrams, H. E., Ross, D. M. and Stearns, N. M. (1991) 'Presenting a diagnosis of cancer: patients' views', *Journal of Family Practice*, 32 (6): 577–81.

Ritchie, S. (1992) 'A Declaration of Rights for people with cancer', *Journal of Cancer Care*, 1 (2): 69–72.

Robinson, J. and Yee, L. (1991) *Focus on Carers*. London, Kings Fund Centre.

Salvage, J. (1985) *The Politics of Nursing*. London: Heinemann.

Seale, C. (1991) 'Communication and awareness about death: a study of a random sample of dying people', *Social Science and Medicine*, 32 (8): 943–52.

Sewell, G. and Wilkinson, B. (1992) '"Someone to watch over me": surveillance, discipline and the just-in-time labour process', *Sociology*, 26 (2): 271–89.

Smart, B. (1992) *Modern Conditions, Postmodern Controversies*. London: Routledge.

Sontag, S. (1979) *Illness as Metaphor*. London: Allen Lane.

Sontag, S. (1990) *Aids and its Metaphors*. Harmondsworth: Penguin.

Stein, L., Watts, D. and Howell, T. (1990) 'The doctor–nurse game revisited', *New England Journal of Medicine*, 322 (8): 546–9.

Towle, A. (1991) *Critical Thinking: the Future of Undergraduate Medical Education*. London: King's Fund Centre.

Wouters, C. (1989) 'The sociology of emotions and flight attendants: Hochschild's *Managed Heart*', *Theory, Culture and Society*, 6 (1): 95–123.

Wouters, C. (1990) 'Changing regimes of power and emotions at the end of life: Netherlands 1930–1990', paper given at the BSA Sociology of Emotion Interest Group, Birmingham.

6

Organizational Nostalgia – Reflections on 'The Golden Age'

Yiannis Gabriel

I came here at a time when there was very little bureaucracy and a much more laid back approach, but also a dedicated approach. People knew what they were doing, where they were going, why they were here and bureaucracy was to be avoided. People were friendly, generally got on well together, it was an organization, a place worth working for. Today, frankly at times it's . . . like something out of *1984*. It's a cross between George Orwell and Kafka; this is my point of view. (Text 1)

They used to go out on great day-trips like to Leeds Castle and the whole company, like 500 people, would have a medieval style of banquet or a summer party or something. Pete who I work with said that he'd been on two of those, whereas the only summer party I've been to here was a picnic across the road in Hyde Park. I think that it was all a dreadful waste of money taking the whole company to Leeds Castle, I mean it's the customers' money after all. The older ones think about the good old days, but I don't think they mind too much; it was just a nice time that has passed now. (Text 2)

These statements come from two employees of a publishing and research organization. They highlight a generational divide, a divide between old and new. Where the young man sees but waste and irrationality, the old man sees true purpose and value. The divide is cognitive and normative, but above all it is emotional. The older man fails to comprehend how the younger one may actually enjoy what he sees as a *1984*-type nightmare; and the younger man is unable to appreciate the depth of the older man's attachment to the organization that was, his yearning for the past, his nostalgia.

Choosing to discuss nostalgia in organizations may seem idiosyncratic. It may be countered that nostalgia is not an emotion at all, at least not one to compete with driving emotions, such as love, hate, envy or anger. Alternatively, it may be suggested that organizations are not a natural habitat for nostalgia, that one feels nostalgic about one's childhood, early loves or youthful indiscretions, but hardly about one's place of work. This chapter presents a view of nostalgia as encompassing a range of distinct emotional orientations in organizations. I will argue that organizational nostalgia is not a marginal phenomenon, but a pervasive one, dominating the outlook of numerous organizational members, and even defining the dominant emotional complexion of some organizations. It feeds organizational folklore about 'characters' and events, engraved in the collective memory. In addition, nostalgia for an organizational golden age exercises a considerable influence on the way present-day events are interpreted, acting as a rich source of symbolism and meaning. More generally, I will try to show that the study of nostalgia provides a powerful approach to the study of feelings and phantasies (as in the Freudian expression), revealing some of the fundamental complexity and ambivalence of emotional life in organizations.

Background

The study of nostalgia has grown in recent years, as nostalgia itself has assumed a dominant place in Western cultures. Whole sectors of the economy are fuelled by nostalgia. The heritage and tourist industries, a large section of entertainment, music and the arts continuously strive to feed people's yearning for a golden past. In the hands of advertisers, nostalgia has become a tried and tested if over-used device for promoting anything from potato crisps to insurance policies. The film industry has become dominated by endless recycling of themes and archetypes from the past, full of references to classic movies and sequels to not-so-classic ones which then come to be seen as classic. Television forever repeats its own golden oldies. Politicians, like Thatcher and Reagan, built substantial support by mobilizing nostalgia for an earlier era, a mythologized past of authentic values and heroic achievements. The celebration of this past, uncomplicated, innocent and thoroughly sentimentalized, has found its spiritual home in Disneyland, whose consequences reach far beyond the leisure sector (Kaplan, 1987; Schwartz, 1988). As the millenium is approaching, we can anticipate an icon-filled orgy of nostalgia. Very *fin de siècle*.

Under this onslaught, academics have abandoned their highbrow disparagement for the concept of nostalgia and have addressed it along two main paths which have occasionally crossed.[1] Cultural critics have approached nostalgia as a social phenomenon whose causes and functions must be sought in contemporary culture.

Most have criticized nostalgia as the latest opiate of the people, a collective escape from the complexities of the present in times of trouble and change (Williams, 1974; Davis, 1979; DaSilva and Faught, 1982; Wright, 1985) in an idealized vision of the past. A few, however, have tried to defend the way nostalgia resurrects the past (which our culture would otherwise banish) as a 'political and psychological treasury from which we draw the reserves to cope with the future' (Lasch, 1980: xviii). As a militantly anti-modern current, nostalgia has more recently found a more hospitable environment in postmodernism.

A second line of inquiry has been pursued by depth psychology. While Freud recognized that loving memories are a central ingredient of psychological maturity, most of his successors noticed nostalgia as an abnormal condition akin to melancholia, which leads to serious disturbances including guilt and self-reproach for the loss of loved objects (Kleiner, 1970; Werman, 1977; Daniels, 1985; Sohn, 1983; Kaplan, 1987). In its acute forms, nostalgia amounts to a total inability to accept the present and a morbid determination to literally live in the past, as embodied in persons long dead, old movies and old radio programmes.[2]

Organizational theorists, for their part, have steered clear of the concept. This is paradoxical, given that ethnographic research has not been slow in revealing 'nostalgic feelings' in the first-hand testimonies of organizational participants (Terkel, 1985). In my own research I was frequently impressed by the cognitive and emotional gulf that separates old from young organizational members (Gabriel, 1988, 1991a), yet I never thought of nostalgia as being part of this gulf. Along with many other theorists no doubt, I felt an instinctive dislike for a term which has been sentimentalized and trivialized to the point where it can hardly qualify as a concept.

It is ironic then to discover that the word 'nostalgia' originated in medicine, as one of those terms which sought to medicalize a complex of emotional and behavioural disturbances. It was first used by the Swiss physician Johannes Hofer in 1688 to describe the morbid symptoms of Swiss mercenaries who spent long periods away from home. The term derives etymologically from the Greek words *nostos* meaning homecoming and *algia* or pain; it initially signified acute or pathological homesickness, a meaning which it still maintains in some European languages. Until the Napoleonic Wars, nostalgia was seen as a peculiarly Swiss sickness, at times attributed to sudden changes in altitudes or the quality of breathing air. It was only in the early part of the twentieth century that nostalgia was de-medicalized losing its link with the military, and later still that the link with home as a *place* was weakened. Gradually nostalgia found its own anchor in the past, i.e. a *time*, coming to signify a warm feeling of yearning and longing towards that time.[3]

In spite of its connection with the past, nostalgia is not the product of the past itself. 'Almost anything from our past can emerge as an object of nostalgia, provided that we can somehow view it in a pleasant light' (Davis, 1979: viii). People can feel nostalgic for trying, hard and disagreeable times, such as the Great Depression of the 1930s or the Battle of Britain. Present experience in Eastern Europe suggests that some people may be beginning to feel nostalgic for the communist past, as a period of security, togetherness and survival in the face of adversity (Rottenburg, 1991). In this sense, *nostalgia is a state arising out of present conditions as much as out of the past itself.* Its attitude towards the past is highly plastic, growing not out of mere recollection, still less out of a historical inquisition. Instead, the nostalgic past is highly selective, generally idealized and infused with symbolism and meaning. Nostalgia therefore creates a retrospective mythology, something which is at once part of us but not part of the present world, evoking a glowing emotional response and inviting further idealization and embellishment, but resisting historical elucidation.

To this idealized picture of the past, nostalgia compulsively juxtaposes the present, which is almost invariably found emaciated, impoverished and lacking (Davis, 1979: 16). In this sense, nostalgic feelings can profoundly affect our construction and interpretation of present-day phenomena and mould our emotional reactions to them. Within organizations, the current leaders, or the present buildings or even the present products may be compared unfavourably with the past ones. One outstanding feature of nostalgia is that it always selects the terrain so that the past, dressed up and embellished, will triumph over the present. If, for example, the past leaders of the organization are generally discredited and the present ones admired, nostalgic feeling will focus on some other feature of the past.

But if nostalgia approaches the past in this glowing manner, it also affirms that the past is irrecoverably gone; it is part of a 'world we have lost'. In organizational nostalgia, the past is frequently separated from the present through a *radical discontinuity*, a symbolic watershed, which cannot be undone.[4] In some organizations this is referred to as 'the changes' (Gabriel, 1988) and may include the move to a new building, the introduction of computerized technology, a corporate take-over, privatization or a new managerial regime or ethos. Employees who experienced the change from old to new see themselves as radically different from those who joined later, and at times may see themselves as 'survivors' from an earlier age. Their past is a shared *heritage* which binds them together, and excludes those who never tasted life before the fall.

There are forms of nostalgia which are intensely private (Daniels, 1985). They draw on intimate moments of our personal histories, as we remember ourselves, little boys or girls lost in a bewitching world. This chapter does not focus on this Proustian variant of nostalgia. Instead we will approach it as a social phenomenon, whose expressions are often shared with others. People who have shared a past experience, and have a nostalgic disposition towards it, will generally feel close and will tend to reinforce the features noted earlier.[5]

Some Ambiguities of Nostalgia

Nostalgia is not an unproblematic concept. Is nostalgia a pleasant or an unpleasant experience? In some European languages (including Russian, German and Greek), the word 'nostalgia' never shed its disagreeable associations with homesickness. Yet, in English, the word has come to signify a predominantly pleasant experience. Although some people comment on its 'bitter-sweet' quality, the majority indicate that they view nostalgia as a positive, pleasant experience. In spite of the recognition that the past is irrevocably lost, nostalgia, at least in its English usage, refuses to collapse into despair or grief even if, at times, it is tinted by feelings such as self-pity or what the French call *tristesse*. A major paradox presents itself, which I will call the *nostalgia paradox*. In a famous passage of Dante's *Divine Comedy*, Francesca da Rimini, tormented in hell for her illicit passion for Paolo, greets the poet with the immortal words:

> *Nessun maggior dolore*
> *Che ricordarsi del tempo felice*
> *Nella miseria.*

> There is no greater pain
> than to remember, in our present grief,
> past happiness. (Canto V, 121–3)

The truth of this statement seems overwhelming, and yet nostalgia somehow evades the painful consequences of such recollections. The paradox suggested here, which existing literature has failed to raise, is this: how can the memory of a past irredeemably lost be experienced as pleasant?

A further question concerns the status of nostalgia as an emotion. The common identification of nostalgia with a yearning, or a longing (Davis, 1979; Kaplan, 1987) would place nostalgia closer to desire than to feeling. There are indeed times when nostalgia has a motivating edge, for example when we visit places with significant earlier associations. This is what advertisers seek to exploit, whether to entice us to visit heritage parks or to attract us to the 'old-fashioned' taste of Brand X.

Desire *demands* satisfaction, as do the driving emotions, associated with it, such as love, hate, jealousy or rage. The same cannot be said about nostalgia, which cannot be frustrated in the same way that desire can. There is general agreement in literature that the emotional tone of nostalgia is not a loud one, but a contemplative, quiet one. This would place it at the opposite end of the spectrum from those above, an emotion resulting from desire already fulfilled, as if the fact that one has lived through a golden past is by itself the fulfilment of the yearning. Kaplan (1987: 471) has, therefore, suggested that nostalgia may be closer to a mood than an emotion, a psychological orientation which affects the entire ego, lending a uniform colouring to the world, and combining a repertory of affects and behaviours. In the pages which follow, we shall retain the concept of 'nostalgic feeling' to describe a warm and loving orientation for the past or features of the past, a tender yearning towards it, as well as a resigned acceptance of the impossibility of bringing the past back.[6]

Nostalgic Voices from Organizations

In spite of these ambiguities, most of us have no difficulty in understanding intuitively what nostalgia is or when someone is experiencing nostalgic feelings. While some of us may still find it distasteful or 'ideologically suspect', we must recognize that the very dislocation of the word from its original meaning of melancholy resulting from long absence from home indicates that it has filled an important semantic space for which no other word was suitable. What forms then does nostalgia take in organizations? I first became aware of it while transcribing tapes of field interviews which my colleague David Robins and I had conducted in five organizations. These were aimed at collecting first-hand accounts of events which had turned into organizational stories. As part of these interviews, respondents were asked to choose from a list a metaphor which aptly depicted their organization. The list included 'football team', 'madhouse', 'a family', 'machine', 'conveyor belt' and others. The responses varied across different organizations, but one type of response was common among older respondents, who, on seeing the list, would say 'It used to be a family, but . . .' Consider, for example, the response of a personnel officer in a large chemical company, who had been with the company for twenty years:

> I've seen a lot of changes in the company since I came. . . . This is confidential . . . Today we are told we are world class, and we go for this unified image, that we are all one, one big happy family, and in my earlier days with the company I'd have said 'Yes, we were wonderful'. It doesn't seem that way now. People are not quite as friendly as they used to be. [*Long pause*] I mean we had, years ago, we had more time to, *for* people. I mean I suppose it's the old con trick, someone in the management decides that we have far too many staff and they start to cut staff and they cut it to the bone and lose an awful lot of people who had all the experience, who really knew. *And the sort of history of the company . . . is lost.* (Text 3)

The image of the organization as a *family* seemed to be at the heart of nostalgic feeling. Not all of the references to family were prompted by my list of metaphors. A hospital training officer, who had previously worked as a telephonist and a receptionist, said, when asked to describe some memorable incidents of her working life:

> The most significant thing since I started working for the NHS was the closure of the old hospital, because that marked a complete change. They closed it down in 1974. It used to be like a small community, being small, everyone knew each other, everyone helped each other, and if a doctor went out he'd say 'I'm going out, if a patient comes, just sort it out.' The nurses would say 'Do you want a cup of tea?', just like a family. When we came to this big place here, all those same people were spread across the site and when you pass each other, you don't have the same contact. That was quite a change. You walk along the corridor and very often you speak to no-one because you don't know anyone; in the old hospital you would have asked who they were. (Text 4)

This respondent later went on to describe the present hospital as a 'sort of machine, well-oiled but still creaking', further highlighting the distance between what was seen as a bureaucratic present and the warm personal atmosphere of the past.

At the time of the interviews, nostalgia was not part of our research programme, and we never consciously raised it with any of the 126 interviewees. It was while analysing the research material, attempting to classify the stories which we had collected that the theme of nostalgia emerged. Listening to the taped interviews I was first struck by a handful of respondents; virtually everything they said was tinted by nostalgia. The emotional tone of what they said, present in voice timbre and tone, pauses and sighs, as well as the words which they used ('lost', 'gone' etc.), was closer to reverie than to recollection. Whenever they talked about the present, whether about the catering, the furniture, the buildings, the leaders, their colleagues or the general ethos of the organization, they drew unfavourable comparisons with the 'good old days'.

In addition to those interviewees whose nostalgia was overpowering, the majority of interviews with older employees at some point displayed some nostalgic qualities. These employees would not merely recollect important incidents in the organization's history, but would seek to incorporate them in an idealized image of the organization's and their personal, past, charged with a fond feeling of affection and warmth. This contrasted sharply with the exceptional few, who sought to demean and devalue the past,[7] and suggested to me that nostalgia may be studied not only as an individual phenomenon, but also as an organizational one, i.e. as an emotional and symbolic attribute of some organizations, growing organically out of organizational processes. Many organizations, like societies, are seen by their members as having a golden age, belonging to the mythological prehistory rather than to documented history. People with first-hand experience of this age treat it as a personal and a collective heritage, against which they perceive, interpret and judge the present.

Some Elements of Organizational Nostalgia

The five organizations under investigation differed in the extent as well as the nature of their members' nostalgic feeling. One organization, a small consultancy firm which had only been in existence for a short while before the research, had none detectable. In a publishing and research organization, nostalgia was a marginal phenomenon; few of those interviewed had been with the company for more than five years. Nostalgic voices in this organization (like Text 1) tended to get lost in the buzz of everyday life. In the remaining three organizations, however, a chemical multinational, a utility and a hospital, nostalgia played a pivotal role in the emotions and perceptions of the numerous older and longer-serving employees. As nostalgia was not part of the planned research, it is not possible to compare its representations at the corporate level. What can, however, be done is to identify certain elements which act as foci of nostalgic feeling.

Buildings

First, the physical *buildings* of the company. The experience of the chemical firm is instructive. This company had moved away from its historic building in the centre of London for a number of years, while the building was radically refashioned. When the company moved back, while outwardly remaining the same, the building's interior was unrecognizable. A senior executive said:

> The old building was like a gentlemen's club, long dark corridors, heavy oak doors, but during the seventies recession we had lost a lot of staff and the rest were rattling like peas in a pod. When we moved out, I found people I didn't even know existed and I'm supposed to know everyone in the building. Everyone at that time worked in their distinct little cells, and the idea was to make the culture of the organization much more open; we would have an all-glazed environment, so that it would appear more open. I have my own personal views on whether it happened, but I'd rather not risk them. . . As for my staff, a lot of them don't like the modern architecture, can't open the windows, we have a high incidence of sickness, headaches. Don't know if this is psychological, psychosomatic or the 'sick-building syndrome', but the staff personalize their work environment a lot more than they did in the old building. They didn't use to have all these fluffy toys around. (Text 5)

The old building acted as a powerful source of nostalgic feeling for those staff who had lived and worked in it. A supervisor who had worked for the company for twenty years said:

> When we moved back, I liked the cleanliness of it, the smell, the new desks. I still like the building concept but I find it difficult to work in . . . I think that the ceilings are too low. The old building was a 1920s building, very elegant, *it was a shame to lose a lot of that*. (Text 6)

Another supervisor, with thirty years' service, had more extreme views.

> I hate it [the building], I loathe it. It's a lovely building to come in and walk around and say 'Isn't it wonderful!' To work in it it's hell, nothing goes right. . . The idea was that there should be an atrium, where there used to be just a light well, sort of white lavatory tiles on

it, an unused space, just open. They decided to turn it into usable space, originally they were going to have trees, then they said it was going to be too noisy. So they carpet it, it's quite stunning if you look from the eighth floor, but from the working point of view it's no good. The idea was that we'd all feel part of a whole, you could see everybody, but you don't. All you can see is the people in the corridors, or you look at the fishtanks, the offices that line up the atrium, half of the time they are empty, so that's depressing! (Text 7)

In addition to the difficulties of living and working in an exposed environment over which one has little control, employees in some corporate buildings experience another source of dissatisfaction. Corporate culture theory has viewed the ostentatious lavishness of corporate headquarters as an emblem of corporate might, much as the cathedrals of the past stood for the might of God and his representatives on earth. For those who have to work in such environments there is a contradiction between the outward opulence of the building and their lifeless, spiritually impoverished qualities.

In the chemical firm in question, the new building carried a potent symbolism, but for many the symbolism was very far from that intended by the architects and the corporate image-makers. Far from corporate splendour, the new building came to stand for a corruption of the old values. Outwardly the same, the building's new interior affronted people's sense of authenticity and epitomized the hollow rhetoric of PR. The atrium, intended to symbolize corporate openness, came to stand for what many of the older staff felt to be the spiritual void at the heart of the organization. Under such circumstances, the old building's dark corridors, ironically, came to symbolize authenticity and community.

I liked the look of the new building when I first walked in, very impressive. But the offices, the way that they are organized, you don't see an awful lot of people. Where we are you might not see anyone all day. It is quiet. Conducive to work, but not conducive to gatherings or anything like that. The old building, well it was antiquated, but it had *character*, while this has no character, *and this is also how I feel about people*. There used to be birthday parties in our offices, Christmas parties, whereas now, they don't have impromptu get-togethers any more. (Text 8)

Leaders

If the physical set-up of an organization acts as a powerful symbol evoking nostalgic feelings, so do the organization's *leaders*. In two of the organizations I studied, earlier leaders had left a powerful legacy against which present leaders were assessed and found lacking. The old leaders had been heads of the family, in contrast to the technocratic or even macho styles of management of the present ones. The following quote interweaves two nostalgic themes to reinforce a comparison with the present: disaffection with the physical premises (absence of bar in the new building) and affection for the departed leader:

> He'd come to the bar most days and have a pint and he might have a packet of crisps and a pork pie or something like that. And he would come and sit down with anybody, it might just be a secretary, someone who'd just started that week. He would put himself in their shoes. He probably learnt more about what went on in the company from these conversations . . . you never see the current chairman, he never comes down. There is no bar anyway. It was a place where you socialized. *So we've lost this these days.* (Text 9)

Similar feelings for the retired chairman were expressed by numerous members of that organization:

> The nice thing about Sir Roy, I didn't have many dealings or *any* dealings in fact, but he was always around, he was quite visible in the dining room having egg and chips for lunch, or in the bar having a pint and people would go and talk to him if they wanted. No matter what he did while he was in power, he always seemed a very human person. Sir Roy was different from all the other chairmen I've known. Although I didn't see him every day someone would say 'Oh yes, I saw him in the bar having a sandwich', so yes, that made me feel different, just the fact that he was around. The current chairman, I wouldn't go back home and say 'The chairman was having egg and chips today'; he doesn't. I don't feel I know him at all. (Text 10)

I collected no fewer than eighteen stories about Sir Roy, a Falstaffian figure, nearly all of them having him talking to people in bars, lifts or dining-rooms. A sense of bonhomie and familiarity characterizes these portraits. Sir Roy was by all accounts a 'character' and *characters* form focal points of nostalgia.[8] They readily come to embody the whole spirit of the golden past, become its champions and its emblems. Characters are memorable, they are unpredictable, they stand out from the crowd and provide a key for a temporary escape from bureaucratic uniformity, predictability and order.[9]

Other 'Characters' and Departed Colleagues

But characters who attract nostalgic feelings are by no means always leaders. Colleagues who departed often form the subject of fond reminiscences, as if their departure was equivalent to their having died. These are instances when nostalgic feeling is most tinted with sadness, melancholia or even mourning.

> Julie was a caring person and would take time to listen to me and then a few days later she'd pop round and have a chat. These days there is not so much time to have a chat with somebody. She'd organize things. She was secretary of the social club and organized events making sure that everyone got involved. A lot of people felt like I feel about her. The space is not available now for recreational activities in this building. There are just two squash courts. (Text 11)

> The financial officer who was here before Mr Walmsley, Mr Green, he was brilliant with everybody, he used to come every Christmas to our office party, and eat awful sausage rolls that we'd made and still look pleased about it. The last time he came, he made me do a waltz with him, he was really a nice guy. (Text 12)

> I've been here for a long time and I've seen the atmosphere change. In the days, ten years ago say, I have still some friends now that I made here then. But the numbers of friends I have now, I can count them on the fingers of one hand. One of the women that used to work here, she is someone who I always look back on, when I look at how it used to be here when it was good fun. She plus another girl are the two people I think of when I think 'It was good in those days when such and such a person was around.' If I look back at the company when it used to be fun to be here, they are the sort of people I think of. (Text 13)

Such quotes weave the departed characters with other nostalgic themes, such as the building and the social functions. In spite of their different emotional content, they highlight *caring* and *altruism* as central features of the organizational golden age. These are features which are prominent in many nostalgia, contrasted to the contractual, cash nexus of the present.

Consider the following two accounts which focus on this theme. They come from two women working in the same department of a utility, dealing with telephone inquiries from customers. Jackie Simpson painted a positively Kafkaesque picture of the present situation in the office, but throughout the interview maintained a cheerful and defiant attitude summed up in the comment: 'It's funny really but when everything is really low, then people decide to have some fun. You are treated like dirt, and you say "Sod it, let's enjoy ourselves, even if we just make fun of each other."' Jackie's proud and outspoken attitude left little room for nostalgia. But when asked for an incident which summed up her experience in the organization, she replied thus:

I used to work for a man, he is at head office now, I was a lot younger then, but to me working, it was my first job and to work here it meant . . . giving a bit and taking a bit. And with him you had that feeling, and I would work a couple of minutes [*sic*!] over. I didn't mind if you had somebody on the phone, you wouldn't get rid of them abruptly just because it was time to go. You wouldn't mind. That sums it up for me. *Then* you wouldn't mind helping. But *now* I just don't like it at all. (Text 14)

This text illustrates the quality of mutuality which was seen as a central feature of the past. This theme recurs in the testimony of Mary Crighton, Jackie's supervisor, a woman who spoke with frustration but also with affection for her subordinates. She had herself had been promoted from being a telephone clerk and now found it difficult to generate much cooperation among her staff.

Everybody now has that selfish streak; my team is all right, but if you ask them to do something 'Ooh!' We talk about the past, we say to the young ones 'You should have been here, when we all used to do this job together and it was good and we used to have good spirit, and we had loads and loads of work, but it had nothing to do with the work, that was loads and loads, but everyone seemed to want to help each other and you would look out for each other and be sympathetic. *It was a different sort of thing.* (Text 15)

The power of such feelings and their familiar quality makes it remarkable that nostalgia has been so little noticed by research on organizations. Space does not permit an illustration of other foci of nostalgic feeling in organizations, but two should at least be mentioned. In contrast to chaotic and irrational rules and procedures of the present, the organization's golden past is seen as one of order and reason; it is as if all the bureaucratic absurdities and the vexations which result never existed at that time (see Text 1). Second, the technology of yesteryear is seen as permitting individualism and creativity in contrast to today's deskilling and routinized systems. This applies especially to pre-computerized information systems which often attracted nostalgic feelings in my research.[10]

To summarize. A number of objects have been identified which attract nostalgic feeling in organizations; these include the physical buildings of the organization, the leaders, departed colleagues, and social functions. In all cases, these are compared favourably with their equivalents of the present time and found richer, more authentic, more meaningful. However, the nature of what I have until now referred to as nostalgic feeling is not constant. The affects, though generally contemplative, range from pride to self-pity, from sadness to joy; most are tinted with some melancholy, at times verging on mourning. In most cases, nostalgia appears to make the present more bearable, but in some it puts today's realities in grim relief. What is constant is idealization and simplification, the experience of the past as a personal heritage, emphasis on community and harping after a quality of authenticity.

Nostalgia and Identity

Organizational nostalgia combines a powerful but variable affective component, a cognitive reconstruction of the past, i.e. its idealization, and a symbolic enrichment, i.e. mythologization. Psychologically, it is most accessible as a component of *self*, that valuable but precarious web of truths, half-truths and fictions which surround the entity which we familiarly refer to as 'I'. Davis (1979: 34) recognized that, as a dimension of identity, nostalgia increases our sense of self-worth. No matter how low, infirm or powerless we are now, we take heart from earlier glories and grandeurs. The world may have changed but no one can deny us our past. We too were there and experienced the golden age. Having met a famous person, having participated in a historic event, having tasted life before the fall become treasured possessions. Kaplan (1987: 473) has rightly pointed out that the memory of such experiences is treated with devotion and veneration.

This gives us a clue to what we called the nostalgia paradox, namely the pleasurable recollection of a past irredeemably lost. The rarer, the more unique the experience, the greater its value. Just as a collector of stamps takes greater pride in the rarest items he/she possesses, or even the rarest items he/she *once possessed*, in nostalgia we take special pride in our most unrepeatable experiences. Consider the football fan who saw England win the 1966 World Cup, the opera enthusiast who attended Maria Callas' last historic performances of *Tosca* in London, or the ageing hippy whose identity was shaped at the famous Woodstock pop festival. Being able to say that they were present at these legendary occasions becomes all the more valuable a part of their heritage, the less likely it is that they will be repeated. Idealization is comprehensible in this context. The details of the events may be less significant than the fact that one was 'there'. The discontinuities which separate those experiences from the present become psychologically beneficial, by enhancing their uniqueness and therefore their value.

The experiences above become all the more powerful as sources of identity, when juxtaposed to the 'dire state' of English football, operatic singing or youth culture of today.

Nostalgia then provides a vicarious fulfilment of what Schwartz (1987) calls the 'ontological function', the individual's need to see him/herself as someone of value, summed up in 'being somebody is good, being a "has been" is bad' (1987: 328). Nostalgia enables a has-been to become somebody again. Nowhere is this clearer than in the example given by Schwartz' mentor, Ernest Becker:

> Anthony Quinn in his great role in *Requiem for a Heavyweight* earned his inner sense of self-value by constantly reminding himself and others that he was '*fifth*-ranking contender for the heavyweight crown'. This made him *somebody*. (1962: 84)

What types of experiences become the foci of nostalgic feeling? Though they may have the qualities of rarity and uniqueness, it is unlikely that acutely pleasurable experiences can easily feed nostalgia later on. If they become the object of nostalgic recollection they are likely to be heavily weighed by melancholy feeling.[11] Discontinuity in such cases weighs as loss; instead of adding to the psychic value of the memories, transforming them into personal treasures, it poisons and destroys them. The loss of an admired chairman, as we saw earlier, may inspire nostalgia. The loss of a loved friend or a treasured child does not. *Nostalgia is not a way of coming to terms with the past (as mourning or grief are), but an attempt to come to terms with the present.* Unless the loss has been psychologically conquered, and this requires strength, nostalgia cannot adopt it as its material.

More mildly pleasurable experiences and less dramatic discontinuities can more easily act as generators of nostalgic feelings and reconstructions. Such experiences may act like faded holiday photographs, old theatre programmes or family heirlooms, no longer triggering specific reminiscences, but rather representing *icons* of a unique symbolic and emotional cosmos. Overwhelming experiences leave powerful memories, traumas, repressions; moderately pleasurable ones can evade the rigours of *memory* and feed the plastic medium of *phantasy*. It is therefore, not as memories, but as *phantasies about the past through which we seek to come to terms with the present, that nostalgia works its spell.*[12]

Organizations as Terrains of Nostalgia

While the neglect of emotional life in organizations has been rightly criticized (Hochschild, 1983; Hosking and Fineman, 1990; Flam, 1990a, 1990b), it is easy to make the opposite error and exaggerate the freedom and strength of emotions in organizations. If emotions in organizations are managed, tempered and defused, that only helps to make them fecund grounds for nostalgia. The modest satisfactions and successes of organizational life can, after some years, begin to feed nostalgic narratives, in a way that violent passions cannot. Equally, however, the very nature of *present* experiences in many organizations further enhances nostalgia. The discontents of today, in other words, find partial but effective consolation in gentle reverie of yesteryear.

To summarize: it is unlikely that nostalgia will feed on a past of extreme pleasure and extreme disappointments, preferring for its source material modest pleasures and enchantments; equally, nostalgia offers most effective consolation for modest disappointments and disenchantments, rather than for severe traumas and psychic injuries. And organizations, by their very nature bureaucratic, impersonal, emotionally cauterized if not emasculated, harbour the types of disillusionments and discontents for which nostalgia can supply effective consolation, namely injuries to our *narcissism*.

Impersonality is a key ingredient of our experience of organizations ever since our first day at school, when leaving our mother's coveted embrace, we proceeded to become one of many, a number on the register, a face among unknowns. Impersonality is a fundamental affront to our narcissism. From being unique members of a family, organizations from school onwards consign us to the status of cogs, important or critical perhaps, but dispensable and replaceable. I shall not develop this point here, but its relation to nostalgia must be clear. For in its very insistence on community, family spirit, characters, warmth, personal care and protecting leaders, nostalgia seeks to undo the painful effect of entering a world of impersonal organizations, *as if the organization of old was nothing but an extension of our loving, caring family*. And in so doing, nostalgia seeks to reinvigorate our ailing narcissism.

To be sure, nostalgia is not the only or even the most powerful mode of consolation available. I have dealt elsewhere (Gabriel, 1991a, 1991b) with manifold symbolic avenues open to people in finding consolation from the injuries sustained by their narcissism in the course of life in organizations. Humour, folklore, fantasy, ritual, detachment, cynicism and routine in their different ways accomplish not dissimilar ends, namely providing temporary relief from the rigours of organizational controls, a symbolic means for turning powerlessness into control and a source of meaning in relatively meaningless situations. Nevertheless, the role of nostalgia as a palliative should not be underestimated, notably for older members. For nostalgia essentially resurrects the selfsame narcissism, towards which the modern corporation is so injurious, the narcissism of the time when we could convince ourselves that we were both unique and the centre of a loving world.[13]

Nostalgia, the Ego-ideal and Injured Narcissism

Nostalgia is but one attempt to recreate the blissful unity of primary narcissism. In the celebrated essay which introduced the concept of narcissism, Freud (1914) singled out as a central feature of narcissistic processes, the raising of an ideal ego. 'To this ideal ego is now directed the self-love which the real ego enjoyed in childhood. The narcissism seems to be now displaced on to this new ideal ego, which, like the infantile ego, deems itself the possessor of all perfections' (Freud, 1914: 74). In the conclusion of that essay, Freud noted that the *ego ideal* is 'of great importance for the understanding of group psychology. Besides its individual side, this ideal has a social side; it is also the common ideal of a family, a class or a nation' (Freud, 1914: 81).

Schwartz (1987) elegantly adds 'organization' to the list and provides a cogent justification for doing so, at least as far as highly 'committed' organizational members are concerned. These partici-pants are willing to sacrifice personal and family lives and are prepared to commit grossly unethical and criminal acts in the interest of the organization. In exchange, the organization offers them an *organizational ideal*, an idealized image of themselves quite untainted by the failings of incompetent officials or the envy of outsiders, pledged to a noble, immortal and anxiety-free future. This organizational image of perfection then becomes the shared ideal of each member, sustaining their individual ego ideals. They too are perfect, inasmuch as they are part of a perfect organization. They too are immortal, as members of an immortal organization. As a member of an organization whose death is inconceivable, the individual too becomes immortal. Threats to organizational survival are seen as personal threats against one's self. Consider, for exam-ple, the uproar generated when government action threatens to put an end to a long-standing organization, like the British Broadcasting Corporation. The end of the BBC, following the review of its charter, would be experienced by its constituency (and especially by its own members) as death. Part of themselves would die the day the initials BBC were replaced by CCB, or CBB or some other neologism.[14]

Schwartz' organizational ideal possesses a utopian, almost millenarian, hue, a true heir to the religious promise of salvation in a future paradise. The use of overtly religious rhetoric, like organizational 'mission', 'visions' of the future, 'charismatic' leadership, indicates that some organizations seek to fashion their mythological ideals after the messianic prototypes of Judaism and Christianity. This may apply to revolutionary parties (hoping to save the world through political action), but in the case of modern corporations it stretches one's credulity, though not perhaps the faith of the most blinkered organizational participants. I have argued elsewhere (Gabriel, 1991b) that for many, an alternative solution to the same problem, i.e. the injurious effect of organizations on narcissism, is the erection of an organizational *malignant*, a grotesque caricature of all the undesirable qualities, summed up in metaphors like 'This place is a madhouse/nightmare.' The individual or group may then derive considerable narcissistic satisfaction from demeaning the organization, celebrating its failures and deriding its absurdities, and placing themselves morally and intellectually above it. The ego ideal is here constructed through its opposition to the organizational malignant; in a nightmarish world, where everything is evil, anything that stands for opposition, denial and defiance easily becomes the object of idealization (as do, for instance, those who resist an occupying force). In many organizations, narcissism is restored by such a demonizing of the present, evident in large areas of organizational folklore. For example, in one organization, the suicide of a hospital cook was seen as conclusive proof of management malevolence. Symbolically, the suicide stood for murder: 'They drove him to it' was the message I received from several of his colleagues. Anyone standing up to 'them' was automatically the object of idealization and admiration (Gabriel, 1991c).

What I am suggesting here is that nostalgic idealization of the past represents a parallel solution, which in the case of some, but not all, organizational members can go hand in hand with the demonization of the present.[15] Individuals who are too disillusioned, too inquisitive, too rational or simply too old, to 'buy' the organization's own ideal, to internalize it and make it their own (like Schwartz' 'committed participants'), may create an alternative ideal, one built not around galvanizing utopias for the future, but around the warm and loving reconstructions of the past. The use of the family metaphor and constant allusions to togetherness, solidarity, caring and purpose are linked not to a future paradise but to a lost one, a time and a place when all biological and psychological needs were met. This was a time when individuals were characters rather than impersonal agents, when they worked together under strong but just leaders, when they prevailed against adversity by pulling together, when relations between them were sincere and authentic, when life was exciting, unpredictable and yet secure. In proclaiming this idyllic past, nostalgia marks the triumphant idealism of the spirit over the discontents of the present. 'Man needs to supplement reality by an ideal world,' wrote F. A. Lange (quoted in Bettelheim, 1990: 107). Like great art then, nostalgia ennobles human experiences, lifts them above the mundane realities of everyday life and gives them a higher and finer quality.

Perhaps, an alternative solution should be added here if only because it stands in such sharp contrast to nostalgia. In addition to individuals idealizing the future (Schwartz' 'organizational ideal') demonizing the present (organizational malignant), or idealizing the past (nostalgia), on occasion one meets individuals who demonize the organizational past. The term 'nostophobia', coined by Davis (1979), comes to mind here. I can provide only one brief but vivid illustration, from a supervisor in the chemical organization, at the end of a twenty-five year career in the selfsame department which spawned numerous nostalgic texts, including some quoted earlier. The contrast of this account with the earlier ones is astonishing, yet it only underlines the malleable nature of phantasy.

> When I joined the organization, it was more like a school and the supervisors' word was law; it was really quite terrible, all the ladies were called by their surnames, it was just horrid. . . Very stern and regimented. When I joined, of course, I had a slight Northern accent. I was told I would be given a month's trial and in that month I had to lose my Northern accent. But I needed the job, so I lost the accent. . . Supervisors in those days were a different breed of people. Tartars! (Text 16)

Although demonization of such power was far outweighed by nostalgic recollection in the organization in question, I would suggest that demonization and idealization are processes that frequently operate in tandem as solutions to the problem of narcissism created by organizations; even Schwartz' idealization of the organization is implicitly complemented by *xenophobia*, the demonization of what lies outside the organization, i.e. interfering state agents, competitors, unappreciative public, as well as their representatives *within* the organization, i.e. the fifth column.

Conclusion

It will by now have become apparent that organizational nostalgia tells us more about the discontents of today than about the contents of yesteryear. Like humour, but in a radically different way, it seeks to provide a symbolic way out of the rigours of bureaucracy, seeking to re-enchant a long disenchanted world. Having lost faith in the future, it idealizes the past, constructing an ego ideal out of what has been rather than about what should become. The myths fomented by nostalgia, like most myths, are wish-fulfilling self-delusions, partial satisfactions in the realm of phantasy of real desires. And like most myths and self-delusions, nostalgic phantasies rarely engage reality-tempting falsification. Within organizations their illusory nature can be safely preserved; nostalgic phantasies and myths serve modern organizations well enough.

In particular, we examined how nostalgia seeks to offer partial consolation for the injuries sustained by our narcissism in organizations, though as a general cultural phenomenon it is no doubt related to the wider disenchantment with the present, and the loss of enthusiasm for the future, whether this should be seen in technological, political or moral terms. Within organizations, nostalgia acts as a cause of an emotional gulf between those with first-hand experiences of the golden past, and those without. This reinforces many other divisions.

In closing this chapter we may offer a tentative evaluation of nostalgia. Is nostalgia good or bad? Rationalists have traditionally disparaged it (a) for its clouding of critical faculties, its proclamation of a set of often infantile illusions and its enmity to true historical inquiry, or more commonly (b) for the ease with which it becomes appropriated, trivialized and exploited by capital's 'merchandisers of meaning'. I feel that a more equivocal evaluation is in order, for nostalgia is a deeply equivocal phenomenon. In as much as it provides a groundrock of loving memories, a life that has been worth living and a source of meaning, ennobling us and enabling us to endure present malaise, nostalgia is good. Its implications should not be pre-judged as conservative and regressive. Many radical movements and many noble causes have been sustained by myth or phantasy of golden age in the distant past (Lasch, 1980: xvii). To be sure, as consumer the individual may be vulnerable to attempts to control his/her nostalgia, manipulated and exploited. But as an organizational participant, his/her nostalgia is harder to control, as the earlier quotes indicate. In this sense, nostalgia may be part of the 'unmanaged organization', those aspects of organizational life, emotion and symbolism which resist attempts to control them through impersonal procedures by management. The unmanaged organization is a kind of organizational dreamworld in which people engage in all kinds of unsupervised, spontaneous activity, where they can distort reality in the interest of pleasure, where emotion prevails over expedience. The chief force of this terrain is phantasy and its landmarks include stories, jokes, myths, gossip, nicknames, graffiti and cartoons (Gabriel, 1991c).

Finally, when compared with some other psychological mechanisms addressing the same needs, namely blind nationalism, hate-filled xenophobia, cynical withdrawal, or slavish conformity to the organization, nostalgia strikes me both as benign and honourable. If only through the means of inappropriate symbols and fictitious images of the past, it seeks to reintroduce idealism in organizations, to maintain a much-needed plurality of voices and views and to vindicate a set of alternative values in organizations, from those of profit, rationality, efficiency and domination.

Notes

Part of the field work presented here was carried out by the author and David Robins with the help of ESRC grant No. R000232627; I would like to acknowledge with gratitude the help and useful suggestions offered by Steve Fineman, David Robins and Howard Schwartz.

1. Cf. Lasch on 'fear of nostalgia' (1984: 65); this describes well the intellectual's aversion to the concept.
2. There is a third path which has little to offer the present discussion, that of marketing. Marketing has taken the nostalgia of the masses as a fact and has sought to understand how specific products may be planned, packaged and presented to maximize their nostalgic appeal. See, for example, Moriarty and McGann (1983), and Unger et al. (1991).
3. For etymology and history of the term 'nostalgia', see Kaplan (1987) and Davis (1979).
4. It could be that the greater the discontinuity which separates us from the time which forms the object of nostalgia, the more recent that time can be. For example, some individuals in Eastern Europe are nostalgic about a very recent past, because of the magnitude of discontinuity between it and the present.

5. The question of whether a person who did not partake of the initial experience may partake in the nostalgic feeling towards it is an open one. My view would be that there is a considerable overlap between fond and yearning feelings for situations we experienced first hand and those we experienced via the descriptions of our parents, great authors (like Homer or Scott) and great artists. For example, Homer may create in his readers, whether young or old, an acute nostalgia for the heroic times.

6. Nostalgia, as a form of yearning for the unattainable which combines idealization with abasement, has much in common with the now obsolete form of 'courtly love', dating from the twelfth-century troubadours. This combined idealization of the beloved lady, the inferiority of the lover, a recognition of the unattainability of the quest, as well as the refusal to collapse into despair and anguish. See Lindholm (1988).

7. See Text 16.

8. Note how the old building in earlier quotes was seen as having 'character'.

9. This is not to say that some current organizational leaders are not seen as characters. Two of the organizations I studied were led by individuals whose eccentric behaviour and unusual foibles attracted much gossip and fuelled organizational folklore. What, however, makes 'old characters' different from 'current characters' is the unequivocally warm feeling they attract, which is evident in the stories recounted about them, like the ones above. By contrast, stories about current leaders seen as 'characters' usually present them as faintly ridiculous or threatening figures.

10. Fearful (1992) has observed the deep gulf existing in an office between employees who joined before the introduction of computers and those who joined since. While she does not use the concept of nostalgia, her research suggests that pre-computerized technology, allowing greater scope for discretion and initiative, can act as a focus of nostalgic feeling in some organizations, polarizing the two groups of employees.

11. Freud observed that: 'Hardly anything is harder for man to give up than a pleasure which he once experienced. Actually we can never give anything up; we only exchange one thing for another' (1908: 143–53). According to this view, acutely pleasurable experiences can hardly form the material of nostalgic recollections.

12. Psychoanalytic theory often distinguishes unconscious 'phantasies' (such as those involved in nostalgia) to conscious 'fantasies' or daydreaming (including fanciful inventions).

13. This is *not* the New Narcissism vividly portrayed and criticized by Lasch. The New Narcissist is self-consciously and militantly anti-nostalgic, living only for the present and having little time for sentimental diversions from the past. Far from being psychologically hurt by bureaucracy, he often thrives and prospers in it, just as the bureaucracy prospers on his services. (Lasch, 1980; Gabriel, 1982). The very impersonality of bureaucracy sustains him and protects him. Unlike the New Narcissism which derives from secondary narcissism (trying to cancel out the disappointment of rejected object love), nostalgia resurrects primary narcissism, seeking to restore the original state of oneness with the world. The golden age of the organization may then be seen as an attempt to recreate the blissful unity of mother and child.

14. See Sievers (1990).

15. See Text 1 for an extreme instance.

References

Becker, E. (1962) *The Birth and Death of Meaning*. Harmondsworth: Penguin.

Bettelheim, B. (1990) *Recollections and Reflections*. London: Thames & Hudson.

Daniels, E. (1985) 'Nostalgia and hidden meaning', *American Imago*, 42 (4): 371–82.

Dante, A. (1984) *The Divine Comedy*, Vol. 1: *Inferno* (tr. Mark Musa). Harmondsworth: Penguin.

DaSilva, F. B. and Faught, J. (1982) 'Nostalgia: a sphere and process of contemporary ideology', *Qualitative Sociology*, 5 (1): 47–61.

Davis, F. (1979) *Yearning for Yesterday: A Sociology of Nostalgia*. New York: Free Press and London: Collier Macmillan.

Fearful, A. (1992) 'The introduction of information and office technologies: the great divide?' Paper presented at the 10th International Aston/UMIST Labour Process Conference, Aston University, 1–3 April.

Flam, H. (1990a) 'Emotional "Man" I: the emotional "man" and the problem of collective action', *International Sociology*, 5 (1): 39–56.

Flam, H. (1990b) 'Emotional "Man" II: corporate actors as emotion-motivated emotion managers', *International Sociology*, 5 (2): 225–34.

Freud, S. (1908) 'Creative writers and daydreams', in *Standard Edition*, Vol. 9. London: Hogarth Press.

Freud, S. (1914) 'On narcissism', in *Standard Edition*, Vol. 14. London: Hogarth Press.

Gabriel, Y. (1982) 'Freud, Rieff and the critique of American culture', *Psychoanalytic Review*, 69 (3): 341–66.

Gabriel, Y. (1988) *Working Lives in Catering*. London: Routledge & Kegan Paul.

Gabriel, Y. (1991a) 'Turning facts into stories and stories into facts: a hermeneutic exploration of organizational folklore', *Human Relations*, 44 (8): 857–75.

Gabriel, Y. (1991b) 'Organizations and their discontents: a psychoanalytic contribution to the study of corporate culture', *Journal of Applied Behavioural Science*, 27 (3): 318–36.

Gabriel, Y. (1991c) 'On organizational stories and myths: why it is easier to slay a dragon than to kill a myth', *International Sociology*, 6 (4): 427–42.

Hochschild, A. (1983) *The Managed Heart*. Berkeley: University of California Press.

Hosking, D. and Fineman, S. (1990) 'The texture of organizing: organizing process', *Journal of Management Studies*, 27 (6): 583–604.

Kaplan, H. A. (1987) 'The psychopathology of nostalgia', *Psychoanalytic Review*, 74 (4): 463–86.

Kleiner, J. (1970) 'On nostalgia', *Bulletin of Philadelphia Association of Psychoanalysis*, 21: 11–30.

Lasch, C. (1980) *The Culture of Narcissism*. London: Abacus.

Lasch, C. (1984) *The Minimal Self*. London: Pan Books.

Lindholm, C. (1988) 'Lovers and leaders: a comparison of social and psychological models of romance and charisma', *Social Science Information*, 27 (1): 3–45.

Moriarty, S. E. and McGann, A. F. (1983) 'Nostalgia and consumer sentiment', *Journalism Quarterly*, 60 (1): 81–6.

Rottenburg, R. (1991) 'Socialism needs the entire person'. Paper delivered at the 8th International SCOS Conference, Copenhagen.

Schwartz, H. S. (1987) 'Anti-social actions of committed organizational participants: an existential psychoanalytic perspective', *Organization Studies*, 8: 327–40.

Schwartz, H. S. (1988) 'The symbol of the space shuttle and the degeneration of the American dream', *Journal of Organizational Change Management*, 1 (2): 5-20.

Sievers, B. (1990) 'Thoughts on the relatedness of work, death and life itself', *European Management Journal*, 8 (3): 321-4.

Sohn, L. (1983) 'Nostalgia', *International Journal of Psycho-analysis*, 64: 203-11.

Terkel, S. (1985) *Working*. Harmondsworth: Penguin.

Unger, L. S., McConocha, D. M. and Faier, J. A. (1991) 'The use of nostalgia in television advertising: a content analysis', *Journalism Quarterly*, 68 (3): 345-53.

Werman, D. (1977) 'Normal and pathological nostalgia', *Journal of American Psychoanalytic Association*, 25: 313-20.

Williams, R. (1974) *The Country and the City*. Oxford: Oxford University Press.

Wright, P. (1985) *On Living in an Old Country: The National Past in Contemporary Britain*. London: Verso.

PART III

EMOTIONS AND THE POLITICS OF DIFFERENCE

7

Emotive Subjects: Organizational Men, Organizational Masculinities and the (De)construction of 'Emotions'

Jeff Hearn

This chapter explores emotions in organizations by focusing on organizational men and organizational masculinities. To write on this is an exciting, if somewhat daunting, prospect. One major theme is the contradiction between the dominant social construction of men as 'unemotional' and the deconstruction of men and men's 'emotions' in organizations. Whereas social constructionism takes a phenomenon, in this case men's emotions in organizations, and seeks to explore the social forces that construct or account for that phenomenon and the forms it takes, deconstructionism attends to the social, and particularly discursive, elements that account for that phenomenon in the first place. As such this latter view contends that men's emotions, like emotions in general, do not have any unmediated existence. Instead men's emotions persist in discourse(s), that is, structured, but not fixed or given, relations of meaning and meaning construction in language and other forms of text and communication. A second theme, and sometimes a contradiction, is the relationship between personal experience and analysis: to write accurately on emotions involves an acknowledgement of the emotion of that process. Emotions are sites for further emotions: just as sex is sexy, so emotions are emotional. Clearly I am also part of, not immune from, that which I am writing (about).

Unemotional Men, Unemotional Organizations

Conventional wisdom often constructs both men and organizations as 'unemotional'. In much dominant discourse, both organizational and academic, men are constructed as the 'unemotional' ones relative to women. In recent literature on men, and especially that which has been labelled confusingly and ambiguously as 'men's studies' (see Hearn, 1989a), men have been constructed as 'unemotional' (or relatively so) compared with women (Farrell, 1974; Seidler, 1992). Similarly, while the private domains are dominantly constructed as receptacles of emotions, including men's emotions, organizations are portrayed as unemotional places. In such dominant views men in organizations are likely to be doubly unemotional. Like most clichés, there is some truth in both of these characterizations.[1]

It is important to neither underestimate nor overestimate the import of conventional wisdom on men and emotions in organizations. For one thing, men 'at work' are generally not expected to display certain categories of emotion, especially those associated with women or those that are conventionally assumed to be 'what women show'. Indeed in one sense this is a very real and pervasive influence on how men behave in organizations, and how men do or do not 'show emotion' there. For example, it is uncommon in many organizations for men to cry, and when men, particularly famous men, such as politicians or sportsmen do, this can easily become newsworthy in its own right. What is remarkable is not so much that men cry, but that this crying is itself seen as remarkable. Men are assumed not to show fear, sadness or even joy; anger may, however, be thought to be appropriate for men at least in some organizational settings. So already here there is some break in the accepted wisdom that organizational men are unemotional. More generally, organizations, and men in them, are being increasingly recognized as emotional or potentially so (Flam, 1990a, 1990b; Albrow, 1992).

The fact that men often behave very differently from women, often have more formal power than women, and so on, does not mean they are necessarily less or more emotional than women. Not only are men far from unemotional, and organizations far from unemotional arenas, but men can be deconstructed as just as emotional as women and organizations can be deconstructed as just as emotional as non-organizational arenas respectively. In this view men are often seen as not being emotional enough, or repressing emotion. Yet surely this is misleading. An alternative construction is that men are too emotional, too much out of control (or indeed too much in control), especially when it comes to anger, sexuality and violence.

Getting Emotional: Getting Personal

To write about men, emotions and organizations is to experience the obligation to get emotional, the sign of redemptive discourse. For like Foucault's commentary on sexuality (1988: 16), there is, in talking of emotions, the obligation, experienced or perceived, to tell the truth about oneself, or at least to talk about 'the truth'.

Rather than pretend to abstract myself from that process I shall acknowledge my presence within this discourse by 'telling the truth' (or at least some stories) about my own emotional experiences in organizations. The problem is not so much what to say or what to drag from any organizational mires, but what not to say. There are too many examples to tell the (full) truth. Being in an organization often can be and often is emotional.

Two Meetings: One Angry, One Fearful

Picture a staff meeting – a meeting of peers, well at least in theory. On the agenda is the advertising of a new post, replacing a temporary one with a permanent one. The discussion centres around the appropriate job description for the new post – should it reflect the strengths of the temporary incumbent or some other set of 'ideal' characteristics? It hovers between such characteristics and the performance of the present worker. At this point a staff member begins to run down that performance. I explode: 'Fucking hell'. I am truly angry – but the outburst is partly a surprise to me and partly very deliberate. It is over before I realized what I had done; yet it is also designed to make clear my disgust of the rubbishing, whatever the outcome on the specific issue. I have the long view in mind whatever happens in this particular case.

This meeting is more formal: it is to decide on the impact of financial cuts on different workgroups, including my own. I do not say a word. The meeting is scripted and interventions could be counterproductive. The meeting is one of anxiety and fear for me – like going to a hostile interview. In fact that is almost what it is. The overall feeling is of more powerful men controlling others – women and men. I feel I'm in the hands of management.

While in the first case crisis and conflict with peers led to anger, in the second crisis and conflict were combined with hierarchy and subordination inducing fear and anxiety.

Two Rituals: One Sad, One Joyful

A year after a student dies, a memorial meeting is held during lunchtime. At the end of the meeting I walk onto the corridor where I work, tears streaming. I feel very sad. A colleague and I embrace. We walk to a room for a cup of tea, just as going from a burial to a wake.

At a graduation party a group of postgraduate students give me a picture as a thank you present. It is a print designed by the sister of one of them. I feel joyful and grateful, not least because of the fact that it is a complete surprise.

What am I to make of these four incidents? Well, several things. First, writing about them is also a *rather emotional process*, slightly rather than massively. Reconstructing an emotional memory or a memory of emotion can itself be emotional. This is clearest in the 'recall' of trauma. Secondly, both the events and the associated emotions appear both distant and immediate. Both seem somehow inevitably emotional and yet *arbitrarily*, even randomly, so. I could have chosen a thousand other incidents. It is as if in some situations emotional responses are automatic, and yet at the same time they are created as whims, as all situations are emotional or potentially so. Thirdly, the events selected are moments of relative *drama*. While routine is often constructed as relatively 'unemotional', and ritual as ambiguous, so drama, especially high drama, is unavoidably emotional (Morris, 1972; Hearn, 1977). In addition, these personal accounts refer to emotions in a number of different ways. For example, the experiences described did appear to involve what are in several senses unusual physiological changes – unusual for me, especially at work, and compared with my usual physiology. On the other hand, in describing them, I am invoking categories of 'emotion' in a variety of ways: they are part of my retrospective construction of myself, masculinities and organizations (Kippax et al., 1988).

These stories could thus be said to 'work' in a number of ways: they partly repeat the Foucaultian imperative to 'tell the truth'; they are also a personal illustration of 'a man having feelings at work' (a happening that is ironically noteworthy). However, more significantly, they show the effects of the contextualizing of feeling and emotion; some of the social rules of men's display of emotions; the historical features and memories that 'make' feelings; and moreover the way that memory work may create further new emotions (often emotions upon emotions) (Crawford et al., 1992).

So What Are Emotions?

Having dispelled a few myths around men and emotions, and given some brief accounts of my own emotional experiences in organizations, it may be useful to explore a little further what might be understood by emotions. This is intended as a background to the subsequent discussion and deconstruction of emotional organizational men.

A useful starting point is Koestler's (1967: 226) definition of emotions as 'mental states accompanied by intense feeling and involving bodily changes of a widespread character'. 'Emotions' do, at least sometimes, refer to relative changes in physiology, for example, when an angry man gets very hot or a fearful man shakes (Darwin, 1965). However, the physiological approach to emotions does obscure a number of difficulties. First, such physiological experiences and their perception are still *relative* to the culture and context in which they occur: what would count as an emotion in one context, would not in another.

Second, the category 'emotion' may be used to suggest a mis-leadingly sharp break with 'non-emotion' (Duffy, 1941). As Eichler argues,

> We must cease to compartmentalise qualities of action as if they were mutually exclusive. Most predominantly, we must cease to treat rationality and emotionality . . . as two mutually exclusive qualities of actions and must instead treat them as separate continua that vary independently and can be applied to any simple action. (1980: 121)

So while emotions may well be linked to relatively extreme mental and physical states, they are also *social* and *ideological* constructs (Hochschild, 1975; Harré, 1986) that *simplify* and *dilute* contradictions from thought, feeling and action. Anything can be 'emotional' just as anything can be 'sexual' (Plummer, 1975). Emotions are formed in emotions.

Accordingly, emotions have to be understood in their social context and in relation to social theory, be it behavioural exchange, conflict, symbolic interactionist or other theories (Gordon, 1985). For this reason, the search for a watertight definition of emotion(s) is likely to be misguided. It is the methodological status of the category, 'emotion', that is more important than substantive precision (Hearn, 1983b): what is of most interest is how the concept of 'emotion' is used or invoked rather than the search for definitions, either in general or in particular.

It is partly for this reason that emotions can be and have to be understood in a variety of socially constructed ways. Emotions can be defined as *responsiveness*, how one feels 'inside'; as *feelings about* feelings, what might be called 'orientation'; as *behaviours* or 'expressiveness'; as *situations* in which emotions are felt and as *social structures*. Allen and Haccoun (1976) have identified how in their empirical research, differences between women and men were greatest in relation to the *expression* of emotions, for anger, fear, joy and sadness. Females were found to express more direct emotions of all four types to males, while males expressed more joy and sadness to females, but more anger and fear to other males. However, as regards internal feelings or responsiveness, differences were least for anger and greatest for fear and sadness, with women feeling more of these than men. For these reasons, it is not possible to chart a simple contrast between women's and men's emotionalities: these are social context specific.

More arguably, 'emotions', that is, the idea of 'emotions', are usually defined within discourses of gender. Nancy Chodorow (1979) and many others have noted that: 'Emotions and feelings tend to be associated with the mother and the feminine' (Seidler, 1992: 20). Conversely, the lack of emotion and of feelings might tend to be associated with 'the father' and 'the masculine'. Yet both of these are cultural, discursive *associations*: for indeed the ideas of 'the feminine' and 'the masculine' themselves are cultural constructions (Eichler, 1980; Moore, 1987).

A discursive approach to emotions and gender opens up a whole number of new questions. Emotion is no longer just physiological experience or change but is a matter of cultural constructions. This includes questions of what counts as 'emotion', and how 'emotions' interrelate with construction of gender. For example, a particular action or experience might be defined as 'firm', 'decisive' and 'rational' if constructed in relation to a man, and as 'bossy', 'emotional' and 'irrational' in relation to a woman. Cultural and discursive constructions are also fundamental in the structuring of 'emotions' in relation to 'individuals' and 'social context' or 'social structure'. For example, emotion is often characterized as something that happens *to* people, something that is directed from elsewhere (either something external such as a managerial crisis or something internal such as an unresolved personal conflict) *onto* the person (Liddle, 1993). In this sense emotion is a category that reproduces a *separation* of the person, in this case the organizational member, from external life and internal life. Accordingly, emotions are a product of the segregation of the person. This separation may often be reinforced by an assumption of the individual being *impelled*, indeed *moved*, by such emotions, thus removing a sense of responsibility from that 'individual'. This is particularly important when men may claim that they are not fully in control of their emotions, as with anger and violence. As Liddle points out there are many metaphors to describe this – 'falling in love', being 'swept away by passion', 'consumed' by rage or jealousy, 'overcome by anger'. The emotions overwhelm the individual who operates between the internal and the external, and accordingly may impel action between these two realms. In such ways emotions are often constructed as operating in the same sort of hydraulic fashion that has often been ascribed to sexual urges, as in the supposed 'uncontrollability' of 'normal male sexuality' (Coveney et al., 1984).

It is important to recognize emotion as both structured, that is, organized in and through social structures, and at the same time *done* in practices and practical situations. As such, while emotion is structured it is not determined. Not only are emotions open to interpersonal *negotiation*, to individual constructions, response and indeed choice, but emotional presentations can be determined corporately and organizationally.

The fact that emotions may often be *constructed* as happening *to* people, and are *structured* in discourses does not mean that emotions are not enacted or practised. Indeed, on the contrary, it is more helpful to see discourses as both *producing* people assumed to be 'subjects' that are or are not emotional, and *produced by* people assumed to be subjects. In both senses subjects do emotions, they do not just happen 'automatically'; they have to be *done*.

Emotions can be understood as sets of acts and practices within various 'emotional' regimes. These acts and practices form and are formed by subjects, which are themselves constructed as emotional or unemotional – they are indeed emotive subjects. The relationship of subjects to acts and practices and to emotions is, however, not necessarily direct or simple. Subjects, acts, practices and thus emotions are ranged across alternative positions, locations and strategies within these 'emotional' regimes. These alternatives include embracement, ambivalence, doubt, resignation, resistance, reflexivity, as well as intrapersonal conflict and reinterpretation of meaning over time. In addition, emotions may be done in relation to other emotions – as with fear of becoming depressed or joy at not being fearful. Thus emotions are formed differentially in social contexts, including organizations; life histories, both personal and organizational; and moments. Indeed emotions often appear to be focused on the particular, especially particular moments in time. These are all social discursive constructions.

To summarize this section, it is necessary to emphasize that emotions, men and organizations, are all social mediations and socially mediated. Both the 'unemotional' and the 'emotional' models of men in organizations present dangers of not sufficiently recognizing the social mediation of the categories of 'men' and 'emotions'. Instead the relationship of men, emotions and organizations is itself socially mediated. There is no such thing as immediate, unmediated experience of emotions. There is nothing intrinsic to social contexts, situations, including organizational contexts and situations, that makes them or people there 'emotional' or 'unemotional'. To put this another way, all social and organizational contexts and situations and all people, including men, may be constructed as 'emotional' all the time. What is valuable is the social, organizational and societal construction of contexts, situations, organizations, experiences, different people, and indeed what is meant by emotions in the first place. Or as Hegel might have put it, all knowledge of emotion is intersubjective, is a matter of desire (rather than disinterested cognition) that is structured around power, and is dialectical (Game, 1991: 8).

Emotions are always present in all human activity, in the sense that there is always the potential for emotions and for calling something 'emotion'. Similarly and paradoxically, emotions are always absent, in the sense that there is always the potential for no emotion and for not calling something 'emotions'. What might be called emotions in one situation may not be in another. What might be called emotional if referring to a woman might not be if referring to a man, and vice versa. While emotions are ubiquitous what is called emotions are socially constructed. Emotions are not just any one thing.

Deconstructing Emotional/Organizational Men

In the light of these complexities, how are we to make sense of the relationship of men, organizations and emotions? To do so involves drawing on a number of concepts. I have already explained the importance of discourse and mediation: men, masculinities, organizations and emotions do not exist in some unmediated form. They are all socially and discursively mediated, partly through each other, both the other concepts and other men, masculinities, organizations and emotions.

Furthermore, deconstructing the relationship of men, organizations and emotions necessitates attention to social structure and societal context, and particularly patriarchal relations of *power and dominance.* These social relations of organizations are themselves emotionalized, that is, constructed as emotions. The operation and experience of organizations entails emotion, men's emotions. Accordingly, these processes of emotionalization are considered in terms of the emotions of *organizational power, organizational process* and *organizational labour* respectively. Inevitably, there is throughout a concern with the construction of gender, not as some fixed or determined process but as sets of formations in discourses, with forms, structures, variations, contradictions, inconsistencies and ambivalences.

More precisely, throughout this chapter there is a continuing tension between a materialist and a discursive approach to men's emotions in organizations. On the first count, men are materially involved in the control of others' emotions, in the control of emotion labour, and in the creation of others' anger, fear and sadness. Others here include women, children and other men, each other. Through those processes men's emotions are structured – the emotion of control, the emotion of controlling others' emotions, and the emotion of controlling emotion labour. This is most clearly seen in the emotion/labour of men who are managers.

The discursive approach is based on the assumption there is no pre-given logic to the association of gender and emotions, and thus men and emotions. Men's 'emotions' can be invoked 'anywhere, anytime, anyhow'. Having said that, discourses are themselves forms of power; they are formed by material relations, as described above, and they constitute material relations.

These two approaches may appear at first different and discrete, yet they are not. The material is discursive; the discursive is material. Men's emotions are both materially structured and discursively arbitrary.

Organizational Men/Organizational Masculinities

Men in organizations are still men: men in organizations, organizational men, are still part of the social category of 'men' and the gender class of men. What this means is that organizational men have political interests with other men, benefit from being 'men' regardless of their own personal choices or interests, and may, in some cases and particularly as owners, managers, professionals, trade union officials and informal leaders, act on behalf of 'men' and other men, and be leaders and articulators of men's political interests against women (see e.g. Walby, 1986, 1990; Hearn, 1987, 1992b; Grint, 1988).

This collectivity of interest between organizational men and men more generally should not obscure the intense differences, differentiations and variations there are between men and their different men's interests. These include amongst many others, differences by age, (dis)ability, economic class, 'race'/ethnicity, region, religion, sexuality. This applies both within and outside organizations. Thus organization men are also divided by these and other kinds of differences.

While men are a social category, masculinities are social constructions of what it is to be a man: individual signs and institutional indications that this is a man. The idea of 'masculinity' has often been used to suggest that there is 'something' masculine that is contrasted with 'femininity' that accordingly is feminine. In contrast, in recent years there has been increasing recognition of both the plurality of *masculinities* and the domination and subordination of particular masculinities – hence the notion of hegemonic masculinity, that is taken-for-granted, dominant forms of masculinity that are powerful partly by virtue of overt dominance and partly through their taken-for-grantedness (Carrigan et al., 1985; Connell, 1987; Brittan, 1989).

Masculinities are shown in a wide range of ways within organizations – what might be called organizational masculinities. These vary according to organizational position, power and status, as well as combinations of differences that involve both organizational definitions and other social differences, such as age, (dis)ability, economic class, 'race'/ethnicity and sexuality. Organizational masculinities are themselves very diverse, simultaneously representing both masculinities and organization(s) through the actions and appearances of particular men.

Organizations in Patriarchies/Patriarchal Organizations

Organizations, including all-women organizations and feminist organizations, have to be understood in the context of men's societal domination – patriarchy or patriarchies (Hearn, 1992b). Having said that, there are clearly different forms of patriarchy, such as public patriarchy or private patriarchy, and furthermore, there are diverse locations of organizations within patriarchies. Accordingly, in analysing organizational men and emotions it is necessary to locate that organization within its patriarchal context: what is the kind of societal patriarchy? where and how is the organization located, for example, as part of the state? what is the kind of organizational patriarchy? what form does it take? does it involve the direct domination or the exclusion of women? is it based on solidarity or competition between men, or both? how is all this maintained and reproduced?

Within public patriarchy – or public patriarchies, as I prefer – more and more areas of women's lives are controlled by men *in the public domains*. This includes not just paid work, manual and mental labour, legal status, care and caring, citizenship and client-hood in relation to the state, and sexuality, but also emotions, emotionality, and the very construction of 'the person' (Hearn, 1992b). Men are thus historically structured and defined through the control of the public domains over emotions and hence the construction of 'men', ourselves. These social processes of public patriarchies are reproduced primarily through organizations. And public patriarchies in organizations and elsewhere are lived, emotional experiences of women and men.

The remainder of this chapter details some of the ways in which men's emotions may be deconstructed: as organizational power, organizational process and organizational labour.

The Emotions of Organizational Power

In discussing emotions, there is often, indeed usually, a tendency to be accommodating to emotions, to accept their individuality, their uniqueness and, to some extent at least, their amoral irrespon-sibility. But there is no reason why this should be so; no reason why emotions should be seen as less social than any other phenomena or any less amenable to critical analysis. The fact that something is emotional does not mean it is to be more readily condoned or accepted. This is especially important when focusing on men – when we put men's emotions or emotionality alongside men's power and dominance. So when men are emotional, it may be a way of showing and continuing dominance, as, for example, with anger; or a way of continuing dominance despite the emotion, as, for example, when men are sad or cry and yet continue being dominant; or a way of contradicting or changing or reducing dominance, as, for example, when men admit to fear of other men, as a prelude to behaving differently with men. Whatever the case, there is no necessary correlation between men's experiencing or showing of emotions and loss of power. Dominating, including being violent, can certainly be a very emotional experience for men. Indeed, in contrast to the notion of the 'inexpressive male' previously discussed, there is often the problem that men 'show' too much emotion.

So how might such structural relations of gender dominance within patriarchies relate in simple terms to the experience of

emotions by women and men? This is merely a preliminary statement prior to a consideration of some of the complexities of the
situation.

In patriarchal organizations, men are *likely* to experience joy
with the reinforcement of that domination. This is most clearly
seen when men celebrate winning a sport, whether a local league
or a World Cup, or winning a war. The highest prize in patriarchies is usually beating other men; dominance over women is
taken for granted, and therefore usually less valued, less a source
of joy. Furthermore, the coincidence of the *expectation* of
dominance and the *experience* of dominance is likely to produce
joy for men; and in turn sadness, anger and fear for women. This
is likely, for example, when men's violence to women goes unchal-
lenged in an organizational setting. In some cases the experience of
dominance may be so acute and painful as to produce an apparent
deadening of emotion. Conversely, in such patriarchal organizations, the challenging of men's violence, or the assertion of
women's power, is likely to bring a disjunction between expectation and experience for men, and thus sadness, anger and fear for
men. Meanwhile, women in that situation may be likely to
experience joy. These structured relations are summarized in Figure
7.1:

	Coincidence (of expectations and experiences)	Disjunction (of expectations and experiences)
Men's emotions	Maintenance of dominance (Joy, fear?)	Challenge from women's solidarity (Anger, sadness, fear)
Women's emotions	Dominance of women (Anger, sadness, fear, deadening?)	Successful challenge by women's solidarity (Joy, anger)

Figure 7.1 *Coincidence and disjunction in patriarchal organizations*

In anti-patriarchal or feminist organizations, the inverse pattern
may operate. The assertion of women's power represents a coincidence of expectation and experience for women and thus the
further experience of joy. Men in that situation may experience
sadness, anger and fear. The challenging of that power of women
will be likely to effect sadness, anger and fear for women, and joy

for men. On the other hand, it could be that feminist organizations work on quite different principles to those that might be the inverse of patriarchal organizations, for example social networks and webs rather than power over others (Carroll, 1984).

These structures of emotion can only be thought of as a rough guide. For emotions are not produced by some mechanical calculus, and indeed patterns of dominance by men are severely complicated in several ways. Firstly, there are many ways in which men's dominance and maintenance of dominance bring their own negative emotions. Most obviously, this is the case with negative emotions, especially sadness (withdrawal) and anger (engagement) to maintain or reinforce dominance. Negative emotions may also be enacted for other reasons. For example, sadness may be experienced by men in positions of dominance in relation to loss either within the organization, such as distance from other people in the organization, or outside the organization, such as the reduction of relationships with friends and family. Anger may also be felt not only in terms of maintaining control but also in terms of dissatisfaction in work or home. As Bannister and Fransella note: 'Hostility is the continued effort to extort validational evidence in favour of a type of social prediction which has already been recognized as a failure' (1971: 35).

Secondly, men's relations with each other are characterized by a complex mixture of solidarity and competition, with the associated emotions of joy, when these are realized and sadness, anger and fear when they are challenged or threatened. For example, men's competitive relations may often involve various forms of fear – fear of losing in competition, fear of dominating too much and thus destroying solidarity, fear of loss, fear of being dominated. Thirdly, men's relations both with each other and with women are diversified by oppressions other than gender, such as economic class, age, ethnicity/'race'. Men may be further differentiated from each other through such oppressions: similarly men's relations with women may be complicated by such oppressions as when, for example, women managers or owners are in authority over men workers. Here again there are the bases for further emotions representing the reinforcement or challenge to such social relations.

Fourthly, various combinations of gender classes (of women, and of men) and the various differentiations of women and men in organizations make for immense possibilities for the experience of contradictory emotions (for example, joy and sadness, anger and fear), contradictions within a particular emotion (both enjoying fear as excitement and disliking fear as threat), and ambivalences about emotions both in general and specifically. The construction of 'emotions' as elements of organizational masculinities may be intensely *contradictory*: both non-emotional and emotional; both fearful and sad; both joyful and angry. Maintaining apparent non-emotionality may itself be intensely emotional. Organization men, professionals, managers and others may all have to work hard to maintain the appearance of 'non-emotionality'. In addition, there are the complex and perhaps confusing experiences of individual men, with their own idiosyncratic biographies and psyches, their own tendencies to conform or to be exceptions from their particular social group.

The Emotions of Organizational Process
If you are still convinced that men are less emotional than women, try going along to a pop concert or a football match – or even the Olympic Games. In these situations men are commonly and definitely emotionalized, that is, constructed as (potentially) emotional. This is not just an individual matter but is a social structural phenomenon; it persists not as some expression of individual personality but as a set of structural relations within which individuals are located. Sometimes this is given clear audible or visible form, as in the chanting of the crowd or the performance of a 'Mexican wave'. Indeed one way of understanding the construction/deconstruction of 'emotions' in organizations is to see organizations not so much as arenas for the *expression* of emotions, as places and spaces, both physical *and* social, that may be *emotionalized*. This means that in different organizations, different people, activities and events may be subject to processes of emotionalization – of framing and interpretation of them in terms of various emotions.

Organizations are dominantly constructed as instrumental arenas. Accordingly, instrumentality is dominantly separated off from the category of emotion. Thus both are ideological in their reduction of contradictions. The very separation of emotions from other social life can itself be seen as an example of the compartmentalizing nature of patriarchies, and indeed other systems of oppression, such as senocracy (adult rule), imperialism, capitalism and heterosexuality. Because of these compartmentalizing processes, particular organizations, people, parts of organizations or types of people, may be emotionalized, that is, constructed as emotional, in paradoxical contrast to dominant organizational instrumentalities.

At this point it may be useful to introduce the question of

the interrelationships of bureaucracy, men's power and emotions. While bureaucracy is often characterized as emotionless, this does not do full justice to Weber's original formulation, and his concern for affectivity in society (Albrow, 1992). Instead bureaucracies, like organizations more generally, are likely to be places of emotion – where, as recognized by Merton (1952), 'timidity, defensiveness, harshness and resentment are part of the daily round' (Albrow, 1992: 319). Rather it is the development and construction of bureaucracies that have been heavily dominated by and associated with men's power and 'masculine' thinking (Bologh, 1990; Morgan, 1992; Hearn, 1992b). For this reason, constructions of bureaucracy have often misleadingly played down the practice of emotions there.

Thus while it is clearly completely inaccurate to equate either organizations or men's actions with instrumentality, and women's actions with emotionality, what is of interest is the organizational *association* of these phenomena in discourses. So how does this emotionalization of organizations and men take place despite, or perhaps because of, their dominant supposed association with instrumentality and non-emotion? Organizations, organizational settings and organizational histories are characterized by their formation in discourse, indeed generally in oral discourse.

> Organizational history is largely oral history . . . It is communicated through stories. Stories reflect and create people's social realities. They focus primarily on the emotional relationships among people in an organizational setting, as well as on the monumental events which help to make these associations more dramatic and memorable. (Tommerup, 1988: 319)

Emotional organizational men construct and are constructed by those stories, which are simultaneously organizational and emotional.

Organizations are thus also complex interrelations of 'work' and 'play'. The organizational construction of 'play' may often even reinforce 'work' and work values (Whyte, 1956; Fine, 1988). The process of work may be experienced as deep sadness, loss and alienation; it may also, however, be experienced as a source of engagement, joy in the busy flow of work (Csikszentmihalyi, 1975; Fine, 1988) and humour (Roy, 1959–60; Collinson, 1988). There is also sometimes a lack of clarity in the boundary between 'work' and 'play' in and around organizations (Hearn, 1977; Dandridge, 1988). In such a way, while 'work' may be indirectly emotionalized, 'playtime' is directly and unambiguously the emotional zone, as in the legendary 'office party'.

Men may be emotionalized, that is, constructed as 'emotional' or potentially so, at particular times, such as initiation ceremonies or retirement 'dos'; in particular organizational sites, most obviously meetings; in particular organizational processes, such as office politics or gossip more generally. Men may also be emotionalized in various external promotions of organizations – in advertising, marketing, publicity and so on. Additionally, men in organizations, organization men, are especially emotionalized in the conduct of sexuality and violence.

The significance of sexuality and violence in the construction of men's emotions in organizations has been well documented (Hearn and Parkin, 1987; Collinson and Collinson, 1989). Sexual process is often constructed for men as emotional process. This is particularly relevant in the complex interaction of heterosexuality and hierarchy within what are seen as 'normal working relations'.

An interesting example concerns the complex interplay of tasks and emotions in management, supervision, tutoring and mentoring. If 'successful', supervision is likely to involve close, even intimate, working relationships; in so doing the supervisory task may become more characterized as an emotional relationship. Depending on the gender of the participants, their sexualities, and the dynamics of power, such relationships may also have a sexual or sexualized character (Hearn and Parkin, 1987; Bushardt et al., 1991; Baum, 1992). Where the supervisor (looking over) is a man and the supervised (looked over) a woman, there is particular scope for the abuse of power within heterosexual dynamics with men more often misinterpreting friendliness and emotional interchange for sexual interest. If 'unsuccessful', supervisory dynamics may well become characterized by fear and anger. Either way, in hierarchical supervision, power, emotion and sexuality may be major themes.

The conduct of actual sexual relations between men or between men and women, who are organizational members, is likely to bring a whole variety of emotions – both for the participants and for others. A number of studies have shown how managers and peers may respond negatively to the part played by women in such relationships (Quinn, 1977; Schneider, 1984), particularly in terms of conflict with ('rational') organizational rules and imperatives (Horn and Horn, 1982). Much less well documented are the responses of people subject to the power of others who are in sexual relationships, including those who are in a client or customer relationship to organizational members.

Matters become yet more complex when sexual relationships in organizations also involve identifiable physical violence. There is a gradually growing body of knowledge about what may happen when sex and men's violence come together in organizational contexts. Interestingly, such actions are likely to produce various emotional responses from women and other men in the organization. I have received reports from five organizations where staff who have persisted in arguing that such sex and men's violence is a problem for management have then themselves been treated as the problem. In one organization, which I have observed at close quarters, the men responded in a variety of ways to the violence of one of their men colleagues to a woman client of the organization. Most did not appear to see this as a particular problem for them as colleagues, nor as something needing a public response from them, preferring to leave it to management to sort out: one became ill, another favoured forgiveness, a third kept a very low profile, a fourth gave solidarity as a man and a friend, and another thought that 'due process' elsewhere should take its course. Two other men (of whom I was one) did see it as a problem – since it undermined the whole basis of the organization's activity. Moreover, even apparently non-emotional responses were immensely emotional, as intense feelings ebbed and flowed, and public statements of procedure were accompanied by private outbursts of emotion, not least between men.

Despite these kinds of dramatic events, organizational process is generally mundane. The life of organizations is emotional and emotionalized throughout. This applies no more than in the emotional relationships that often exist *between* men in organizations. Men may band together, seek out each other's company, and develop strong emotional attachments with other men (Collinson, 1992). Support, flattery, reassurance, intimacy, competition, and thus emotion are part of ordinary organizational relations between men. As such, these may frequently also have a, not so hidden, erotic or sexual element (Hearn, 1992b). Men's organizational relations with other men are often charged with desire, both collectively and individually. Sometimes this is made more explicit, as in the 'lads' night out' or in organizational horseplay (Hearn, 1985). More usually, men's organizational relations are implicitly characterized by a male homosexual subtext (Wood, 1987). This usually fairly blatant desire by men for the company and promotion of other men exists in tension with the 'male sexual narrative' (Dyer, 1985) and dominant heterosexuality of most organizations.

The emotional life of organizations is also elaborated through the relationship between individual men's private and domestic lives, and men's organizational positionings. For example, men who see an organization as their prime source of friendship and support may relate emotionally to it very differently from men who see an organization more instrumentally. In such ways organizational masculinities and men's emotions are both a public and a private affair. They are constitutive of masculinities; it is not that primordial, private masculinities are somehow modified within organizations.

The Emotions of Organizational Labour

In addition to the emotions of organizational power and of organizational process, there is the business of the labour and the tasks of organizations, and how they also may be emotionalized. Clearly the social construction of 'emotion(s)' and emotions in organizations is unevenly arranged throughout society. In particular, certain arenas of society, which might be summarized as 'reproduction', are constructed as 'emotional'. These include birth, death, nurture, regeneration/degeneration, sexuality, violence, and therefore men's relationship to these 'emotional arenas'. Within these emotional arenas there are specific points or moments of reproduction (O'Brien, 1981; Hearn, 1982, 1983a, 1987), which may be constructed as the sites of the most emotional experiences, and the greatest scope for the complete satisfaction and complete dissatisfaction of *desires*. These may be the *times* of drastic or significant change in reproductive process or the period after that change or sometimes the time of anticipation of that change – of acute coincidence and disjunction between expectations and experiences. Such intense phases of reproduction may be sites for emotional construction, development and expression in a more extended way. Indeed reproduction and reproductive process are themselves founded on material, emotional labour. On the other hand, the construction of 'emotions' may act as a metaphor for reproduction, and the immensely variable experiences that surround it. Similarly, what is called 'the subjective', and even 'the unconscious', may be considered as a metaphor for reproductive process.

Individuals who live in one emotion all the time, or who experience great depths of a particular emotion or combination of emotions, or who convert a certain emotion into action, may experience special problems for themselves or may create special problems for others. Anger may become violence, sadness depression, fear paralysis or flight, and joy ecstasy. Such emotions/actions may become the emotional labour for others to be done directly or managed indirectly, as when bereavement or loss is managed in medical organizations.

These emotional sites and emotional arenas are the grounds in and upon which are established and developed organizations, for example medicine, law, religion, sport. These specialist organizations are structured around the organization of the emotions. In these organizations men typically have positions of power, authority and leadership over the organizations and over emotions and emotion work or emotion labour.

Men's presence in such organizations symbolizes organization, and organization symbolizes power, power over emotions and emotion work. This is clear in men's presence as church leaders, psychiatrists, doctors, lawyers; such organizational masculinities are based in the control and management of the emotions of others, both 'clients' in emotional or potentially emotional states, and emotional workers such as nurses (Hearn, 1982, 1987).

These emotional arenas are also subject to other developments, with the further historical growth of organizations that specialize in different ways in emotional material. These include hospitals, organizations of medics, midwives and other health workers, health authorities, undertakers, boxing boards of control, sports clubs and associations. In these again men characteristically take distinctive locations as managers and controllers, for example as sports managers and coaches, as well as sometimes specializing in emotion work there.

Furthermore, more powerful men often characteristically manage emotion labour and at the same time avoid emotion labour. Such men control the emotion labour of women and less powerful men, who themselves may manage the emotions of 'others', as clients, patients, lay people, members of the public. This is itself often associated with what is called 'self-control' of the men themselves, the control of their own emotions. This avoidance and control of men means that for some men at least the construction of organizational masculinities is premised on a lack, a distance, from emotion and emotion labour. Such organizational masculinity is an inverse – it is *not* something; rather than being something, its presence is formed in absence.

In organizations which do not specialize in emotional arenas, emotion work is still an important aspect. Indeed in all organizations there are *social differentiations* of men and the construction of organizations – through emotion work, emotion management and the presence of emotion in other kinds of work. In particular there is wide variation in the organizational contexts that legitimize emotions, both their expression by men and their attribution to men. For example, organizational legitimation is variable for men's use and maintenance of anger, according to class, status, hierarchical position, occupation, as well as the assignment of age, 'race', sexuality, and so on. This is documented by Game and Pringle (1983) in terms of the legitimation of the anger of men doctors towards or in contrast to women nurses.

In one sense all organizational work, membership and presence is emotion labour. And this applies as much to men as to women. Indeed the quality of being in an organization – organization-ness – is itself a form of emotion and emotion labour. This is perhaps clearest when we consider the emotion labour that is a taken-for-granted part of specific organizational masculinities. For example, men shopfloor workers may routinely care for, engage with, yet resent, even hate, 'their' machinery; men office workers may place heavy emotional investments in the 'seriousness' of their work or alternatively, and sometimes simultaneously, treat it as an object of fun, to be joked about, and 'reduced' in stature; men managers may specialize in doing people work in all manner of 'masculine' ways. In all these cases men present organizational masculinities, and so show themselves to be men. The experience and construction of emotions has to be placed in the context of the experiences of organizations – of organization-ness. This is not just in the exercise of liberal restraint or culturally prescribed norms but in the very emotional experience of what it is to be in an organization, to organize and be organized.

The case of management is particularly instructive. Management is still predominantly done by men, and men's power is still maintained by management (Hearn, 1989a, 1992a, 1992b). Whether the management of the professions, the state or business, management is centrally concerned with the management and control of emotions, both of others and the self. Of special importance is the relationship between the construction of 'control', both self-control and control of others, and 'emotions' including anger and sadness for men in many organizational situations. Managers who are centrally involved in the business of managerial control may also be beset by excessive anxiety about that control or about how to 'balance' control and masculinity (Dixon, 1976; Lears, 1981; Filene, 1986; Hearn, 1992b: 166, 246–7). This is illustrated no more clearly than by the case of Frederick Taylor (Kakar, 1970; Morgan, 1986). As such, management is a kind of emotion labour managing emotions, yet often constructed as non-emotion(s). Management, men and emotions are inextricably bound together in power. Accordingly, men are not specifically 'unemotional' in organizations or elsewhere. The construction of 'emotions' pervades men's presence in organizations in diverse ways, including the very construction and definition of organizational masculinities.

No Conclusions

It is customary to conclude with conclusions – to close off, to close down, to seal the script, to seal emotions. Instead I offer no conclusion (cf. Flax, 1990) other than an acknowledgement of the emotion of discourse (cf. Grosz, 1987). Accordingly, I feel obliged to say a little about my own emotional/organizational life, my own emotional being-in-organization. I have a very strong emotional presence in my own employing organization. I have worked there since 1974, quite a long time. I can hardly describe it as an overwhelmingly happy experience, yet I am very attached to my organization, perhaps overattached, a place to love and to gain power and status. So I find it difficult if things do not go as I would like – I find it personally hurtful, as I feel a great care and sense of caring towards the workplace that I happen to have inhabited. Over recent years I have felt quite a lot of pessimism about my organization, for several reasons: conflicts at work, distress and disappointments, the movement of universities towards a much nastier and much more reactionary educational system, the end of an era, sadness and loss, crisis and danger. While men's dominance persists in universities as elsewhere, it is not monolithic or undifferentiated – there are hopes, opportunities and fertile groves of change – against patriarchies. Patriarchies and patriarchal organizations can contain the seeds of their own destruction; signs of positive and emotional change. Altogether, this is quite an emotional mix. The strength of emotional perspectives on organizations, and in this context organizational men and organizational masculinities, is that they accommodate the subtleties and depths of structured power, as well as the subtleties and intimacies of personal experience.

Notes

I am grateful to David Collinson and Elizabeth Harlow for discussions on the issues raised in this chapter, to Wendy Parkin and Stephen Fineman for comments on an earlier draft of this chapter, and to Sue Moody for typing the script.
1. Accounts of 'organization men' as 'unemotional' are sometimes presented positively, as, for example, in much malestream theories of organization,

management and leadership, where good management is assumed to depend on being rational, strategic, controlled, 'unemotional'. A rather similar kind of account is sometimes presented more negatively, in which men's supposed 'unemotionality' might be seen as a loss or even a block to organizational functioning, and accordingly women are encouraged into management to bring that missing quality (see Adler and Izraeli, 1988: 4–7). Both positive and negative accounts can draw on a wide variety of theoretical traditions including biological and nonbiological, cognitive or psychoanalytic development, Parsonian social systems theory of 'the family', 'sex/gender differences' and 'sex role socialization'. A dominant theme of these various literatures is the 'inexpressive male/man' (Sattel, 1976): the significant question is whether this is (seen as) worse for women or for men themselves – in other words does men's 'inexpressiveness' damage women or men, or indeed both? Such analyses are usually premised as linking emotions and their expression with measures of masculinity and femininity (Constantinople, 1973). These kinds of connection are ideologically unproven and distorted. It is now clear that women are not simply 'more emotional' than men (Jacklin and Maccoby, 1974, 1975). Indeed 'objective personality' and 'subjective personality' are not statistically significantly differentiated between women and men (Durkin, 1978).

References

Adler, N. J. and Izraeli, D. N. (1988) 'Women in management worldwide', in N. J. Adler and D. N. Izraeli (eds), *Women in Management Worldwide*. Armonte, NY and London: M. E. Sharpe. pp. 3–16.

Albrow, M. (1992) 'Sine ira et studio – or do organizations have feelings?', *Organization Studies*, 13 (3): 313–29.

Allen, J. G. and Haccoun, D. M. (1976) 'Sex differences in emotionality: a multidimensional approach', *Human Relations*, 29 (8): 711–22.

Bannister, D. and Fransella, F. (1971) *Inquiring Man. The Theory of Personal Constraints*. Harmondsworth: Penguin.

Baum, H. S. (1992) 'Mentoring: narcissistic fantasies and Oedipal realities', *Human Relations* 45 (3): 223–45.

Bologh, R. W. (1990) *Love or Greatness? Max Weber and Masculine Thinking – A Feminist Inquiry*. London and Boston: Unwin Hyman.

Brittan, A. (1989) *Masculinity and Power*. Oxford: Blackwell.

Bushardt, S. C., Fretwell, C. and Holdnak, B. J. (1991) 'The mentor/protégé relationship: a biological perspective', *Human Relations*, 44 (6): 619–39.

Carrigan, T., Connell, R. W. and Lee, J. (1985) 'Toward a new sociology of masculinity', *Theory and Society*, 14 (5): 551–604.

Carroll, S. J. (1984) 'Feminist scholarship on political leadership', in B. Kellerman (ed.), *Leadership – Multidisciplinary Perspectives*. Englewood Cliffs, NJ: Prentice-Hall. pp. 139–56.

Chodorow, N. (1979) *The Reproduction of Mothering: Psychoanalysis and the Sociology of Gender*. Berkeley, CA: University of California Press.

Collinson, D. L. (1988) '"Engineering humour": masculinity, joking and conflict in shop-floor relations', *Organization Studies*, 9 (2): 181–99.

Collinson, D. L. (1992) *Managing the Shopfloor: Subjectivity, Masculinity and Workplace Culture*. Berlin: de Gruyter.

Collinson, D. L. and Collinson, M. (1989) 'Sexuality in the workplace: the domination of men's sexuality', in J. Hearn, D. L. Sheppard, P. Tancred-Sheriff and

G. Burrell (eds), *The Sexuality of Organization*. London and Newbury Park, CA: Sage. pp. 91–109.

Connell, R. W. (1987) *Gender and Power*. Cambridge: Polity.

Constantinople, A. (1973) 'Masculinity–femininity: an exception to a famous dictum?', *Psychological Bulletin*, 80 (5): 389–407.

Coveney, L., Jackson, M., Jeffreys, S., Kay, L. and Mahoney, P. (1984) *The Sexuality Papers. Male Sexuality and the Social Control of Women*. London: Hutchinson.

Crawford, J., Kippax, S., Onyx, J., Gault, U. and Benton, P. (1992) *Emotion and Gender. Constructing Meaning from Memory*. London: Sage.

Csikszentmihalyi, M. (1975) *Beyond Boredom and Anxiety*. San Francisco: Jossey-Bass.

Dandridge, T. (1988) 'Work ceremonies. Why integrate work and play?', in M. O. Jones, M. D. Moore and R. C. Snyder (eds), *Inside Organizations. Understanding the Human Dimension*. Newbury Park, CA: Sage. pp. 319–31.

Darwin, C. (1965) *The Expression of the Emotions in Man and Animals* (1872). Chicago and London: University of Chicago Press.

Dixon, N. (1976) *On the Psychology of Military Incompetence*. London: Jonathan Cape.

Duffy, E. (1941) 'An explanation of "emotional" phenomena without the use of the concept "emotions"', *Journal of General Psychology*, 25: 283–93.

Durkin, J. J. (1978) 'The potential of women', in B. A. Stead (ed.), *Women in Management*. Englewood Cliffs, NJ: Prentice-Hall. pp. 42–6.

Dyer, R. (1985) 'Male sexuality in the media', in A. Metcalf and M. Humphries (eds), *The Sexuality of Men*. London: Pluto. pp. 28–43.

Eichler, M. (1980) *The Double Standard. A Feminist Critique of Feminist Social Science*. London: Croom Helm.

Farrell, W. (1974) *The Liberated Man*. New York: Random House.

Filene, P. G. (1986) *Him/Her/Self. Sex Roles in Modern America*, 2nd edn. Baltimore, MD: Johns Hopkins University Press.

Fine, G. A. (1988) 'Letting off steam? Redefining a restaurant's work environment', in M. O. Jones, M. D. Moore and R. C. Snyder (eds), *Inside Organizations. Understanding the Human Dimension*. Newbury Park, CA: Sage. pp. 119–27.

Flam, H. (1990a) 'Emotional "Man": I: the emotional man and the problem of collective action', *International Sociology*, 5 (1): 39–56.

Flam, H. (1990b) 'Emotional "Man": II: corporate actors as emotion-motivated emotion managers', *International Sociology*, 5 (2): 225–34.

Flax, J. (1990) *Thinking Fragments. Psychoanalysis, Feminism and Post-modernism in the Contemporary West*. Berkeley, CA: University of California Press.

Foucault, M. (1988) 'Technologies of the self', in L. H. Martin, H. Gutman and P. H. Hutton (eds), *Technologies of the Self, a Seminar with Michel Foucault*. Boston: University of Massachusetts Press; London: Tavistock. pp. 16–49.

Game, A. (1991) *Undoing the Social. Toward a Deconstructive Sociology*. Milton Keynes: Open University Press.

Game, A. and Pringle, R. (1983) *Gender at Work*. Sydney, London and Boston: Allen & Unwin.

Gordon, S. L. (1985) 'Micro-sociological theories of emotion', in H. J. Helle and S. N. Eisenstadt (eds), *Micro Sociological Theory. Perspectives in Sociological Theory*. Beverley Hills, CA: Sage. pp. 133–47.

Grint, K. (1988) 'Women and equality: the acquisition of equal pay in the Post Office 1870/1961', *Sociology*, 22 (1): 87–108.

Grosz, E. (1987) 'Feminist theory and the challenge to knowledges', *Women's Studies International Forum*, 10 (5): 475–80.

Harré, R. (1986) *The Social Construction of Emotions*. Oxford: Blackwell.

Hearn, J. (1977) 'Toward a concept of non-career', *Sociological Review*, 25 (2): 273–88.

Hearn, J. (1982) 'Notes on patriarchy, professionalisation and the semi-professions', *Sociology*, 16 (2): 184–202.

Hearn, J. (1983a) *Birth and Afterbirth: A Materialist Analysis*. London: Achilles Heel.

Hearn, J. (1983b) 'The professions and the semi-professions: the control of emotions and the construction of masculinity'. Paper presented at British Sociological Association Conference 'Gender and Society', University of Manchester, Bradford, April. Mimeo: University of Bradford.

Hearn, J. (1985) 'Men's sexuality at work', in A. Metcalf and M. Humphries (eds), *The Sexuality of Men*. London: Pluto. pp. 110–28.

Hearn, J. (1987) *The Gender of Oppression. Men, Masculinity and the Critique of Marxism*. Brighton: Wheatsheaf; New York: St Martin's Press.

Hearn, J. (1989a) 'Leading questions for men: men's leadership, feminist challenges and men's responses', *Equal Opportunities International* 8 (1): 3–11.

Hearn, J. (1989b) 'Reviewing men and masculinities – or mostly boys' own papers', *Theory, Culture & Society*, 6 (3): 665–89.

Hearn, J. (1992a) 'Changing men and changing managements: a review of issues and actions', *Women in Management Review*, 7 (1): 3–8.

Hearn, J. (1992b) *Men in the Public Eye. The Construction and Deconstruction of Public Men and Public Patriarchies*. London and New York: Routledge.

Hearn, J. and Parkin, W. (1987) *'Sex' at 'Work'. The Power and Paradox of Organization Sexuality*. Brighton: Wheatsheaf; New York: St Martin's Press.

Hochschild, A. R. (1975) 'The sociology of feeling and emotion', in M. Millman and R. M. Kanter (eds), *Another Voice: Feminist Perspectives on Social Life and Social Science*. Garden City, NY: Doubleday/Anchor. pp. 280–307.

Horn, P. and Horn, J. C. (1982) *Sex in the Office . . . Power and Passion in the Workplace*. Reading, MA: Addison-Wesley.

Jacklin, C. N. and Maccoby, E. E. (1974) *The Psychology of Sex Differences*. Stanford, CA: Stanford University Press.

Jacklin, C. N. and Maccoby, E. E. (1975) 'Sex differences and their implications for management', in F. E. Gordon and M. H. Strober (eds), *Bringing Women into Management*. New York: McGraw-Hill. pp. 23–38.

Kakar, S. (1970) *Frederick Taylor: A Study in Personality and Innovation*. Cambridge, MA: MIT Press.

Kippax, S., Crawford, J., Benton, P., Gautt, U. and Noesjirwan, J. (1988) 'Constructing emotions: weaving meaning from memories', *British Journal of Social Psychology*, 27 (1): 19–33.

Koestler, A. (1967) *The Ghost in the Machine*. London: Hutchinson.

Lears, T. J. J. (1981) *No Place of Grace. Antimodernism and the Transformation of American Culture 1880–1920*. New York: Pantheon.

Liddle, M. (1993) 'Gender desire and child sexual abuse: accounting for the male majority', *Theory, Culture & Society*, 10 (4): forthcoming.

Merton, R. K. (1952) 'Bureaucratic structure and personality', in R. K. Merton et al., *Reader in Bureaucracy*. Glencoe, IL: Free Press. pp. 361–71.

Moore, H. (1987) *Feminism and Anthropology*. Cambridge: Cambridge University Press.

Morgan, D. H. J. (1992) *Discovering Men*. London and New York: Routledge.

Morgan, G. (1986) *Images of Organization*. Newbury Park, CA: Sage.

Morris, J. (1972) 'Three aspects of the person in social life', in R. Ruddock (ed.), *Six Approaches to the Person*. London: Routledge & Kegan Paul. pp. 70–92.

O'Brien, M. (1981) *The Politics of Reproduction*. London: Routledge & Kegan Paul.

Plummer, K. (1975) *Sexual Stigma, an Interactionist Account*. London: Routledge & Kegan Paul.

Quinn, R. E. (1977) 'Coping with Cupid: the formation, impact and management of romantic relationships in organizations', *Administrative Science Quarterly*, 22 (1): 30–45.

Roy, D. (1959–60) '"Banana time": job satisfaction and informal interaction', *Human Organization*, 18 (4): 158–68.

Sattel, J. W. (1976) 'The inexpressive male: tragedy or sexual politics?', *Social Problems*, 23: 469–77.

Schneider, B. (1984) 'The office affair: myth and reality for heterosexual and lesbian women workers', *Sociological Perspectives*, 27 (4): 443–64.

Seidler, V. J. (1992) 'Rejection, vulnerability, and friendship', in P. Nardi (ed.), *Men's Friendships*. Newbury Park, CA: Sage. pp. 15–34.

Tommerup, P. (1988) 'From trickster to father figure: learning from the mythologization of top management', in M. O. Jones, M. D. Moore and R. C. Snyder (eds), *Inside Organizations. Understanding the Human Dimension*. Newbury Park, CA: Sage. pp. 319–31.

Walby, S. (1986) *Patriarchy at Work*. Cambridge: Polity.

Walby, S. (1990) *Theorizing Patriarchy*. Oxford: Blackwell.

Whyte, W. H. (1956) *The Organization Man*. New York: Simon & Schuster.

Wood, R. (1987) '*Raging Bull*: the homosexual subtext in film', in M. Kaufman (ed.), *Beyond Patriarchy. Essays by Men on Power, Pleasure and Change*. Toronto: Oxford University Press. pp. 266–76.

8

The Public and the Private:
Gender, Sexuality and Emotion

Wendy Parkin

This chapter focuses on issues of gender, sexuality and emotionality at 'work'. Four illustrative settings are described: paid work in a university, paid work in a social services department, paid work in a residential establishment and unpaid work in the family. In some of these settings, in which I have direct experience, I feel a different person. This will be explored in terms of the divisions between paid work and unpaid work; types of work undertaken; organizational type (public or private); and organizations as locations of oppression and discrimination. The new position of gender and sexuality in organizational theory (Hearn and Parkin, 1983), and recent feminist scholarship, will be used to explore interconnections between gender, sexuality, emotionality and organization.

Public and Private: Gender and Sexuality

The public/private divide is the starting point – of crucial importance in the analysis of gender relationships (Elshtain, 1981). The public world of paid work – organizationally based and politicized – is often contrasted with the private and personal world of the family and the domestic, perceived as relatively apoliticized. Clark and Lange (1979: xiv) describe this division as two spheres of life: 'Sphere A is the sphere of the 'productive' or 'political' activity, of 'public' life and the sphere of reason. Sphere B is that of women, is that of 'non-productive', 'non-political', 'merely reproductive', 'private', 'natural', and emotional activity.'

Many tasks which were historically located in the domestic sphere – the production of goods, health care, midwifery, education – have moved into organizations such as factories, hospitals and schools (Ehrenreich and English, 1979). Health and welfare bureaucracies have taken over many traditional family roles, while also becoming part of the state intervention into family life.

The public/private divide can be regarded as a useful way to explore gender divisions of domination, particularly men's domination of women's lives. This occurs through the gender divisions of labour, management, power, authority and leadership in organizations. Such divisions tend to promote the interests of instrumental, white male, heterosexuality and rationality and devalue women's roles – particularly the domestic ones of cooking, cleaning or caring. Men also dominate in the realm of the domestic/family. The public/private divide also suggests subtle mechanisms of control: women are consigned to the private sphere – the apolitical, the sexual, the emotional. Women have the 'expressive role', men the 'instrumental'. The expressive role encompasses physical care of dependent people and of men. In sum, a gendered division of labour divides emotions and the way they are expressed, by whom and where.

Not surprisingly, perhaps, the move from the domestic sphere to the public sphere of paid work can give a woman a different sense of self and emotionality. In both spheres men tend to dominate, and women's domestic and caring role is devalued. However, there is often a presumption that, when entering the public realm, it is entry to the world of goal-directed organizations, the world of politics, the world of dispassionate reason, and the world of the 'productive'. This world has always been gendered, though it has not always been thought of as such. Indeed, as Flax (1987) observes, only recently have scholars considered the possibility that there may be at least three histories in every culture – 'his', 'hers' and 'ours'.

Gender was not regarded as an issue until put on the organizational agenda by women. Likewise sexuality, which was perceived as belonging in the private realm of the family. The sense that organizations are arenas of powerful sexual and emotional politics emerged through feminist studies of sexual harassment (Farley, 1978; MacKinnon, 1979) and theorizing on sexual politics (Millett, 1971; O'Brien, 1981). The paradox of 'organizational sexuality' (Hearn and Parkin, 1987) is that, far from being excluded from the workplace, sexuality is an integral part of organizational life – whether through, for example, sexual liaisons, 'pin-up' calendars, jokes, bodily states such as premenstrual tension or pregnancy or menopause.

Because sexuality, as an organizational issue, has been developed by feminist analysts, it can lead to the assumption that sexuality, like gender, is an issue only for women; something introduced by women from the private realm where it supposedly belongs. But this ignores the prevailing and powerful discourse of the 'male sexual narrative' and its fundamental interconnectedness with male gender powers in the public and private domains. When women's sexuality and bodily states are the focus of attention then the power of the male heterosexual sexual drive can easily be ignored. So, for example, it can be taken for granted that sexual advances should be welcomed by women in organizations.

An analysis of the male sexual narrative 'exposes' the organizational world as one where men dominate through leadership, status, hierarchy, authority, management, power and language. The literature speaks of the 'entry of women' into management (Gordon and Strober, 1975). No literature addresses the entry of men because they are already there and they set the agenda. Not only do they dominate through these processes, they also dominate the sexual and emotional agenda, most profoundly by not perceiving they have one and that the sexual agenda is that of women. However, it is mainly men who put pin-ups on the wall, exploit boss–secretary relationships (Pringle, 1989), develop sexist shop-floor humour (Cockburn, 1983). The most ridicule is often reserved for women who challenge sexist language such as 'manpower', 'chairman', 'blue and white collar', possibly because of the fundamental relationship of language to power.

The interplay of gender powers and the male sexual narrative is revealed in the terminology of 'policy thrusts', 'targeting', 'scoring', 'rising to the challenge', 'virility'. Davis, et al. (1991: 22–3) focus on the assumptions about emotionality in such discourse, particularly the splitting of power from love. In the public sphere of power, love is suggested to be out of place or irrelevant. Love can be seen as dangerous to power in this analysis, especially 'in the upheaval brought about by the "scandalous" love affairs of politicians and the way in which love affairs between bosses and employees tend to cause trouble'.

'Affairs' in organizations can be seen as threatening, and not just when they involve top politicians. If affairs are 'found out' it is often the women who are sacked, transferred or demoted (Hearn and Parkin, 1987). For example, in a recent case where a woman was dismissed for having an affair with her boss, the company stated that 'she had infringed her contract of employment, which demanded *she* behave in a seemly and proper manner and should resign' (*The Guardian*, 1992; my emphasis). It is women's sexuality, not men's, that is seen as a potential threat to organizational discipline (Cockburn, 1991: 27). Not only are women seen as the 'takers in' of sexuality, they are seen to take in irrationality to organizations (Broverman et al., 1981; Pringle, 1989). The problematizing of women and their sexuality could thus be extended to women as the holders and purveyors of emotions, equally problematized in organizations. Thus the body politics of women in organizations may be constructed around emotionality and men's around rationality.

I would like to illustrate some of these issues with case examples. Each reveals how the gendering of emotions is differently constructed, and politicized, in contrasting public and private settings.

Case Study: the Domestic/Private

The domestic is the realm of mostly unpaid work and inhabited by those unemployed in paid work for a variety of reasons: dependent children, older and dependent older people; disabled and ill people together with those who do the caring, mainly women. Here is the 'rightful' place for sexuality, the expression of emotions merged into the social construct of 'expressive women'. My own domestic 'career' has incorporated a number of roles and innumerable emotions about this construct which constitutes 'doing the emotional work' in the family.

Arguably, as for many other women, my 'domestic career' has determined my 'public career' with my 'female narrative' of career break, career change, part-time and temporary work and reduced promotional opportunities contrasting with 'male narratives' of more full-time permanent posts and enhanced career prospects (Hearn and Parkin, 1987: x). This questions the supposed 'apolitical' notion of the domestic career as women are constructed in the 'public' by their domestic role. A young woman relative removes her wedding ring before going for a Head of Department interview and carefully rehearses responses to indirect questions about her domestic status and likelihood of having children. My personal experience of seeing a less qualified person obtaining a permanent post which I had applied to job-share demonstrates the political nature of the private realm as it profoundly affected my public career, or lack of it. Also demonstrated is the emotional nature of the public realm as I experienced the frustration, anxiety and anger of continuing temporariness. Thus, the emotions of the public arose out of the politics of the private.

Case Study: the Public

While my role in the domestic has determined my career path in the public, there are many aspects of my private world to be left behind when I enter the public, particularly sexuality and the expression of emotions. With the recognition of the power and paradox of 'organization sexuality' the false dichotomy around sexuality has been exposed. Similarly, we now need to explore the assumptions around the emotionless public world. In the public world I hold two separate posts in two different settings in each of which I feel different and also experience and express different emotions. Rather than entering an 'emotionless' sphere it is an exploration of not only how the 'context organizes the mind' (Jones, 1989: 26) but also how 'the context organizes the emotions'. As with sexuality, this is a two-way process with sexuality and emotionality both constructing and being constructed by the organizational context.

One setting is a local authority family centre where I practise as a social worker and work with young children and families; the other setting is a university where I have a Senior Lectureship in Social Work and Applied Social Studies. Both posts are permanent. The differences between the two settings in effect will refer to gender and sexuality, different organizational structures and geography, the types of work undertaken, management, and the notions of teams.

The two settings have marked differences. Both are in the public world but the family centre could be seen as being in an ambiguous position. The family centre building is a three-bedroomed house with kitchen and bathroom, a suitable domestic setting for children and parents who may attend for several hours. The word 'family' in the title along with the setting can give rise to ambiguity as to its purpose – which is firmly within the public realm, and part of state intervention into family life within the legal framework of Child Protection. Many users of the service initially perceive the centre as being 'independent' and not part of Social Services and where children and families will be kept together at all costs. This misperception is understandable in approaching a house with the word 'family' in its title.

This ambiguity is not present in the university setting where the building and its purpose are clearly part of the public realm. The family centre, although part of a large state bureaucracy, is a small unit, geographically isolated from other parts of the bureaucracy, whereas the university campus is large and its subunits are obviously part of a larger whole. Internally there is the relative privacy and isolation of single rooms or the maximum of two people to a room, though this has a gender and class gradient as the cleaning staff have no base room, clerical/secretarial staff can have several sharing rooms, temporary lecturers having access to a room but no desk, fractional lecturer appointments sharing rooms and full-time academic staff having sole occupancy of rooms. In the expression or containment of emotions this geographical distribution has some people, usually women, more publicly on view than others.

At the family centre, five of the six staff occupy an upstairs room as an office with little or no privacy. The unit is so small there is rarely anywhere to go in the building as other rooms are in use for work. As well as one's expression of emotion being constantly on view, this very close working proximity on a regular basis generates emotions and feelings which are quite different from occupying a single or shared room at college. At the family centre the closeness can be supportive but also irritating with feelings of having no control over what feels like constant scrutiny. At the college there is more feeling of distance, autonomy, control and privacy. At the family centre the person with sole occupancy of a room is the clerical/administrative person who often finds her room the one place where people can sit and express negative feelings. This puts this person at the hub of the emotional life in the centre. Such a role reflects the way that secretaries as 'office wives' can not only be used to run errands for male 'bosses', make their tea, remember family birthdays but also undertake some of the emotional support work: 'protecting their charges from unnecessary interference and strain, making tea, buying presents, even cleaning their bosses' false teeth' (Miles, 1983: 199). This emotional support work is perceived as women's work but necessary for the smooth running of the organization and often also takes place in informal networks over tea, in corridors, in toilets and washrooms. Here in the places where people may 'complain about the boss' comes together the gendered, emotionalized and sexualized world of the organization. These informal networks are as crucial for those researching the emotions world of organization as to those researching the sexualized world.

The type of work undertaken in the university and the family centre gives rise to different emotions, not that one setting has unemotional work and the other has emotional work. In the family centre setting there is daily contact with people in severe distress – parents who are separated from their children, women and children physically and sexually abused or neglected, lives spent in care, lives affected by mental illness, drink and drugs. In social work, there is contact with physical and emotional pain and distress in the face of which the worker is encouraged to demonstrate a professional front in order to be strong for the person seeking help. Workers who cry with clients, show shock, anger, dismay or who are themselves overwhelmed by the client's feelings are seen as unprofessional (see also Fineman, 1985). In psychodynamic terms the worker may be at the receiving end of a range of negative emotions from clients in the 'transference' process where the worker represents to the client a feared or disliked or lost figure from the past. Inside, the worker will be experiencing a variety of emotions, as their shared humanity with clients means they are not immune in their professionalism from feeling shock, anger and upset when listening to accounts of physical and sexual abuse. In this sense the work is 'emotionally charged' and certainly different from an assembly line job where interaction is with colleagues and management but not with the end product in an emotional way. Another dimension of the social work task is a recognition of emotionality being present within the discourse of subjectivity. Many social work clients are perceived in their objective status, 'client' being one such status.

> One can characterise social work as straddling a split between internal subjective states, such as pain, want, suffering, love and hate, and objective characterisation in that they are awarded statuses, such as old age, crime, debt, handicap, illness and madness. The knowledge produced under social work's regime of truth is one which describes a process whereby these individual states and objective statuses are transformed into a social subject. (Philp, 1979: 92)

This work of reaching the subjective experience of objective statuses is particular to social work forms of knowledge and so there is an emotionality that is situation specific – not in the uniqueness of the emotions, but the means by which they are aroused. In this sense the form and nature of the work is an important variable in the production of emotions.

Another organizational variable is style of management. Both organizations have bureaucratic and professional structures. In Social Services departments frequent confusion arises in having workers supervised by managers who are professionally qualified but whose task is usually the bureaucratic one of work flow, time and person management, and appraisal. In the university, the management structure is less immediate and obvious with colleagues having administrative responsibilities rather than management ones. In both settings management structures are male dominated. In the university setting, the stresses and emotional states are more around personal responsibility for time management, workload, research activities, teaching styles and curriculum development. This is changing and the emotional climate will change as staff appraisal, more control over time management, large student numbers with distance learning are all introduced. The practice setting is more obviously managed with workload and work performance closely scrutinized. There is blurring between accountability, management and support, with workers often unwilling to share their emotions with managers for fear of being seen as weak or 'over-identifying' with clients (see also Fineman, 1985). These emotions, often arising from the nature of the work, are often, in my experience, shared more freely at the peer group level, sometimes to the point of organizing 'semi-private realm' support groups held outside office hours and aimed at the giving and receiving of emotional support. The wider 'encounter' and 'co-counselling' movements have been part of a sensitivity towards workers' emotions and the need for their expression. This form of emotional support for workers is not in the mainstream of organizational life but seen as a private realm activity.

Within the context of the management/supervisory relationship feedback is given on work performance with encouragement to see this as 'objective' guidance on the task and not to be 'taken personally' (Hawkins and Shohet, 1990). This concept of 'not taking things personally' is, I suggest, a false notion of human emotionality: the idea that one can separate off part of oneself that will not be affected when given negative feedback. This view separates person from feelings, professional self from emotions, and is the basis for a spurious and damaging duality which can make people feel vulnerable and inadequate when they do take things personally. In Personal Construct Theory terms (Fransella and Dalton, 1990), if the notion of 'not taking it personally' was construed then a robot and not a person would be the end product.

Inevitably the gendered nature of management generates an emotional climate as do other oppressive aspects of management structures. Groups oppressed by class, gender, age, sexuality, ethnicity or disability find this oppression mediated through management structures. In rational terms management should be fair, impersonal and impartial, whereas in reality management structures reflect wider power structures with a different 'emotional atmosphere' depending on whether one is one of the oppressed or one of the oppressors.

In both work settings there are team meetings. The notion of teams can conjure up a view of a group of people in the workplace where emotions can be shared and expressed. Both team meetings are essentially task focused with worker needs and issues having low priority. In the family centre clients are discussed, but in terms of group supervision or planning of the work rather than focusing on staff feelings and emotions. If a team is not functioning well then outside consultants may be used to focus on 'team dynamics' when expression of emotion is encouraged as a way of engendering change. This is to enable the team to perform its task better rather than to facilitate the team as a forum for expression of emotionality (though the expression of extreme emotionality is often a by-product of team development). The literature on teams and teamwork does not demonstrate and focus on feelings and emotions.

A book on teams (Larson and La Fasto, 1989) outlines key features of success: a clear elevating goal; results-driven structure; competent team members; unified commitment; collaborative climate; standards of excellence; external support and recognition; and principled leadership. At the family centre the Larson and La Fasto criteria were used to explore team performance but in addition other models of team development were used to specifically include experiential training. The notion of 'experiential' carries connotations of feelings and emotions, though suggests again a false separation between the view that some work is 'experiential' and gives rise to feelings and other work does not. In this work, training focuses on exercises aimed at arousing emotions to reflect the therapeutic work undertaken with clients. The starting point for the assessment of such therapeutic work is to assess the feelings and emotions one is experiencing as a way of identifying problems and issues in the work undertaken. This starting with emotions and finishing with problems and issues is unusual. Organizational work usually leaves out the feelings and emotions to focus just on problems, issues and tasks.

I have outlined some of the differences between the two work settings and have attempted to explain differences in emotional content and atmosphere. The one feature left out is the emotionality of simultaneously holding two such posts when at times each one can be a refuge from the other but the very holding of two such different and demanding posts can lead to feelings and emotions arising from this joint enterprise. These feelings were not unlike those discussed by Bastian and Blyth in their study of 'two organization' employees:

> 'two hierarchies, two sets of section meetings, two "in" trays, two sets of admin. staff, telephonists, coffee cups, "Christmas parties", leaving parties, temperamental photocopiers . . . the list is endless!' Another clear area of concern appeared to be the marginality of respondents to each of the organisations. . . Not surprisingly therefore, respondents reported their experience of isolation and being 'on the fringe'. (Bastian and Blyth, 1989: 23)

This study reflects my own experience of an 'emotional weighting' resulting from moving between two settings with regular adjustments from the emotionality of one to the emotionality of the other and where two halves add up to more than one. It also links with the regular daily move from public to private where concerns for a client or student are replaced by concerns about children left with other carers and the guilt of once again getting home late!

Case Study: Merging Domains

An organizational setting for emotional work is that of residential establishments, often called 'homes'. There are homes for older people who privately mourn their loss of independence, own homes, and partners. They are places where loss is an ongoing issue as people die. But in the everyday running of such homes, bodies are hidden, death is denied, mourning and grief with the concomitant emotions denied, in the belief that residents (and staff) are not to be reminded of their own demise. There are homes run on similar bureaucratic lines for people incapacitated through illness and disability. There are homes for children, often statutorily removed from home. When upset, some children find their 'keyworker' is not there. A young child when asked who looked after her replied, 'whoever is on duty'. The majority of staff in residential establishments are untrained and not professionally qualified for the task of helping residents with their deep emotional pain and distress, arguably exacerbated by the loneliness and isolation of the setting itself.

The focusing on this setting arises out of previous research into issues of sexuality and gender in residential settings (Parkin, 1989). This was undertaken through questioning students on residential placement as to how issues of sexuality were dealt with through training, guidelines for behaviour and organizational policies. At the time, there were, as there have been subsequently, scandals concerning the sexual abuse of children and sexual harassment of staff in children's homes. The students had considerable anxiety about how to deal with sexuality but found, with few exceptions, they were given no guidance, had no rules and there were no written policies and little training. Sexuality is an emotional issue and experience, compounded when adult and children's sexuality is exploited and abused in a setting presumed 'safe'.

The setting emerged as having an ambiguity which contributed to the possible exploitation of residents and staff. In the public/private divide residential establishments are not clearly defined. They are in the public but use the language of the private such as 'homes', 'house parents', 'uncles', 'aunties'. Many of the tasks of cooking, cleaning and intimate caring are of the domestic realm and pay and conditions of service reflect the devaluing of the domestic within the public realm. Stacey and Davies (1983) conceptualized 'intermediate zones' which straddle the public/private divide and which Parkin (1989) developed to analyse the way sexuality and sexual exploitation were dealt with in residential establishments. Parkin explored how these establishments were presented as models of 'homes' and caring but actually blurred with models of 'total institutions' and control. This blurring and merging of models leaves an unclarity in which power and decision-making processes can exploit relatively powerless and vulnerable adults and children. Public realm rules can change to private realm rules in establishments called 'homes' but staffed and run more like total institutions and infrequently inspected. Issues of sexuality and sexual exploitation were thus confused by the ambiguity of the setting, as arguably will be issues of emotionality and their expression: not just the emotional misery, deep hurt and distress of sexual abuse but the whole gamut of the emotional miseries of dependence and loss.

Case Study: Death and Mourning

As sexuality is seen as a private issue, so can death and mourning. Although most deaths take place in hospitals or residential establishments in Western society, Kubler-Ross (1970) in her study of the terminally ill, found doctors unwilling to acknowledge they had dying patients in their care. This denial of death in the public realm has parallels with the denial of sexuality so that the emotions of grief and mourning are assumed to belong to the private realm, as is sexuality.

Recent research on death has focused on the recognition that death is part of the public realm but located in particular discourses, a discourse being defined in the Foucauldian sense as a system for the possibility of knowledge or 'structures of knowledge through which we understand, explain and decide things' (Parton, 1991). Death, according to Prior (1989) has always been present in the discourses on demography and pathology, with their search for the cause of death. The hospice movement has widened the debate around death and care of the dying within the medical profession.

It could be argued that the hospice movement has brought death into the public realm or, alternatively, that the hospice movement is another example of an intermediate zone between public and private. In the hospice there is care for the dying and a recognition of the need for emotional work. Its location is often in voluntary organizations with fund-raising for survival. It is certainly not part of mainstream medicine. Rather than allowing death and grief into the public realm, it is relocated into the 'merging domains' and back into the private where teams of hospice-based nurses care for dying people at home. Many of these nurses are trained in counselling as well as nursing care, a recognition of the need for training in the handling of emotions. A study examined the stress of working with dying or critically ill people in intensive care units and hospices. It particularly looked at the difference between these two groups of nurses in the way they handled the emotional work. Hospital nurses dealing with the critically ill were significantly more job dissatisfied than the hospice nurses (Cooper and Mitchell, 1990).

The emotions around grief and mourning have a gender division which, in the context of nursing the dying, can approximate to the professional splits between nurses and doctors with nursing seen as a semi-profession (Simpson and Simpson, 1969) and politicized as such (Twomey in Salvage, 1985):

He came on to the ward at ten
I was right, he said.
leukaemia
I said he'd got leukaemia, didn't I?

Are the parents here?
Nurse – go and see.
She went, running.
Yes, they're here she said, breathlessly

I'll break it to them, he said
decisively
and broke them

And left the nurse with the pieces.
But she wasn't trained to cope with broken lives
She was only trained
to fetch the stethoscope.

This politicization of nursing and its designation as a semi-profession is gendered. Historically, nursing has been a woman's profession. Nursing tasks have reflected a discourse on caring and the 'sanitary' (Abbott and Wallace, 1990). Nurses have had responsibility for the cleanliness of the wards and the patients, and would offer care in the manner of a good Victorian mother. The doctor, however, would be schooled traditionally in scientific/medical discourse, and patient welfare would be under his or her ultimate direction. Abbott and Wallace see this distinction between nurses and doctors as the reason nurses have had such difficulty in being seen as autonomous practitioners. The task and gender distinctions still persist in divisions of labour and emotions concerning death and dying. The nurse counsellor is an example of the emotional tasks being seen as the work of women, as are a wide range of caring tasks.

Medicine is strongly professionalized and one of the traditional male-dominated professions. Women are entering the profession in increasing numbers but few break through the 'glass ceiling' to higher-status posts in hospitals. The ethos is of control of emotions as part of being professional, even though the daily activity is dealing with people in pain and distress. Patients are encouraged to be brave in the face of pain and distress. Doctors do not demonstrate feelings. In a popular TV medical soap opera a trainee woman surgeon showed distress when assisting at her first mastectomy and was sent out of the theatre to be told later, by a male consultant, that she was a professional first and a woman second. If she continued to show distress it would be considered that she wasn't 'up to the job' (see also Howell, 1979).

This view of the need to hold on to strong or negative emotions is a feature of organizational life in general. The impersonal, hierarchical rational/legal basis of bureaucracies, and the socialization into professionalism, are features of organizational life which contribute to the suppression and denial of feeling and emotion. When emotions are expressed such as upset, grief, anxiety, worry, then these are channelled to be dealt with in the private realm. A manager of a recently bereaved employee felt personally sympathetic when the woman returned to work but was too upset to function effectively. The bureaucratic 'allowance' of compassionate leave was used up, no holiday allowance was left, so the woman was advised to obtain a sick note if more time needed to be taken. This possibly fairly typical example shows an attempt to confine emotion to the 'private' while also pathologizing it into an illness to be dealt with bureaucratically.

> Just as we discount the symbols of mourning, because they no longer have a universal meaning, so we discount loss, because it is merely private and particular. . .
> This belief that loss can be made good by substitution is, I think reinforced by the predominantly bureaucratic organisation of contemporary, industrial society. The crucial administrative structures no longer depend upon familial structures, but on the co-ordination of impersonal functions. Bureaucracies are impregnable by death. At worst it robs them of experienced talent which may be scarce. The organisation is hardly disturbed – the dead man's replacement is already waiting. A bureaucratic society, therefore, need not prescribe the passage of mourning: death creates no crisis in corporate life. So we come to perceive grief as a sickness because in terms of the dominant principles of our social organisation, the unwillingness to replace a vacated role promptly is as much an aberration as the unwillingness to substitute for a missing satisfaction. (Marris, 1986: 90–1)

The Public: Discourses of Emotions

The recognition that organization theory, or theorizing in the public domain, gives little consideration to emotions has similarities with the lack of attention given to gender and sexuality. Fineman argues that:

> The limited consideration of emotion in organization theory results from a desire a] to separate conceptions of people from those of organizations, b] to reify the organizations, c] to separate processes of rationality from those of emotion, and d] a cultural, especially Western male, predilection to suppress, deny or minimise the role of emotions. (1991: 5)

Emotions are recognized as being part of the public in the 'fairly gross emotional categories of job satisfaction and stress' (Fineman, 1991: 11). This leads to exploration of other categories or discourses for the location of emotions: 'Furthermore, positivism, and its attendant scientific rationalism guides the investigator's hand in most early, and much present organizational research.'

The private realm is seen as the repository for emotional life as well as sexuality. Both are difficult to research in organizations for a number of reasons including the problems of prevailing research methodologies; their introduction by women into organizations and their problematization; and the organizational control of emotions. This emerges as a 'male emotional narrative' which has obvious links with the male sexual narrative in defining the organizational context for sexuality and the expression of emotion, and in controlling women's emotions as another dimension of the exercise of asymmetrical gender powers.

The work on the social organization of death (Prior, 1989) demonstrated the discourses in which death is located in the public realm. Similarly, emotionality is located and often confined to certain discourses. The interplay of knowledge formation and power is demonstrated in the way discourses develop and form new ways of exercising control. Parton (1991: 5) argues that:

> Foucault's primary objective was to provide a critique of the way modern societies control and discipline their populations. Sanctioning the knowledge-claims and practices of the new human sciences – particularly medicine, psychiatry, psychology and criminology – what Ingleby [1985] and Rose [1985] refer to as the 'psy' complex.

Power is exercised in the confining of knowledge to certain discourses as it is exercised in the 'mobilization of bias' to keep certain issues, for example, gender, sexuality and emotions, off the organizational agenda (Bachrach and Baratz, 1963). To locate emotions and emotionality it is necessary to discover the discourses in which they are marginalized, trivialized, controlled and overlooked.

One discourse is that of the 'extra-mural' which is a very indirect way of recognizing that organizational politics is influenced by personal feelings and values. This notion is demonstrated in the work of Morgan (1986: 149), who represents each individual who enters the organization in terms of three interconnected circles of vested interests – task, career, extra-mural. Because they frequently overlap, they become part of the daily political negotiations and decision making of the individual even before they meet up with other individuals with whom they have to negotiate:

> Most often the balance between task, career and extra-mural is an uneasy and ever-changing one, creating tensions that lie at the center of political activity. The fact that the areas of complete convergence of interests is often small . . . is one reason why organizational (or task) rationality is such a rare phenomenon.

Only indirectly, through the recognition of the rarity of task rationality, is there reference to other influences on decision making. Task and career are part of the organizational agenda, but the recognition of the 'extra-mural' acknowledges that, within the organization, people's 'personal values and life style' are not left behind in the domestic.

Emotionality is part of organizational life but this recognition comes from a number of sources, not mainstream organization theory. Look up the index of organization theory textbooks and 'emotion' and 'feelings' are absent (see also Fineman, 1991). Gergen (1992) describes the romanticist discourse of the nineteenth century giving way to the modernist understanding of the person in the twentieth century and now to postmodernist thinking. However there are still romanticist legacies in organization theory. These include psychoanalytically based theories of the organization with emphasis on unconscious dynamics, work of Jung on archetypal bases of action; human need based theory; human potential perspectives; leadership and personal resources; and Japanese management theory emphasizing bonds between organizations and their members. In these romanticist legacies is, arguably, the location of another discourse for emotions seen as 'residual' legacies compared with modernist discourse with its emphasis on objectivity, rationality, scientific thinking and use of the machine metaphor.

> Yet, as postmodern consciousness sets in, the empirical process is redefined. Rather than correcting the language of understanding, primary research is typically justificatory. It proceeds on the basis of assumptions, or discourses, already shared within the scientific sub-community, and generates evidence that is interpreted within this restrictive discursive domain. Because it commences with theoretical views already intact, whatever data are produced by the research will inevitably be named or defined within this theoretical spectrum. In this sense the theoretical perspective is self-fulfilling; all that exists does so by virtue of theoretical definition. Research results do not stand as separate and independent vindicators of position; they are essentially reification devices for positions already embraced. (Gergen, 1992: 213)

In the modernist discourse it is clear that emotions are not part of the language as they will not fit into 'positions already embraced'.

Social constructionist perspectives (Fineman, 1991; Mangham 1988) and the interactionist perspectives in the paradigm analyses (Burrell and Morgan, 1979) stress the importance of meaning and subjectivity. In the radical humanist perspective, also of the paradigm approach, the focus is on the way the subject internalizes oppression and feels and acts accordingly. Subjectivity is thus another discourse in which emotionality is located. The notion of 'the experiential' is another. It could be argued that both are marginalized and overlooked as is the 'fading romanticist legacy' that has no part of organizational life. However, the new emphasis on subjectivity has arisen through feminist scholarship and research which looks at the importance of sexual politics and gender issues. Stanley and Wise (1979) are frank about their personal feelings in their study of obscene phone calls. Feminist scholarship has criticized malestream theory and malestream research. Feminist issues are also marginalized in organizations, leading to a double suppression of issues around emotionality as the discourses from romanticism and the discourses from feminism – both of which emphasize the subjective – are marginalized. So it is clearer why issues of emotionality are absent from organization theory: it is not just that there are 'shadows of rationalism and masculinism in the marginalization of emotions' (Fineman, 1991: 4) but that masculinism and rationalism are central.

Like 'organization sexuality' the recognition of organization emotionality through the acknowledgement of its discourses leads to questions about the nature of emotionality, its links with organizational politics and power, and its relationship to the male sexual narrative and gender powers. As being found out is seen as the real offence when 'affairs' take place in organizations, perhaps the real 'offence' for emotions is not the holding of them but the demonstration of them, especially strong ones and negative ones. 'Social norms help regulate and order the emotional turmoil: there is a "right" time, place and face for most feelings' (Davis et al., 1991: 22).

The Public and Control of Emotions

This chapter has focused on the links between the problematizing of gender and sexuality in organizations and the problematizing of emotions. Emotions, like sexuality, are assumed to be located in the private or marginalized in discourses within the public. This leads to forms of social control over emotions; keeping control of one's emotions is perceived as strength in the organizational setting.

The need to be 'emotionally strong' or keep emotions under control, to function in an organization can be considered in the context of organizations as creating and reproducing various structural oppressions of people on grounds of, for example, class, gender, race, age (dis)ability and sexuality. Oppression is a term used here to describe structures of power which exclude certain groups of people from organizations or unjustly prevent them from achieving any power or status within the organization. Different groups have different experiences of oppression, with the politics of one 'category' often developing without reference to other 'categories'. In reality they are interconnected so that, for example, a black woman could struggle simultaneously with racism and sexism.

Recently increasing attention has been paid to the politics of disability (Oliver, 1990; Morris, 1991). As with all oppressions, attention focuses not only on the oppressed group but also on those in power who can stereotype, label and oppress. When researching the interconnectedness of oppressions in organization, Hearn and Parkin (1992a) noted that 'able-bodiedness' is one of the fundamental categories around oppression in that it is taken for granted in organizational life that people possess their senses, are mobile and physically well and strong. Analogously, we find that emotional strength is a prerequisite of functioning in an organization and those who show their feelings are categorized as emotionally weak. Men who express emotion are seen as even weaker and 'like women'.

Cost-effectiveness and increased throughput in organizations leads to increased workloads; more stress and more distance between users and providers. In this context emotional and physical strength are taken for granted. Stress and emotion are seen in terms of personal weakness and not as a result of organizational structures and pressures. In particular the structures of male rationality may construct and control emotionality through defining emotional strength in terms of male rational norms. The male gender powers, already underpinned by the male sexual narrative (Hearn and Parkin, 1987) are further strengthened by the male emotional narrative which defines, determines and controls what is meant by emotionality.

The recent growth of counselling services inside the workplace is a way in which emotions are dealt with, controlled and confined. Employees can be wary of such services inasmuch as they may symbolize 'not being up to the job', and their use may be reported back to people who can give or withhold promotion (see also Newton et al., 1993). This consigning of emotions, and their expressions, to the counselling arena is often a further way in which the expression of strong emotion is stigmatized and pathologized. 'Expressions like "to become emotional" still have the connotation of a lack of control over emotions, of being swept away by them. Expressions like these are reminiscent of this very danger *and* of the rigid social control that served to counter it' (Wouters, 1992: 245; italic in original). Emotions, grieving, illness and stress are confined in the private realm or dealt with in the public realm through counselling services which have connotations of weakness and stigma. In this way emotions are controlled by those in power defining what is meant by emotionality, and then imposing a pathology on expression of emotions which do not fit the criteria of organizational strength.

The Public and Emotionality of Harassment

Stanley and Wise (1979) described their feelings when researching obscene phone calls and their subjective experiences were a recognition of the emotionality of doing the work. The links between gender powers and the male sexual narrative were developed by Jeff Hearn and myself in the writing and research of *'Sex' at 'Work'* (Hearn and Parkin, 1987). The emotional impact of the work came at the end with separate conclusions reflecting the different subjective experiences of undertaking the research.

For Wendy
Jeff Hearn's account of the impact of the research for him parallels mine in the way that the development of the research has also been a development in awareness; mine has been a developing awareness of the depth, intricacy, complexity and enormity of the oppression of the male sexual narrative. . . A further profound revelation has been the growing awareness of the extent of sexual harassment through imagery, symbolism and language. (Hearn and Parkin, 1987: 161, 163)

For Jeff
Indeed . . . it is the attempt to understand and change myself and other men that has increasingly become the motivation for this study. (Hearn and Parkin, 1987: 157)

Similarly, two accounts of the emotional experience of reviewing *In the Way of Women* (Cockburn, 1991; Hearn and Parkin, 1992b) were written, as Jeff and I experienced different emotions as we read of the many exercises of power used by men to resist women's equality in organizations.

The experiences of inequality for women in organizations are wide ranging: blocked promotional opportunities; dual labour market; control of time and space; pin-ups on walls; sexual innuendo and jokes; unwanted bodily contact; forced sexual contact. The emotional cost of such experiences is firstly through the experiencing of negative emotions such as anger, disgust, fear, anxiety, blame and guilt. There is an emotional cost too in the need to suppress such emotions. A woman may hear a sexist joke which the men think is funny but may cause the woman to feel anger. Accusations of 'losing one's sense of humour', 'being unable to take a joke', 'over-reacting' are commonplace. Depending on her place in the organization a woman may challenge, show anger, ridicule or politely smile and hide her feelings. All of these are emotional costs of sexism and sexual harassment, and are women specific in this context. It is not that men do not experience such emotions, but for women the emotional costs arise from asymmetrical power relationships. The false duality of men as 'emotion-less' and women as 'emotion-full' in organizations is a further potential source of harassment, as is the view that men are in control of their emotions and women in an 'essentialist' sense do not have their emotions (any more than their sexuality) under control. The harassment of the out-of-control male heterosexual sex drive can then be ignored.

This duality between 'emotion-less' men and 'emotion-full' women highlights, in its extreme polarization, not only the gendered nature of emotional life in organizations but questions about what is meant by emotionality in organizations. I know I feel different at work from the way I feel at home. The emotions are not different but the move from the private realm to the public realm moves me into a context in which emotions and their expression are created and perceived differently. Asymmetrical gender power relations are common to both domestic and work realms but 'organization is precisely and uniquely the means by which power is effected' (Cockburn, 1991: 17). Men are not emotion-less but experience love, joy, pain, hurt, anger, loss, humiliation, for example. I believe that women's reasons for experiencing some of these emotions however, are different from men's and a direct result of unequal gender power relationships. The primary way in which I feel different in different settings is not just because of different structures, kinds of work, management styles, public and private, but because of the problematized construction of me as an emotional, sexualized woman.

The 'backlash' view that feminists have made the world a worse place for women is countered by Faludi (1992) who

> documents the frightening magnitude of the power and wealth mobilised to undermine women's struggles for equality and to erode women's

rights. . . With humour, precision and wit *Backlash* authoritatively maps out the many-sided fight against feminist goals waged by business, political, legal, evangelical and above all media establishments throughout the 1980s – alongside many men's personal resistance to women's battle for independence and parity. (Segal, 1992)

Faludi counters the view that we are in a postfeminist era. Hearn and Parkin (1992a) recognize one of the contradictions of post-modernism between the content of the message and the medium of the message where the medium is the *real* message. They see the message as that of postmodernism (or postfeminism) but the medium remains firmly modernist, rational malestream, using existing power structures and hierarchies. The reality continues to be defined through the same modes as before.

Conclusion

White male hegemony extends not only to occupation and control of positions of leadership, power and authority but to control of sexuality and emotional climates. The persistence of spurious dualities around public/private, sexual/asexual, rational/irrational, male/female, task/process, unemotional/emotional, are part of this hegemonic control. The development of postmodernism, post-feminism and poststructuralism can also be perceived as the control of theory when the real message is the medium which persistently remains white, male and middle class.

Emotionality is more difficult to construct and define than sexuality but is also inextricably linked with gender. The male sexual narrative has been argued as underpinning male gender powers. The emotional narrative of organizations can also be perceived as part of such gender powers, with the male emotional narrative of 'stiff upper lip', suppression of emotions and seeking of emotional satisfaction through sexuality being the organizational norm. It is also part of organizational control which helps to support the male patriarchal/fratriarchal hegemony.

References

Abbott, P. and Wallace, C. (1990) *The Sociology of the Caring Professions*. London: Falmer Press.

Bachrach, P. and Baratz, M. S. (1963) 'Decisions and nondecisions: an analytical framework', *American Political Science Review*, 57 (3): 632–42.

Bastian, P. and Blyth, E. (1989) *Joint Appointments in Social Work Education*, CCETSW Paper 27.2, Practice Teaching Series.

Broverman, I. K., Broverman, D. M., Clarkson, F. E., Rosenkrantz, P. S. and Vogel, S. F. (1981) 'Sex-role stereotypes and clinical judgements', in E. Howell and M. Boyes (eds), *Women and Mental Health*. New York: Basic Books.

Burrell, G. and Morgan, G. (1979) *Sociological Paradigms and Organizational Analysis*. London: Heinemann.

Clark, L. M. G. and Lange, L. (1979) *The Sexism of Social and Political Theory*. Toronto: University of Toronto Press.

Cockburn, C. (1983) *Brothers. Male Dominance and Technological Change*. London: Pluto.

Cockburn, C. (1991) *In the Way of Women. Men's Resistance to Sex Equality in Organizations*. London: Macmillan.

Cooper, C. L. and Mitchell, S. (1990) 'Nursing the critically ill and dying', *Human Relations*, 43 (4): 297–311.

Davis, K., Leijenaar, M. and Oldersma, J. (eds) (1991) *The Gender of Power*. Newbury Park, CA: Sage.

Ehrenreich, B. and English, D. (1979) *For Her Own Good. 150 Years of the Experts' Advice to Women*. London: Pluto.

Elshtain, J. B. (1981) *Public Men, Private Women*. Oxford: Martin Robertson.

Faludi, S. (1992) *Backlash*. London: Chatto & Windus.

Farley, L. (1978) *Sexual Shakedown*. London: Melbourne House; New York: McGraw-Hill.

Fineman, S. (1985) *Social Work Stress and Intervention*. Aldershot: Gower.

Fineman, S. (1991) 'Organizing and emotions'. Paper presented at 'Towards a New Theory of Organization' conference University of Keele 3–5 April.

Flax, J. (1987) 'Postmodernism and gender relations in feminist theory', *Signs: Journal of Women in Culture and Society*, 12 (4): 621–43.

Fransella, F. and Dalton, P. (1990) *Personal Construct Counselling in Action*. London: Sage.

Gergen, K. J. (1992) 'Organization theory in the postmodern era', in M. Reed and M. Hughes (eds), *Rethinking Organization. New Directions in Organization Theory and Analysis*. London and Newbury Park, CA: Sage. pp. 207–26.

Gordon, F. and Strober, M. (eds) (1975) *Bringing Women into Management*. New York: McGraw-Hill.

The Guardian (1992) 'Company wrong to sack woman for having an affair with boss', 25 April.

Hawkins, P. and Shohet, R. (1990) *Supervision in the Helping Professions*. Milton Keynes: Open University Press.

Hearn, J. and Parkin, W. (1983) 'Gender and organizations: a selective review of and a critique of a neglected area', *Organization Studies*, 4 (3): 219–42, repr. in A. Mills and P. Tancred (eds) (1992) *Gendering Organizational Theory*. Newbury Park, CA: Sage.

Hearn, J. and Parkin, W. (1987) *'Sex' at 'Work'. The Power and Paradox of Organization Sexuality*. Brighton: Wheatsheaf; New York: St Martin's Press.

Hearn, J. and Parkin, P. W. (1992a) 'Organizations, multiple oppressions and postmodernism', in M. Parker and J. Hassard (eds), *Postmodernism and Organization Theory*. London: Sage.

Hearn, J. and Parkin, W. (1992b) Review of *In the Way of Women* by C. Cockburn (1991), *Sociology*, August: 515–17.

Howell, M. (1979) 'Can we be feminists and professionals?', *Women's Studies International Quarterly*, 2: 1–7.

Ingleby, D. (1985) 'Professionals as socialisers: the psy complex', in A. Scull and

S. Spitzer (eds), *Research in Law, Deviance and Social Control 7*. New York: JAI Press.

Jones, S. (1989) 'Child care and the state', *Context*, 3 (Autumn): 26–8.

Kubler-Ross, E. (1970) *On Death and Dying*. London: Tavistock.

Larson, C. E. and La Fasto F.M. J. (1989) *Teamwork: What Must Go Right/What Can Go Wrong*. Newbury Park, CA: Sage.

MacKinnon, C. A. (1979) *The Sexual Harassment of Working Women*. New Haven, CT: Yale University Press.

Mangham, I. (1988) *Effecting Organizational Change*. Oxford: Blackwell.

Marris, P. (1986) *Loss and Change*, revised edn. London: Routledge & Kegan Paul.

Miles, R. (1983) *Danger! Men At Work*. London: Macdonald.

Millett, K. (1971) *Sexual Politics*. London: Virago.

Morgan, G. (1986) *Images of Organization*. Beverly Hills, CA: Sage.

Morris, J. (1991) *Pride against Prejudice. Transforming Attitudes to Disability*. London: Women's Press.

Newton, T., Handy, J. and Fineman, S. (1993) *Alternative Perspectives on Occupational Stress*. London: Sage.

O'Brien, M. (1981) *The Politics of Reproduction*. London: Routledge & Kegan Paul.

Oliver, M. (1990) *The Politics of Disability*. London: Macmillan.

Parkin, W. (1989) 'Private experiences in the public domain: sexuality and residential care organizations', in J. Hearn, D. L. Sheppard, P. Tancred-Sheriff and G. Burrell (eds), *The Sexuality of Organization*. London: Sage.

Parton, N. (1991) *Governing the Family*. London: Macmillan.

Philp, M. (1979) 'Notes on the form of knowledge in social work', *Sociological Review*, 27: 83–111.

Pringle, R. (1989) 'Bureaucracy, rationality and sexuality: the case of secretaries', in J. Hearn, D. L. Sheppard, P. Tancred-Sheriff and G. Burrell (eds), *The Sexuality of Organization*. London: Sage.

Prior, L. (1989) *The Social Organization of Death*. London: Macmillan.

Rose, N. (1985) *The Psychological Complex: Psychology, Politics and Society in England 1869–1939*. London: Routledge & Kegan Paul.

Salvage, J. (1985) *The Politics of Nursing*. London: Butterworth Heinemann.

Segal, L. (1992) 'The empire strikes back', *Everywoman*, May: 20–1.

Simpson, R. L. and Simpson, I. H. (1969) 'Women and bureaucracy in the semi-professions', in A. Etzioni (ed.), *The Semi-Professions and their Organization*. New York: Free Press.

Stacey, M. and Davies, C. (1983) *Division of Labour in Child Health Care: Final Report to the S.S.R.C. 1983* (Dec.). Coventry: University of Warwick.

Stanley, L. and Wise, S. (1979) 'Feminist research, feminist consciousness and experiences of sexism', *Women's Studies International Quarterly*, 2: 359–74.

Wouters, C. (1992) 'On status competition and emotion management: the study of emotions as a new field', *Theory, Culture & Society*, 9: 229–52.

9

Narcissistic Emotion and University Administration: An Analysis of 'Political Correctness'

Howard S. Schwartz

The term 'political correctness' (PC) entered American public discourse in a *New York Times* article by Richard Bernstein (1990). Discussion was then taken up by a large number of periodicals representing a wide range of opinion and intellectual level. Thus, *Time* and *Newsweek* had cover stories, but so also did the *New Republic*, the *Atlantic* and the *New York Review of Books*. In almost all instances, the discussion was critical.

Bernstein described PC in the following way.

> there is a large body of belief in academia and elsewhere that a cluster of opinions about race, ecology, feminism, culture and foreign policy defines a kind of 'correct' attitude toward the problems of the world, a sort of unofficial ideology of the university. . .
>
> Central to pc-ness, which has its roots in 1960s radicalism, is the view that Western society has for centuries been dominated by what is often called 'the white male power structure' or 'Patriarchal hegemony.' A related belief is that everybody but white heterosexual males has suffered some form of repression and been denied a cultural voice. (Section 4:1)

He adds

> But more than an earnest expression of belief, 'politically correct' has become a sarcastic jibe used by those, conservatives and classical liberals alike, to describe what they see as a growing intolerance, a closing of debate, a pressure to conform to a radical program or risk being accused of a commonly reiterated trio of thought crimes: sexism, racism and homophobia. (4:4)

Reaction to the charge of 'political correctness' was not long in emerging. Central among the themes used by those charged with these questionable practices were that, in the first place, the charges were false – that there had been no widespread infringement of free speech – and second that the charge of political correctness was, itself, an attempt to silence debate. According to this view, the charge of PC came from those in the academy, and their confederates elsewhere in the power structure, whose power was being threatened by new forces, previously suppressed, who were now demanding their place in the institution's power structure.

At a conference at the University of Michigan held to 'dispel the myths associated with PC', panellist Jon Weiner, professor of history at the University of California at Irvine and contributing editor of the *Nation*, said: 'They project a world that does not exist on the college campuses today. . . Undergraduates at Irvine saw the *Newsweek* story, came to me and said, "Gee do we have thought police on our campus?" ' (Zielinski, 1991: D2). Richard Campbell, a conference organizer and professor of communications at the University of Michigan said this: 'There's a lot of exciting changes going on in the nature of the university and the nature of society . . . Some people feel threatened by these changes' (Zielinski, 1991: D1). Panellist Julianne Malveaux, a columnist and teacher of Afro-American studies at the University of California, Berkeley, was more explicit. The attack on PC, she said, is 'the white males' last gasp. . . PC is a code word for: They're taking over our campus' (Bates, 1991: A7).

This theme was adumbrated in a document labelled 'Statement on the "Political Correctness" Controversy' which was 'issued by a special committee appointed by the president of the [American] Association [of University Professors]' and published in the AAUP magazine *Academe*. It begins:

> In recent months, critics have accused American higher education of submitting to the alleged domination of exponents of 'political correctness.' Their assault has involved sloganeering, name calling, the irresponsible use of anecdotes, and not infrequently the assertion that 'political correctness' is the new McCarthyism that is chilling the climate of debate on campus and subjecting political dissenters to the threat of reprisal. For all its self-righteous verve, this attack has frequently been less than candid about its actual origin, which appears to lie in an only partly concealed animosity toward equal opportunity and its first effects of modestly increasing the participation of women and racial and cultural minorities on campus. (Gray, et al., 1991: 48)

But notice that the claim that the attack upon PC comes from morally dubious sources is inconsistent with the denial that PC exists. This point was made in a letter to *Academe* by Charles Fried, a professor of jurisprudence at Harvard Law School. Commenting on the AAUP 'statement', Fried said:

Rarely does a statement, which is wrong in its conclusions, impetus and effect, also carry its own refutation on its face. The statement by Professors Gray, Poston, Stern, and Strohm is such a rare example. Many decry the pressures on American campuses to conform to a standard leftist catechism. They complain that vague and undefined charges of race and gender 'insensitivity' are used to bully them into silence. Professor Gray, et al., respond to this complaint by explaining that the complainers are 'frequently less than candid about its *actual* [emphasis supplied] origin, which appears to lie in an only partly concealed animosity toward equal opportunity. . . .' Thus they carelessly give as clear an example as one would want of the very bullying which Gray et al. deny exists. (Fried, 1991: 10)

Or consider the way the University of Michigan conference, at which numerous panellists denied that PC exists, appeared to an observer:

We sat in auditoriums, facing lecturing teachers; most panels had a tame 'conservative' to be the butt of abuse. One night a *Times* reporter named Richard Bernstein played the goat. Poor doofus, when he tried to explain that the reviled Western intellectual traditions actually spawned the revolutionary movements, he came off sounding like James Brown's *This Is A Man's World*.

So how did scholars receive his arguments? The crowd turned into a hissing, booing mob, egged on by several panellists, including syndicated columnist Julianne Malveaux, who rolled her eyes, snickered, made faces and barked 'bullshit' while others talked. Another panelist told the crowd, after mentioning Jeanne Kirkpatrick,[1] 'You can hiss if you want to.' The crowd complied.

To which the author added:

Imagine yourself a college student in that auditorium, dependent on the moderator for a needed grade. Would you stand up to the hissing, booing mob, given sanction by the podium? Would you challenge the orthodoxy of a professor who boasts that his facts are unabashedly tilted? Would you take on campus radicals and risk being publicly labeled a racist?

Or would you shut up, get the grade and go on to your real major? (Moss, 1991: 12C)

And yet, from the other point of view, even a cursory look at almost any American university faculty will disclose that most of its members are white males. A search of the university bookstore will equally reveal that most of what is studied in these universities is the product of white males. Certainly the selection process which underpins all this represents a form of valuation. And would it not follow that it represents a form of devaluation for those whose services and works have not been selected? And if those who had been devalued felt and expressed a certain anger, who could be surprised?

PC and University Administration

At first glance, the argument over whether or not PC exists appears undecidable. We have here two points of view, each internally consistent, and each intelligently expressed by deeply committed people, convinced of the truth of what they are saying. They talk past each other from within conceptual frameworks that are not commensurable.

Within the postmodern framework the PC controversy appears as a clash between discourses or languages. Typically, nothing is thought to exist outside of language (Derrida, 1974; Rorty, 1989), which gives rise to an epistemological relativism. Within this context, choice comes to be seen as determined by rhetoric.

But putting the matter this way tends to remove the sting from the PC controversy, since it appears to rest the determination of the matter on the question of who can produce the most compelling metaphors (Rorty, 1989). But note that the interlocutor who 'rolled her eyes, snickered, made faces and barked "bullshit" while others talked' was also using rhetoric, as was the 'hissing, booing mob'. And if the mob had threatened to burn down the houses of the anti-PC speakers, that too could have been seen as a rhetorical move.

What needs to be seen is that such rhetorical moves would have been part of the university's administrative process, part of the way it organizes itself. As Foucault (1979) has argued, the questions of power and knowledge are inseparable from one another. What counts as knowledge, within a given culture, is a function of how power is manifested within the culture, and therefore of how that culture organizes itself. The PC controversy is a surrogate for the question of how the university should be run. And if one can grant that administration can be done well or badly, and that this is a different question from that of whose interest is served, one can see that there is something at stake here.

In the present chapter I wish to explore some of the administrative consequences of the Political Correctness controversy, not from a linguistic, but from a psychodynamic point of view. As opposed to the linguistic differentiation, the psychodynamic difference between the PC and the anti-PC frameworks may be seen as a difference in emotions. From this point of view, the sides of the controversy represent alternative paradigms for university administration, based on different emotional processes and structures.

To put the matter very simply, PC represents an expression of narcissistic processes within university administration. Narcissism is an emotional orientation in which others are seen as existing to love oneself, and not as persons in their own right with their own, independent, emotional agendas. PC represents an attempt to take certain groups and to organize university life in support of their narcissism. The aspects of university life which are under attack by PC represent institutional arrangements that recognize that there are independent others outside of anyone's experience who must be accepted as others; and whose independent existence must be given its place within the core of anyone's emotional life.

To put the issue in Freudian terms, PC represents the workings of the *ego ideal*, while the traditional university represents the workings of the *superego*. In the next section, I will briefly develop the psychologies of the ego ideal and the superego. Then I will show how they manifest themselves as the emotional bases for the opposing dynamics of PC and the traditional university.

The Ego Ideal and the Superego

In the beginning of psychological life, boundaries have not yet formed between the infant and the mother, and the infant's mother is its world.[2] The total devotion of the mother to the infant results in the infant experiencing itself as the centre of a loving world. Freud (1957) refers to this experience as 'primary narcissism'. As time goes by, the infant is painfully alerted to the fact that the world does not lovingly revolve around it, and comes to feel isolated and helpless in the face of it. To escape from its helplessness, the child fantasizes a return to the original narcissistic state, to fusion with the mother who was the whole world, the *maternal imago* (Chasseguet-Smirgel, 1986).

The fantasy of this return to the state of narcissistic fusion is referred to by Freud (1955) as the *ego ideal*. The ego ideal represents us as we would best like to be. We would be able to do exactly what we want and have it turn out to our benefit since the world would be structured around our desires. Thus, we could be free and spontaneous without having to worry about the consequences. The ego ideal pictures us as perfectly at home in the world, without anxiety, sure of ourselves, certain of the validity of our behaviour, without doubt or marginality. On the individual level, we can see the ego ideal represented in the concept of success. On the collective level, the idea of a society manifesting the ego ideal lies behind our idea of utopia.

The problem is that, short of psychosis, the ego ideal never comes to be. In reality, we never get to be the centre of a loving world. The world is, in fact, not our mother. It existed before we were born. And it will continue to exist after we are dead. Moreover, if we had never been born, it never would have missed us. Far from being the centre of a loving world, we are always powerless and marginal in the face of a world that is deeply indifferent and dangerous to us.

But the ego ideal is not the powerful fantasy that it is because it has a basis in fact. Rather, it gains its power because we need it to defend ourselves against our very helplessness and marginality. An important task of culture is to maintain the fantasy of the ego ideal while also explaining why, at any given time for any given person, it has not come about. Within modern society the dominant cultural adaptation that has arisen to solve this problem involves the superego.

For Freud, the superego represents the internalization of external constraint to form obligation: the child undertakes to punish itself with guilt for behaviour for which the father would otherwise have punished it. In this way the child learns the rules of morality that operate within its culture; why it must do what it does not want to do. It learns, for example, when it must inhibit its sexuality and aggression and what a fair day's work is. Indeed, it is only through this process that the child comes to make sense of the fact that it has to work in the first place.

Thus, the superego involves a fundamentally different relationship to others, and to external reality generally, than the narcissism of the ego ideal. It is premised on the recognition that others are others, and that they will reward me or punish me as an expression of their own agenda and not in accordance with mine. Under the ego ideal, I experience the external world as part of myself. Under the superego, I experience myself as being part of the external world.

In Freud's account of development, the child is constrained to become like the father, to do something useful and culturally valued, under the supposition that then the child can again become fused with the maternal imago (Schwartz, 1992). In other words, the adoption of the superego enables one to give up the ego ideal temporarily on the promise of being able to earn it later through the performance of one's adult role. The corollary of this, of course, is that if one has not attained the ego ideal it is because one has not done enough that is useful and one needs to do more. One can easily see the value of the superego by reflecting that it both generates culturally useful activity and, at the same time, preserves society from the distortion of reality and the sense of infinite entitlement that narcissism would otherwise generate.

Modern society can be seen to involve an interaction of the ego ideal and the superego. The superego provides the basis both of positive achievement (Rothman et al., 1992) and of the renunciation of immediate gratification. The ego ideal is represented both as a developmental emotional bedrock and as a promise of what will happen if one fulfils one's cultural obligations.

In our culture, the task of acting in accordance with the demands of the superego has traditionally been the role of the male, of the father, who had to act in the world to earn standing with the female, the mother (Schwartz, 1992). With regard to the children, the role of the father was to inculcate the superego by representing harsh external reality within the family so that, by identifying with him, they could learn to cope with it. At the same time, his role was to create a distance between the family and harsh reality so that the ego ideal could operate within the family. The female, by contrast, had the role of bringing up the children and giving them a sense of being the centre of a loving world. In other words, the female was oriented toward maintaining the ego ideal for the children – to give them a deep feeling that they were loved.

The Psychological History of PC

In order to understand PC one needs to recognize that in recent decades the role of the father, the superego, has come to be repudiated. Taking its place has been the domination of the narcissistic psychology of the ego ideal.

It would go beyond the scope of this chapter to give a full account of how this happened. Nonetheless, it seems beyond dispute that PC is a carry-over from the radicalism of the 1960s (for example Kimball, 1990) and in order to get some sense of it, we need to make some sense of the psychodynamics of the time. In doing so, I rely on Todd Gitlin's (1987) excellent chronicle together with my own memory.

Children of affluence, growing up in the 1950s, the people who were to become the radicals of the sixties had an uneasy relationship to the comfort of their surroundings. If they had identified with their fathers they could have felt comfortable in their comfort, since they could have felt that they, in their turn, would earn the abundance that their fathers had earned.

But as Gitlin shows, the times did not lead to identification with the fathers because the fathers were disdained (also see Keniston, 1965). Important books of the time, which Gitlin argues represented a powerful cultural trend, were *The Man in the Grey Flannel Suit, The Organization Man*, and *The Lonely Crowd*. Such books presented an image of the father as one who had sold out, who had lost his freedom by adapting, and all for the purpose of material acquisition. This material acquisition did not seem worth the price to many young people. Hence, they refused identification with the father and retained the freedom he had lost. Still under his protection, they could live in the fantasy of the ego ideal, maintaining their sense of narcissistic omnipotence, which his superego had made possible.

But notice that this refusal to identify with the father made it difficult to form the superego and therefore gave these people no ground on which to feel entitled to their prosperity. Affluence was nice enough, but the guilt that came with the sense of being unentitled was mortifying. This was especially the case when they compared themselves with others who were not so prosperous: black people, working-class people and, later on, people in the Third World. Out of this, during the early 1960s, the nucleus of the group that would form the student movement attempted to reform the superego in a way that would serve as a new basis of entitlement without abandoning their freedom and without having to sustain the guilt of comparing themselves with those less well off.

This reformation was based on the role of the social reformer who championed the ideal of 'participatory democracy' – a form of organization that would be both efficient, in the sense of being able to raise everyone's level of prosperity, and non-hierarchical. This was the heart of what was called the New Left generally, and Students for a Democratic Society in the US, specifically, as its organizational form.[3]

It is very likely that had it not been for the Vietnam war, the impulse that went into the New Left would have had the salutary effect of increasing the level of democratic participation in society and in organizations. Brought into line with the limits imposed by reality, it would indeed have been a reformation of the superego and a real benefit to civilization. The problem with the Vietnam war, and with the awakening to the racial caste system which occurred at the same time, is that it raised the level of guilt beyond what this reformulated superego could readily work off.[4]

The predominant memory I have of that era, and Gitlin shows that this was characteristic of the student radicals of the time, was the belief in the absolute moral depravity of the American pursuit of the Vietnam war, and of the terrible incapacity of the student movement to stop it. To children of affluence, unaccustomed to the idea that they could not get anything they wanted just by wanting it, the idea that they could not stop the war, even though it was dreadfully wrong, was incomprehensible and inadmissible. But there it was! The war was not only wrong, its continued conduct threatened their sense of omnipotence.

The mature response would have been for the students to accept their limitations and do what they could within the constraints set by the world. This would have been activity in accordance with the superego. But the alternative chosen by a good many people at that time was to abandon the superego and give free reign to the ego ideal. This involved abandoning the possibility of action in the real world, in exchange for striking a pose in a fantasy world. By identifying with revolutionary movements abroad, with black militants at home, with the historical figures of world revolution, all defined within a fantasy of The Revolution, young people could sustain their sense of importance. At the same time they could give themselves an enemy whose resistance would explain the difficulty of what they were doing. The only casualty in this was the sense of reality.

For, as Gitlin makes plain, this idea of an impending revolution in the United States was ridiculous. Any serious thought would show the absurdity of the idea. But the idea was an absolute imperative. Anything which called it into question was morally unacceptable. So, caught between the necessity to believe and the sobering influence of realistic appraisal, the students abandoned realistic appraisal. Indeed, they stigmatized and scapegoated it. They came to feel directly threatened by realistic sense, and came to take it as their enemy. It was this realistic sense, insofar as it conflicted with the fantasy of the left, that formed the basis of political incorrectness. But the capacity to internalize real external demands is the basis of the superego. Thus, the enemy they set themselves up against was the superego itself. In what follows I would like to show how this dynamic plays itself out in the current PC conflict.

Dynamics of Political Correctness

The Crime of White Maleness

Perhaps the central emotional thrust of political correctness is the vilification of white (i.e. European) males. It is also the point that most clearly shows the psychodynamics of the process.

Clearly enough, the assault upon the white males and the 'Patriarchy' is an assault against the father. It is a blanket vilification. As Richard Shweder, writing in the *New York Times* has observed, '"white male," dead or alive, is now used as an accusation . . . a slur'. Following with the usual thinking behind the charge, he says, 'The left relishes the usage. It thinks that white males have held center stage too long, that it's time for their victims' (1991: Section 4: 15).

What is peculiar about this attack is that the grounds upon which the centrality of the white males rests is typically not mentioned. Thus, the edifice, not only of Western civilization, but increasingly of the civilization of the whole world, was largely created by white males, certainly in disproportion to their numbers. Science, technology, law, economic institutions, indeed, the university itself – one could go on – are predominantly the products of white male invention and construction. The worth of these products is tacitly granted by those foes of white males who wish to be integrated into the leadership of those creations, for example business organizations, created by the oppressive white males. But there is never any credit given to the white males for their contribution; nor is any gratitude or respect expressed.

The point I wish to make here is not that white males are entitled to some credit. Rather, I want to make a psychodynamic point by trying to understand the significance of the fact that, in the attack, the ground of entitlement is not mentioned. This reveals the difference between the psychology of the superego and the working of the ego ideal.

The superego operates with the currency of respect, not love. The superego presumes the freedom of the other and the voluntary nature of his or her actions. Within the psychology of the superego, when there is an accomplishment, an achievement, we presume that it is something that might not have happened, and that its occurrence was the result of the fact that somebody did it. Respect arises from our belief that an individual did something which he or she might not have done. When Shweder speaks of 'center stage', he is talking about the expression of this respect. The psychology of the superego, then, would assert against the claim of having had too much 'center stage'. 'They earned it.'

Against the claim 'They earned it', within the psychology of the superego, may be asserted 'Their achievements were not that important', or 'This other group deserves more credit', or 'This other group was deprived of a fair opportunity to earn it', or 'They didn't earn it, their ancestors did.' All of these are claims of equity, which may be seen as the way a balance is established between the demands of the superego and the entitlements of the ego ideal. When they are true, they operate as genuine grounds for legitimate grievance. There is, after all, such a thing as inequity. And it is an undeniable fact that numerous important contributions of members of such groups as African-Americans and women *have* often been overlooked.

What distinguishes political correctness from legitimate grievance, from considerations of equity, is the extent to which disputation over who is to be appreciated *denies the validity of the claim of having done something to earn it altogether*. The fact that the claim of earned entitlement is rarely mentioned, let alone denied, indicates that the psychology of the superego has been abandoned here.

What has taken its place is the exclusive psychology of the ego ideal. Within the psychology of the ego ideal one does not gain appreciation through doing something, but by being who one is.[5] The ego ideal operates with the currency, not of respect, but of love. Within the narcissistic world of the ego ideal, good things just happen as if by magic. When they happen to one, they happen naturally because one is so wonderful. They are themselves expressions of love. Earning appreciation through voluntary behaviour does not enter into this.

The corollary of this is that, within the psychology of the ego ideal, if one does not feel loved, if one does not experience the ego ideal, this must be because somebody is bad, with hatred directed toward them as the result. But, as we know, one never gets to be the ego ideal. The ironic result is that the psychology of the ego ideal, which has love as its primary emotional core, gives rise to hatred as the result of its inevitable failure of fulfilment. The question is, where is this hatred to be directed? There are two possibilities: first that one does not belong in the world of the ego ideal because of one's own badness. In this case one feels this hatred as shame. The alternative is that others are bad, in which case one feels humiliated and hates those whom one experiences as causing one's humiliation.

In the former case, it is important to re-emphasize that, if the superego is present, if achievement is valued, one can convert this shame into guilt and use it, not only as the basis of a drive to become good through achievement but as a way of deferring the ego ideal. In this way one can deflate the shame or humiliation which would come from failure to attain it. But if the superego is itself devalued, one can easily understand how the latter case might evolve.

Here, the locus of causality for one's feeling of being unloved is directed outward and one experiences oneself as having been humiliated by those who appear to be valued. In this case, the claim that individuals have earned their respect through their achievement is not seen as a valid claim for positive valuation. Rather it is experienced as an insult, part of the dynamic of oppression which functions to deprive one of the love that should come to one naturally.

From this follows a culture of envy and resentment (Schoek, 1966). Within this culture, those who are experienced as having humiliated one are thought to be evil and one experiences rage and hatred against them. They have stolen the love that properly should come to oneself. The narcissistic fantasy that accompanies this is that if one destroys the forces of evil, then one will become the centre of a loving world.[6]

The result of these dynamics is to redefine the concept of what the university is all about and to reinterpret all of its processes. It turns the university into a setting for a Manichaean battle between the forces of Good and the forces of Evil,[7] between Oppressors and Oppressed.[8] This redefinition has a number of aspects. In the next section, I will discuss a few of them.

Multiculturalism and the Inversion of Valuation

The shift from the psychology of the superego to that of the ego ideal has the effect of delegitimizing achievement as a ground for appreciation. The concept of respect loses its meaning. The claim 'They earned it' comes to seem an expression of racism, sexism, or classism, depending upon who fares badly in the comparison. In a word, it becomes politically incorrect.

By disallowing the claim of earned entitlement, the politically correct devalue achievement as a basis for appreciation, and substitute perceived deprivation. As I have said, the ego ideal does not operate within the calculus of respect, but of love. Appreciation in this world is seen as attaching not to the behaviour, which one may have voluntary control over, but to the person him or herself.

The assertion of previous standards of appreciation, based on achievement, comes to seem to be a way of taking appreciation away from those who truly need it. The traditional hierarchy of valuation within the university is inverted. The pride that previously marked the attainment of approved ends comes to seem as if it has been taken from someone else and deserving, therefore, of stigmatization.

An interesting aspect of this is the effect it has on achievement-oriented minority students:

> many black students seemed ill at ease with their own achievement – as if it were somehow a betrayal of their race. Several admitted they had kept their high school grades secret in order to avoid charges that they were 'selling out.' One pre-med student described having to watch herself when she went home to Brooklyn: 'If I speak in complete sentences, my girlfriends accuse me of putting on airs.' (Jacoby, 1991: 29)

On the other hand, the previously unappreciated, those stigmatized, make their claim to appreciation based on their stigmatization. In this way, the nature of the university's process shifts entirely.

Within the psychology of the superego, the university is an arena of competition for respect based on achievement. Here the university functions as a father, who prepares students to achieve something in the world based upon the differential reward of good versus bad work. If the process is successful, the student internalizes this criticism of bad work, as part of the superego, and goes out into the world where he or she does good work based upon this internalization.

Under the psychology of the ego ideal, the meaning of the university becomes quite different. Here, the university functions as a mother. Or rather, not as a mother but as the maternal imago – the infant's fantasy of what the mother should be. The maternal imago – I shall refer to her as the Mother – does not differentiate among her children on the basis of their achievements. For the Mother, appreciation means, not respect, but love. She loves us perfectly exactly as we are. When life is not perfect for us, we call upon the Mother's love to make it so. Accordingly, it is through our suffering that we call upon her love. She understands our need for love in exactly the way we experience it, and therefore adopts our grievances and validates our resentments. She is our perfect ally in our struggle against those who have Oppressed us and made life less than perfect for us.

Within the logic of the ego ideal, as I have shown, it follows that the cause of the feeling of unappreciation must be that the

Oppressors have stolen their appreciation from the Oppressed. They therefore need to be brought to account. The logic of this principle requires that the Oppressed be loved more in order to compensate, while the Oppressors deserve to be humiliated for their effrontery and their appreciation taken from them. Taken together, what this means is that those who feel unappreciated will be confirmed in their resentments and will be helped to take back the appreciation which has been stolen from them. Then they will feel appreciated and life will be perfect. This is the process that defines the politically correct university.

From this vantage point, we can understand why, instead of a competition for achievement, the students come to engage in a competition for sympathy and even pity. By showing that they have been victimized, oppressed, abused, devalued in the past, the students assert their claims to compensatory appreciation. From this we understand the development of the balkanization of student bodies into hyphenated groups proclaiming their history of oppression and grievance. The African-Americans have their history of slavery and discrimination. The Jews have the history of anti-Semitism and the holocaust. The women have the history of rape and sexual harassment. The homosexuals have homophobia and gay bashing. The white males have a more difficult project, but it is far from hopeless. They can, for example, condemn their ancestors for depriving them of their purity, and in that way join the anti-Oppressor chorus with full fury. All of these, of course, are ways of expressing resentments and legitimizing one's demands for appreciation.

Resentment, because of its narcissistic premise, is a bottomless pit. This explains the curious phenomenon that, at politically correct universities, the absence of serious racism or sexism, for example, does not appear to diminish the intensity of the struggle concerning them. This is suggested by a report on Oberlin College, written for the *New Republic* by Jacob Weisberg:

> To see how obsessed the campus is, one only has to pick up an issue of *The Oberlin Review*. The news, letters, and editorial columns of every issue are full of accusations of racism, sexism, heterosexism, homophobia, 'ableism,' and a host of other insensitivities abhorrent to the disciples of what might be called Oberlinism.

But

> Oberlin has a long liberal pedigree. The college, which first enrolled blacks in 1835, was a stop on the underground railroad. Today it brags of its achievements in recruiting and retaining minority students and

faculty. With the exception of the odd bit of bathroom graffiti, there is little of what anyone outside of a college campus would call racism. But in a perverse equation, perceived racism at Oberlin is inversely proportional to actual racism: the less students see, the harder they look. . .

Last spring two black women were asked to leave an outdoor table at a local bakery because they were eating food bought at a rival restaurant. They initiated a boycott, vowing to make life hell for the racist establishment. 'The ignorance, the audacity, the arrogance, and the racist attitude to do such a thing is what is horrifying to us,' one said in the letter to the *Review*. 'We have got to realize that it is not just the administration and all of the other top brass practicing bigotry. It's the everyday person perpetuating it.' (Weisberg, 1991: 22–3)

The point here is that the Oppressed's ego ideal, never fulfilled, is defined by the Oppression directed against it. It only exists in a state of conflict with whatever it experiences as keeping it from fulfilment. In a way, it needs racism, or sexism, or the like in order to survive as an identity. In the absence of real racism, sexism, or other real assaults, it needs to create them.

Ultimately, what keeps our ego ideal from being fulfilled is reality itself. Interpreting reality itself as Oppression permits narcissism to ensure its permanent continuity, for there is always plenty of reality to fulfil that purpose.

The Redefinition of the Purpose of the University

The whole nature of what constitutes knowledge changes in the politically correct university. Along with it go changes in the ideas of the transmission of this knowledge, in the form of teaching, and the creation of new knowledge, in the form of research and scholarship. From the study of intellectual and artistic achievements, characteristic of the superego, teaching becomes the furtherance of the struggle of Oppressors against Oppressed. Everything that is done is legitimized by reference to its function in this Manichaean battle. The narcissistic premise here is that anything else serves the purpose of Oppression. As Eldridge Cleaver said it, 'If you're not part of the solution, you're part of the problem.'

One consequence of this is the creation of whole programmes and departments whose agendas and definitions subordinate traditional scholarship to overt political activity (Short and Iannone, 1992). Again, we get the whole range of multicultural curricular changes that have been widely reported, for example by D'Souza (1991).

In all of this, we find a disparagement of the idea of great works which is closely related to the disparagement of achievement I have already discussed. The very idea of great works comes to be seen as a technique of Oppression. This is perhaps the saddest element of the multicultural inversion. As D'Souza (1991) has pointed out, multiculturalism does not typically lead to an incorporation of great works from other cultures. Increasingly, it appears to mean an indiscriminate outpouring of material with no serious claim to distinction based only upon its cultural lineage. Thus, we have this:

> 'I couldn't have taught this class 10 years ago,' declares Stanford Prof. Kennell Jackson to an overflowing classroom on the first day of the spring quarter. 'But people don't look at me like I'm crazy anymore – what history does has broadened considerably.' And Prof. Jackson is not exaggerating. 'Black Hair as Culture and History,' his ambitious new upper-level seminar, addresses how black hair 'has interacted with the black presence in this country – how it has played a role in the evolution of black society.'. . .
>
> If not for Prof. Jackson's earnestness, one might mistake the class for a parody of multiculturalism. The syllabus, handed out on the first day of class, includes such lectures as 'The Rise of the Afro' and 'Fade-O-Rama, Braiding and Dreadlocks.' According to this course outline, local hair stylists will visit for a week of discussions. Enrolled students will view the 1960s musical 'Hair,' read Willie L. Morrow's '400 Years Without a Comb,' and Dylan Jones's 'Haircults,' and study the lyrics of Michael Jackson's hit pop single 'Man in the Mirror'. (Sacks, 1992)

The narcissistic premise upon which political correctness operates assumes that nothing exists outside of the struggle against Oppression. In this context, we can understand that everything the university does would be enlisted in the struggle. Here are some examples of the way the politically correct, writing in academic journals, redefine the teaching of composition:

> All teaching supposes ideology; there simply is no value free pedagogy. For these reasons, my paradigm of composition is changing to one of critical literacy, a literacy of political consciousness and social action. (Laditka, 1990: 361)

And, in an award-winning essay:

> [The classroom in composition ought to be considered] a disruptive form of underlife, a forum which tries to undermine the nature of the institution and posit a different one in its place. (Brooke, 1987: 151)

A special element of the faculty's contribution to the transformation of the course of study is worth mentioning in its own right.

This is the denial of reality. As we saw before, in the traditional family the father had the function of coping with external reality. This was the meaning of the superego. Thoroughly repudiating the superego and denigrating its works means that the necessity of coping with external reality must be denied and, indeed, with it must go the idea that there is an external reality that has to be coped with.

From this, we get the idea that each group may define reality however it sees fit, and that, indeed, groups have done so all along. Narcissism sees only narcissism in others, not having the basis for understanding that anything else exists. Thus, denial of an objective reality is seen as politically correct because the assertion of an objective reality was merely a power ploy on the part of the politically dominant group to legitimize and make natural its dominance. From this, we get the fact that peculiar claims concerning history, for example, are not only asserted but taken seriously. This is perhaps most blatant in 'Afrocentric' thought. Thus, for example, a collection of essays called *African-American Baseline Essays* which was adopted by the public school system of Portland, Oregon, maintains, according to C. Vann Woodward, that

> Africa is the mother of Western civilization, that Egypt was a black African country and the source of the glory that was Greece and the grandeur that was Rome. Africans also discovered America and named the waters they crossed the Ethiopian Ocean, long before Columbus. (Woodward, 1991: 42)

When a teacher in Portland, Richard C. Garrett, questioned such things, he was told 'You have your scholarship, we have ours' (Garrett, 1992).[9]

More important, though, is the denial that the laws of the physical universe are not objective but represent, again, only the outlook of the white males. Thus:

> [D]espite the deeply ingrained Western cultural belief in science's intrinsic progressiveness, science today serves primarily regressive social tendencies. [*I*]*ts ways of constructing and conferring meanings are not only sexist but also racist, classist, and culturally coercive.* (Harding, cited in Gross, 1992; emphasis added)

Counterposed to this is an emerging 'feminist' science, based on a feminine communion with the object of study (Harding, 1986). We see in this communion the loss of boundaries between self and other characteristic of the maternal imago. What will be left of the technological capacity of the West if the laws of physics, for example, lose their special place among the universe of possible texts is anybody's guess.

Most widely publicized among the abuses of PC have been restrictions on speech. These have taken place in the classroom. For example, Stephen Thernstrom was pilloried for insensitivity for reading, in his course on race relations at Harvard University, from white plantation owners' journals (D'Souza, 1991). And Ian Macneil, a visiting professor, was denounced by the Harvard Women's Law Association, who repeated their denunciations in letters sent to other universities that might have considered hiring him. His crime consisted, in the first instance, of including in his case book, as an example of the legal 'battle of the forms', a 'sexist' quote from Byron and then for being awkward in his response to the ensuing vilification. The quote was:

> A little still she strove, and much repented,
> And whispering, 'I will ne'er consent' – consented.
> (D'Souza, 1991: 197–8)

More widely publicized has been the proliferation of restrictive speech codes designed to combat 'hate speech'. Thus, the university of Michigan adopted a code that prohibited

> any behavior, verbal or physical, that stigmatizes or victimizes an individual on the basis of race, ethnicity, religion, sex, sexual orientation, creed, national origin, ancestry, age, marital status, handicap, or Vietnam-era veteran status. (cited by D'Souza, 1991: 142)

Because of the obvious danger that such codes would be, as they have been, declared in violation of the First Amendment, a great deal of effort has gone into crafting them so that they would prohibit what is offensive and preserve what is valuable. But such efforts would have to come to naught. They would have to be based on a formal distinction between types of speech. But the real issue for their politically correct authors was never *what kind of* speech is offensive, but *whose* speech is offensive.

> A student newspaper funded by Vassar College termed black activist Anthony Grate, 'hypocrite of the month' for espousing anti-Semitic views while publicly denouncing bigotry on campus. In an acrimonious debate, Grate reportedly referred to 'dirty Jews' and added, 'I hate Jews.' Grate later apologized for his remarks. Meanwhile, outraged that the *Spectator* had dared to criticize a black person, the Vassar Student Association first attempted to ban the issue of the publication, and when that failed it withdrew its $3,800 funding. The newspaper 'unnecessarily jeopardizes an educational community based on mutual understanding,' the VSA explained. (D'Souza, 1991: 10)

The point is that the whole purpose of the politically correct university is to idealize the Oppressed and demonize the Oppressors. This holds true of speech as well as anything else. Symbolic activity which feeds the narcissism of selected groups is not only protected but obligatory. Given the totalizing character of narcissism, anything that conflicts with it is forbidden. This is what the discourse of 'sensitivity' is all about. But put this baldly, it is hard to see how anyone except the most ideological could accept it. And that is the dilemma of those who want to write speech codes.

Finally, we may mention among the abuses of PC, programmes designed to 'fight' racism, sexism, homophobia, and other offences by 'sensitizing' individuals who do not have the right opinions or emotions. A good deal of emotional brutalization may often be seen in these programmes. Remember that a failure to idealize the underappreciated groups is seen as a sign of racism or sexism, or whatever the underappreciated group is. These attitudes do not belong in the loving world of the maternal imago and cannot be allowed to persist at the university. The subjectivity that underlies them is seen as diseased or evil and any steps that eradicate it are seen as legitimate and worthwhile. The methodology here most powerfully involves the infliction of shame.

The Emotional Basis of Political Correctness

An example of this is offered by a student describing his experience at a mandatory 'Diversity Seminar', given to incoming students at the University of Michigan.

> One activity that particularly angered me was called 'Take a Stand.' An imaginary line was drawn down the center of the room. One side is the 'comfortable' side, the other is the 'uncomfortable' side. When the facilitator made a statement, we were to stand on whichever side of the room corresponded to our opinion of the statement. The farther away from the center one stood, the more comfortable or uncomfortable he was.
>
> The first statement was 'Dating someone from another race.' I walked over to the uncomfortable side, and when I turned around, I found myself alone. I was simultaneously confused and embarrassed.
>
> 'You mean all of those people are comfortable with dating people of another race?' I asked the facilitator.
>
> 'Yes,' he replied.
>
> [. . .]
>
> 'Would anyone like to comment on why they're standing where they're standing?' asked the facilitator. Not surprisingly, everybody's eyes were on me.

'Since you asked,' I said, 'one of the many reasons is that my parents would probably boot me right out of the house.' I didn't feel bad about saying this.

One member of the group said 'That's how your parents feel, but how do you feel?'

I feel that I was ostracized from the group because of my beliefs. (Boeskool, 1991)

The issue of shame enables us to turn to one of the more interesting questions about the PC controversy. How does political correctness get its power over its opposition? The stands taken as politically correct are often quite radical and have a great deal of opposition to them among more traditional elements of the university. But these traditional elements are often rapidly and decisively overcome. They often stand quite mute in fact. How does that happen?

In order to make some sense of this, we need first to look at the way face is maintained within society. As Goffman (1959, 1967) has shown us, society may be seen as being a very intricate drama, in which participants present claims for deference based upon a definition of themselves and the situation and others transact a drama in which those claims are maintained. Typically, he notes:

> Each participant is allowed to establish the tentative official ruling regarding matters which are vital to him but not immediately important to others, e.g., the rationalizations and justifications by which he accounts for his past activity. In exchange for this courtesy he remains silent or non-committal on matters important to others but not immediately important to him. (1959: 9)

On the surface, then, we all grant due deference to each other. At least we typically grant each other sufficient deference to validate each others' characters and keep the drama moving. Underneath the surface, or backstage, so to speak, a vigorous process is at work seeking to ensure that the apparently spontaneous mutual celebration taking place on the surface comes off. And this backstage activity involves, on all of our parts, a deep understanding of the ways in which we have to play our roles and other people have to play theirs.

Thus, on the one hand, we stifle a yawn when a story someone is telling is boring to us, and we try very hard not to show that stifling a yawn is what we are doing. On the other hand, we avoid situations where we know that groups who are deferential to us in public may have reason to be discussing us more critically.

We all know that we are playing roles and we have to know this in order for the roles we are playing to come off. But we have this knowledge privately, since the public display is not of the playing of the roles, but of the roles that are being played.

This means that social life is a kind of sleight-of-hand operation, in which we all both know, and do not know, about the performance that we, and others, are putting on. And we maintain this tenuous but necessary balance by asserting our own and accepting each others' privacy.

Political correctness works by denying the right to privacy. The premise of narcissism, after all, is that other people are not entitled to have independent minds. PC turns our private awareness of our inner feelings into a source of shame. To have to try to act in a politically correct manner is to be politically incorrect. As George Orwell put it in *1984*, 'A Party member is required to have not only the right opinions, but the right instincts' (1949: 174). Love of the Oppressed, not the display of love but love itself, is a criterion for one's own moral acceptability.

The alternative to that acceptability is to be the target of rage and scorn. The result of this is that individuals take their own deviation from the public demonstration as indicating that there is something wrong with them. Unable to dispel this impression by admitting their feelings, each participates in the public ritual of agreement, leaving all the others to believe that there is something wrong with them for their own deviation. It is the apparent unanimity of the consensus so formed that maintains this apparent unanimity.

A classic experiment by Solomon Asch (1956) illustrates this dynamic. In that experiment, a subject was required to make the simple perceptual judgement of whether lines were the same or different lengths. But the subject was confronted with the question in a group situation in which the other members of the group had already unanimously made their judgements in an erroneous way. Unbeknownst to the subject, the other members of the group were confederates of the experimenter. The question was whether the real subject would contradict the clear evidence of his senses and go along with group, or whether he would go along with his senses and differ from the group. Strikingly, most of the subjects – approximately three-quarters – conformed.

Thomas Scheff (1990), analysing this experiment, argues that the response which occasioned the conformity, a response felt, incidentally, both by those who conformed and those who did not, was shame: 'the fear that they were suffering from a defect and that the study would disclose this defect' (1990: 90).

He quotes Asch on the subjects who conformed:

> They were *dominated* by their exclusion from the group which they took
> to be a reflection on themselves. Essentially they were *unable* to face a
> conflict which threatened, in some undefined way, to expose a defi-
> ciency in themselves. They were consequently trying to *merge* in the
> group in order not to feel peculiar. (Asch, 1956: 45; cited by Scheff,
> 1990: 90–1; emphasis added by Scheff)

The obvious point is that three-quarters of Asch's subjects, in
an experiment that meant nothing, failed to resist conformity
because they feared it would reveal some undefined 'deficiency'.
What could one expect in the tense political atmosphere of a
university where the 'deficiency' that would be revealed would be,
for example, one's racism, with all the connotations of slavery,
lynchings, and Jim Crow laws that charge brings with it?

The denigration of the father and his role leaves the individual,
especially the male, in the terrible position of being stuck with the
sense of unworthiness which the superego functioned to allow him
to turn into guilt and discharge. And this unworthiness has to be
contrasted with the evident purity claimed by the Oppressed. They
are idealized and perfect.

In the narcissistic world of political correctness, guilt cannot
be seen as being part of the natural limitation of being human.
The game has changed. Guilt, which refers to behaviour, is no
longer the metric of morality. The metric of morality is shame,
which attaches to the identity. Thus, the white male is stigmatized, not for what he does, but because of who he is – a
white male.

Guilt, because it is based upon actions which can be more and
less good, is relative. Moreover, we can make reparations for our
bad actions by doing something good. We do not have to be stuck
with our guilt. Shame, by contrast, is absolute and irredeemable.
It relates to us by virtue of who we are; and we are, and remain,
who we are.

Within the psychology of shame, the only way people can claim
worthiness is to project their unworthiness outward and attack it
as part of the political correctness project. In that way they
become politically correct. Those unwilling to go through this
transformation typically internalize the rage of the politically
correct in the form of depression, and this leaves them without the
sense of authority that they need to resist political correctness.

Conclusion: Withstanding Political Correctness

Understanding the emotional basis of political correctness can go only so far in resisting it. The weakening of the traditional values of the university by shame and rage must have some positive corrective in the form of a sense of the worth of these values. Finding support for the traditional values of the university means finding the value of the father.

Recognizing the value of the father is difficult because it means recognizing our own limitation. The father's function is to reveal to us that the world does not revolve around us, that we are not its meaning. We naturally and inevitably hate him for it. But the sad fact is that the father is right, whether we like it or not. In the world, people appreciate us in accordance with whether we fulfil *their* needs, not in accordance with our needs to be loved. The traditional function of the university, expressing the meaning of the father, is to prepare us to live in that world. The father loves his children, but he knows that his actions toward them cannot be based on sentimentality.

When the university abandons the role of the father and adopts that of the maternal imago, it takes on a responsibility that its love cannot discharge. For the world the politically correct university attempts to create is an emotionally closed universe. It is based on the child's fantasy that the mother is the world. And she is not. There is no room for external reality in this world. This means that she, and the children she raises, will find themselves at war with the external reality that certainly does exist. This war will cause herself and her children greater and greater pain, not to mention the pain they cause in the world they go to war with. She does her children no good service by raising them in this way.

Notes

1. A well-known conservative and, in the Reagan administration, US representative to the UN.
2. The logic of the chapter requires only that motherhood and fatherhood are different roles. It requires no commitment to their usual biological differentiation.
3. Interestingly, as Gitlin observes, many of the early SDS members were the children of former radicals themselves. This was a part of the fathers with which they could identify.
4. It is worthwhile noting that there was an international dimension to the struggle against the Vietnam war. Thus, for example, Bertrand Russell organized an international tribunal to investigate charges of American war crimes (Gitlin, 1987: 268). European students, especially, came to see the Vietnam war as a

struggle of the oppressed against capitalist imperialism. The major representative was the US, but the whole capitalist world was seen as implicated. 'All Power to the Imagination', a slogan of the Paris rebellion of May 1968 (Gitlin, 1987: 241), illustrates well the psychological dynamics I describe here.

5. I use the term 'appreciation' to mean positive valuation, a concept which includes both love and respect.

6. Compare here the Marxist notion that all that needs to be done in order to create a perfect world is to knock off the capitalists. Along these lines, Post (1986) found, in a study of terrorists, that they believed that destroying the establishment would be destroying the source of evil, from which only good could result.

7. Manichaeanism owes its origin to Mani, a Persian philosopher of the third century AD. Psychodynamically oriented readers will recognize Melanie Klein's (1975) concept of 'splitting' here.

8. There is, of course, such a thing as real oppression. But oppressors are not a mythic force of the sort that the psychology of the ego ideal projects. They are simply human beings who have let their narcissism run away with them. I will follow the convention here of referring to the mythic, Manichaean projections with capital letters, leaving the lower case to refer to the real thing.

9. For a discussion of Afrocentric 'scholarship' see Lefkowitz (1992). This is from her account:

> several years ago I had a student who seemed to regard virtually everything I said about Socrates with hostility. . . [H]er instructor in another course had told her that Socrates (as suggested by the flat nose in some portrait sculptures) was black. The instructor had also taught that classicists universally refuse to mention the African origins of Socrates because they do not want their students to know that the so-called legacy of ancient Greece was stolen from Egypt.

But,

> Because Socrates was an Athenian citizen, he must have had Athenian parents; and since foreigners couldn't become naturalized Athenian citizens, he must have come from the same ethnic background as every other Athenian. . . It was as simple as that. (1992: 29–30)

References

Asch, S. (1956) 'Studies of independence and conformity: 1. A minority of one against a unanimous majority', *Psychological Monographs*, 70: 1–70.

Bates, K.L. (1991) 'Politically correct: is it a plot by left or right?', *Ann Arbor News*, 16 November: A7.

Bernstein, R. (1990) 'The rising hegemony of the politically correct', *New York Times*, 28 October, 4: 1,4.

Boeskool, R. (1991) *The Michigan Review*, 10 (1), 5 September: 5, 15.

Brooke, R. (1987) 'Underlife and writing instruction', *College Composition and Communication*, 38, May: 141–53.

Chasseguet-Smirgel, J. (1986) *Sexuality and Mind: The Role of the Father and the Mother in the Psyche*. New York: New York University Press.

D'Souza, D. (1991) *Illiberal Education: The Politics of Race and Sex on Campus*. New York: Free Press.

Derrida, J. (1974) *Of Grammatology*. Baltimore: Johns Hopkins University Press.

Foucault, M. (1979) *Discipline and Punish: The Birth of the Prison*. New York: Vintage.

Freud, S. (1955) 'Group psychology and the analysis of the ego', in *Standard Edition*, Vol. 18. London: Hogarth Press.

Freud, S. (1957) 'On narcissism: an introduction', in *Standard Edition*, Vol. 14. London: Hogarth Press.

Fried, C. (1991) Letter to the editor, *Academe*, November–December: 10.

Garrett, R. G. (1992) 'Portland "essays"', (Letter to the editor), *New York Times*, 3 August: A18.

Gitlin, T. (1987) *The Sixties: Years of Hope, Days of Rage*. New York: Bantam Books.

Goffman, E. (1959) *The Presentation of Self in Everyday Life*. New York: Doubleday/Anchor.

Goffman, E. (1967) *Interaction Ritual*. New York: Pantheon.

Gray, M. W., Poston, L. S., Stern, C. S. and Strohm, Paul (*The Special Committee*) (1991) 'Statement on the "political correctness" controversy', *Academe*, September–October: 48.

Gross, P. R. (1992) 'On the "gendering" of science', *Academic Questions*, 5 (2): 10–23.

Harding, S. (1986) *The Science Question in Feminism*. Ithaca, NY: Cornell University Press.

Jacoby, T. (1991) 'Psyched out', *The New Republic*, 18 February: 28–30.

Keniston, K. (1965) *The Uncommitted: Alienated Youth in American Society*. New York: Delta Books.

Kimball, R. (1990) *Tenured Radicals: How Politics has Corrupted our Higher Education*. New York: HarperPerennial.

Klein, M. (1975) *Love, Guilt, and Reparation and Other Works, 1921–1945*. London: Hogarth Press.

Laditka, J. N. (1990) 'Semiology, ideology, *praxis*. Responsible authority in the composition classroom', *Journal of Advanced Composition*, 10 (Fall): 357–73.

Lefkowitz, M. (1992) 'Not out of Africa', *The New Republic*, 10 February: 29–36.

Moss, C. (1991) '"PC": alive and well at Michigan', *Detroit News*, 23 November: 12C.

Orwell, G. (1949) *1984*. New York: New American Library.

Post, J. M. (1986) 'Hostilité, conformité, fraternité: group dynamics of terrorist behavior', *International Journal of Group Psychotherapy*, 36 (2): 211–24.

Rorty, R. (1989) *Contingency, Irony, and Solidarity*. Cambridge: Cambridge University Press.

Rothman, S., Lichter, S. R. and Lichter, L. (1992) *Elites in Conflict: Social Change in America Today*. Greenwich, CT: Greenwood/Praeger.

Sacks, D. (1992) 'The cutting edge of multiculturalism', *Wall Street Journal*, 29 July: A10.

Scheff, T. J. (1990) *Microsociology: Discourse, Emotion, and Social Structure*. Chicago: University of Chicago Press.

Schoek, H. (1966) *Envy: A Theory of Social Behavior*. New York: Harcourt Brace & World.

Schwartz, H. S. (1992) 'Masculinity and the emotional basis of work', working paper, Oakland University.

Short, T. and Iannone, C. (1992) 'How politicized studies enforce conformity:

interviews with Julius Lester and Elizabeth Fox-Genovese', *Academic Questions*, 5 (3): 48–65.

Shweder, R. A. (1991) 'The crime of white maleness', *New York Times*, 18 August, 4: 15.

Weisberg, J. (1991) 'Thin skins', *The New Republic*, 18 February: 22–4.

Woodward, C. V. (1991) 'Equal but separate', a review of *The Disuniting of America* by A. M. Schlesinger, *The New Republic*, 15 & 22 July: 41–3.

Zielinski, M. (1991) 'The PC attack: conference takes on right-wing challenge to university reform', *Ann Arbor News*, 13 November: D1, 2.

PART IV

DIRECTIONS

10

An Emotion Agenda

Stephen Fineman

What directions are possible for work on emotion in organizations? There are three interdependent areas to consider: questions we should be asking about emotionality; issues of method; and theoretical positioning. I would like to offer some pointers in each of these areas.

Questions We Should Ask

Once the passions, performances and contexts of working life become uncoupled, we begin to lose the sense of emotionality that this volume addresses. We need a *process* and *contextualized* view of emotions. Within such a perspective there are a number of important questions; for example:

What are the essential emotionalities of working? This broad, but very central, question is a response to the vacuum in social science literature on an adequate phenomenology of working and organizing. Emotion researchers have tended towards a segmentalist approach where single-label emotions, or clusters of similar emotions, have been isolated for attention. This can be revealing, but what is missing are the definitions and redefinitions, interlayering of feelings, feelings about feelings, over time and in experiential depth. It is perhaps noteworthy that three contributors to this volume have cited Studs Terkel's *Working* collection of biographies to illustrate their arguments. Despite being seventeen years old, the narrative accounts in the book, together with light but poignant interpolations from Terkel, speak in a rare *whole* way about the feelings of the men and women who opened their hearts to him. There are other possible approaches – to which I will turn later in this chapter.

How does the sharing of feelings change those feelings, and so re-form one's organizational reality? Talking with others about certain emotional experiences is a common, sometimes obsessional, feature of organizational life – often ritualized in regular 'confessions' during coffee breaks or meal times. The point, however, is that the social sharing of emotion can be more than a simple venting of frustrations or a moan session; it can substantially redefine the emotional material and contribute to the emotional texture of the organization. The explicit or implicit work of others symbolically recontextualizes the emotions. In other words, we can feel different about our feelings because we find different explanations for the emotional 'event' (Rime et al., 1991). Organizational culture research has yet to incorporate such issues – a significant omission.

In what ways do decisions unfold over time as a function of the way people *feel*, and *change* their feelings – about themselves, their projects and significant others? How, for example, does anxiety, suspicion, love, and hate take decision making through various paths towards particular outcomes? Such issues are at the heart of the intertwining of cognition and emotion, often falsely separated. Settings such as personnel selection, appraisals, crisis management and layoffs are appropriate for exploration. Each, though rationalized and systematized in the guidebooks, are often full of thinly disguised anguish, doubt, and concern – for some or all of the parties involved. Implicitly, they are highly emotionalized zones where decisions are based on hunches, feeling good, uneasiness, liking, fear of exposure, and so forth; the emotions *constitute* the decision process. But exactly how, and in what forms?

A corollary to the above concerns decisions which have direct moral overtones. As illustrated in some of these pages, people will hurt others, double-deal, cheat, or do worse, if the company ethos supports such behaviours, *and* the cost of not doing so seems too great. Some will act with a cynical shrug; others will feel ashamed, but still conform. We also know that many corporate actors will do things at work that they would not contemplate doing outside of their organizational setting. It is of fundamental importance to emotion research to understand how feelings such as of shame, guilt and embarrassment can become redefined or extinguished. The importance lies in the kind of managerial/corporate actions that may ensue – such as victimizing others, despoiling the natural environment, or purveying dangerous products. An interesting illustrative case is reported in *The Guardian* (19 November 1992). It concerns a 'green' fridge:

A fridge has been developed by two independent German scientists who, on moral grounds, would not countenance the use of ozone-damaging coolant CFCs. They discovered that a particular mixture of propane and butane did the trick nicely, was safe, cheap, and openly available. But meanwhile the giant chemical industry had invested heavily in a different replacement gas (HFCs) which was ozone friendlier than CFCs, but a very powerful global warmer in the long term. Its response to the far safer green fridge was to do everything it could to discredit it and prevent its manufacture.

The logic of commerce, power and vested interest is obvious in this case. But what of the individual executives who knew that they were attempting to crush a product which was much safer environmentally than theirs? What shift of feelings permits what many would regard as an immoral act? How do the political structures and processes of the organization turn and tune emotions? In what settings and circumstances does fear (of what or whom?) challenge or corrupt the emotions which provide inner signals to moral judgement?

What *are* the organization's feeling rules? The common response to this question has been to point to the instructions issued to the hamburger seller, aircraft attendant, professional model or insurance salesperson on how they should create the 'right' impressions in their various occupational settings or moments. But arguably there are other feeling rules, implicit ones; the subtle product of working arrangements and the social history of the workplace. Such unspoken, and largely invisible, rules will regulate a myriad impression-management behaviours, as well as the open expressions of feelings. When, and where, for example, is it appropriate to laugh, cry, sneer or rage? We could fruitfully explore how different settings become emotionalized in different ways; how people learn the emotional codes or rules; and what happens to deviants – such as whistleblowers. For all practical purposes, it is the changes in feeling rules (implicit and explicit) which breathe new life into an organization's culture or subculture, permitting shifts from, say, secrecy to openness, confrontation to collaboration.

Closely linked to the above is the question (hinted at in some chapters of this book) of when and how the expression of certain emotions becomes pathologized.

We could regard all organizations as having zones of expressive tolerance which are likely to vary according to organizational type and part. So, for example, the range and quality of expressive behaviour in the advertising agency could be different from that of the supermarket; and what happens on the production floor of a newspaper can be unlike that of the school staff room. Exploring such emotional differences could be instructive, but even more central for emotion research is to discover how people come to know that they have hit a boundary, what happens when the socially constructed boundaries are breached, and what happens to the breacher (studying rule-breaching is one route to discovering the otherwise invisible rules). Pathologization is one feature of this, where the expression of certain strong emotions – such as anger, moral outrage, grief or stress – is driven to the margins and shadows of the organization. They become defined in terms of 'something really wrong' with the person.

Stress is an interesting example in that the rhetoric associated with its massive popularization ('stress at work is to be expected; but with help you can manage it and feel better') suggests that stress, the disease, is an individualized thing to treat. Organizations which have assimilated this message are often content to quietly acknowledge that being sick or off work for reasons of stress is acceptable – up to a point. Some (complimented on their 'enlightened' personnel policies) offer the services of company counsellors. If stress has 'come out' in this manner, how are other emotions defined and socially controlled? In what circumstances are people labelled 'mad' and ejected from the organization (the passionate whistleblower; the sexually promiscuous)? How are the emotional boundaries renegotiated such that yesterday's dubious or unprofessional outburst is today's acceptable, or even welcome, feeling? Where do shifting societal ideologies (such on the role of women, the meaning of work, sexuality, social class, ethnicity) influence this process?

We should broaden our understanding of how power in organizations affects emotional disclosure, feeling rules, and climates of trust and mistrust. Of all the institutional characteristics, power can be seen to be one of the most influential on how and where people are able to direct and define their feelings. But power should be widened beyond the structural analyses common to many of the sociological paradigms of emotion – to include non-hierarchical, and transactional processes (e.g. Srivasata, 1986; Pfeffer, 1981). I have in mind, particularly, power regimes amongst peers, and power based on informally defined social orders and patterns of deference.

Finally, we are missing the systematic development of the excellent organizational work pioneered by Menzies-Lythe on social defences at work (see Chapter 1). If the organization of work reflects our individual, emotional, disorganization, our working patterns could benefit from the scrutiny of a psychodynamic eye. The force of this argument derives partly from the questions that social constructionism fails to ask. Namely, why the various forms of organizational order take hold at all; whether there is a reason(s) for the infinite variety of social games we create and play; and where the emotions which hold together our organizational processes get their bite. It seems to me that psychodynamic theory (of which psychoanalysis is one discourse) cannot but strengthen the cultural and dramatistic explanations of emotion, not least because it acknowledges that human beings enter organizations with the traces of years of emotionality and emotion work already within them.

At its most basic, therefore, we can explore the emotional 'roots' of people's desire to enter a particular occupation or organization, and the kinds of solace, self-punishment or sense of being that that achieves. We can ask questions about the symbolism of joining particular work and group activities in terms of the biographies of the group members – early longings, confusions and conflicts. It is noteworthy that such historical information is given particular prominence in the recent rash of biographies and autobiographies of 'captains of industry'. They help the reader to frame explanations for recent conduct in ways that link, sometimes compellingly, with earlier emotional development – be it smooth, protected, conflictual or traumatic. Seen this way, the leader's grand achievements or failures are no simple consequence of the rational application (or misapplication) of business skills.

The 'stuckness' of some organizations is a familiar theme in the organizational change literature. It would be instructive to unpick the deeper emotional features of 'resistance' and 'vested interest' using the language and insights of group and organizational psychodynamics. If, as argued in earlier chapters, work organizations fulfil an ontological function – a reason for being – change can touch some of the most enduring concerns of human beings. We have a good case here for bringing together interactionist/social constructionist views on change with psychodynamic ones, to develop more emotion-sensitive models for our change efforts.

Issues of Method – Different Discourses

As researchers of organizational emotions, how best can we gather and communicate our essential subject matter – what it is to 'be emotional', 'to feel' at, or about work? We require a medium, or mediums, which represent and convey feeling in fulsome evocation, timbre and context. The constructions of normal social science do not help very much. At best they offer everyday feeling-labels of the sort peppered throughout this book – anxiety, fear, happiness, joy, gloom, despair, excitement, envy, guilt, shame. . . These do have important associative meanings, but they do not specify the emotional nuances, as contexted in specific work circumstances. Feelings ebb and flow. They are sharp and diffuse. They are sometimes hard to describe, and when they are described they often become 'something else'. So our difficulty is more than an arbitrary issue of methodological choice: the method makes the feelings.

With emotions we are faced with one of the most real, and sometimes most exquisite, features of what it is to be a human being; but at the same time they soon exhaust the descriptive/evocative capacity of written language. This much, of course, we can learn from the struggles of our poets and dramatic novelists, many of whom have a far better grasp of the raw material of emotion than do social scientists. The point was brought home to me when reading a draft version of Yiannis Gabriel's chapter on nostalgia. I was puzzled that his descriptive passages on nostalgia did not *feel* nostalgic. Nostalgia, I realized, was more than a written description of the good old days; it was also a *sense* of longing, a tone of voice, a wistful expression on the face. Conjure up these images (which he now has) and the emotion complex begins to live.

How can we face the task of gathering personal feelings? We can ask people to tell us their organizational stories; we can record dialogue, interactions and non-verbal clues to feelings; we can gather people's introspections; we can use ourselves as subjects. Examples of all these narratives can be found in this book – which represents a fair section of available approaches to qualitative social research. All of them produce words to express what may or may not be what is 'really' felt. We cannot release emotion from the cultural symbols, the languages, that are available to us.

But perhaps we can be more adventurous in our use of available media, such as photographs, drawings and paintings – less conventional vehicles in a word-occupied publication culture. Ulmer (1989) speaks intriguingly of creating a 'mystory'; a discourse which blends orality, print and video, which is always specific to its composer. Here mediums of art and the humanities are used to address the expressive limitations of the conventional written text.[1] The search for emotional 'essence' has taken some sociologists into presenting field data as poetry or as a dramatic play (Ellis and Bochner, 1992; Richardson, 1992). Inventing new expressive forms, or adopting ones from other disciplines, is liberating for the student of emotions. Emotion is de-atomized and restored to something approximating its experiential validity.

Work Feelings – in Process

Multiple narratives enrich the emotional picture, but what is rare is the portrayal of 'real-time' emotions in organizational life. The significance here is that, while some work feelings are programmed through feeling rules for a particular event or situation, many are not; they are spontaneous or improvised.

Capturing emotion in process requires some methodological ingenuity. It lends itself to a 'tracer' form of ethnography where the investigator follows people and their moments over time, *in situ*. Narratives based on live dialogue, stories, observations, diary accounts, taped personal musings and interviews would provide a data-set from which the interlayering and unfolding of emotional experience can be defined. Always, though, the investigator is part of the account; to a greater or lesser extent he or she selects, does the looking, listening, points the camera, edits the tape recording, holds the pen. The challenge of subjectivity research is to acknowledge and honour this intermingling. Ronai (1992) does this with powerful effect in a multiple-layered account of her own work as an erotic dancer. The smells, sights, revulsion and power of her encounters and inner feelings are translated passionately onto the screen of her word processor when she returns home. Sequences are flashed up in loosely connected or discontinuous order and form. In her immediate reconstructions we see something of the conflicting meanings, images and flashbacks that characterize her lived emotions.

Theoretical Positioning – and Conclusion

In Chapter 1 I outlined the growing range of researchers and disciplines that now regard emotion as an appropriate subject to study. Organizational theory can benefit much from the cultural relativity of anthropology and social history; the social texturing and stratification of sociology; and the personal/interactional theories of social psychology and psychodynamics. It is exciting that organizational emotion can be studied through complementary frameworks, and so perhaps escape the grip of a single discipline or single frame. The various disciplinary streams offer concepts (some overlapping) and reference points (often very different) which can be applied to organizational settings and integrated into organizational theory. Organizational theory does not need to invent emotion, as if from scratch. What it needs, though, is an empirical filling out, along the lines already suggested. There is already a stimulating array of emotion-concepts and social models to test out directly, or to use more lightly and imaginatively in the interpretation of grounded data.

It is important that both felt emotion and emotional display are explored. Both lead in somewhat different theoretical directions – the former towards the ontological, the latter towards performance skills. They intersect at the point where social/organization rules determine their expression and shape. Felt emotions have had a very constricted treatment so far in organizational studies, while performance skills appear to be a 'growth area'. There are some conceptual deadends to be avoided. A particular one I have in mind is the neo-behaviouristic approach, where fragments of emotional display are observed, measured and classified, followed by an adding in of organizational 'variables' that may or may not influence the observed patterns (e.g. Rafaeli and Sutton, 1989). While tiny elements of role performances are not without interest, such research wrenches actor from context (instead of the mutuality that I have argued earlier) and places the researcher in an imperial position – in a field where we would do better to close the gap between researcher and researched.

In sum, the emotional field is one the organizational researcher can explore with some joy. It contains an abundance of conceptual riches which, with wise use, can transform our rather grey and tidy picture of people in organizations to one which ranges in emotional colour, passion and individual purpose.

Note

1. At the University of Bath we ask our students to compose 'portfolios' of their learning in organizational behaviour. They are encouraged to experiment with different narrative forms in order to express the processes and passions of the learnings over time.

References

Ellis, C. and Bochner, A. P. (1992) 'Telling and performing personal stories: the constraints of choice in abortion', in C. Ellis and M. G. Flaherty (eds), *Investigating Subjectivity*. Newbury Park, CA: Sage.

The Guardian (1992) 'The Big Chill', 19 November.

Pfeffer, J. (1981) *Power in Organizations*. Marshfield, MA: Pitman.

Rafaeli, A. and Sutton, R. (1989) 'The expression of emotion in organizational life', *Research in Organizational Behavior*, 11: 1–42.

Richardson, L. (1992) 'The consequences of poetic representation: writing the other, rewriting the self', in C. Ellis and M. G. Flaherty (eds), *Investigating Subjectivity*. Newbury Park, CA: Sage.

Rime, B., Mesquita, B., Phillipott, P. and Boca, S. (1991) 'Beyond the emotional event: six studies on the social sharing of emotion', *Journal of Cognition and Emotion*, 5 (5/6): 435–65.

Ronai, C. R. (1992) 'The reflexive self through narrative: a night in the life of an erotic dancer/researcher', in C. Ellis and M. G. Flaherty (eds), *Investigating Subjectivity*. Newbury Park, CA: Sage.

Srivasata, S. (1986) *Executive Power*. San Francisco: Jossey-Bass.

Terkel, S. (1975) *Working*. Harmondsworth: Penguin.

Ulmer, G. (1989) *Teletheory*. New York: Routledge.

Index